Praise for Ann Mariah Cook's *Running North*

"This remarkable chronicle of the grueling Yukon Quest remains a vivid illustration of the soaring potential of both human and canine character."
—*Booklist*

"*Running North* is the kind of book that you don't want to end."
—*The Plain Dealer* (Cleveland)

"A captivating account of her family's participation in the grueling sled-dog race known as the Yukon Quest. . . . A flowing, highly readable style that takes the reader on a journey most will never attempt. . . . This suspenseful, humorous read will have readers anxiously awaiting more."
—*Library Journal*

"An appealing adventure-memoir."
—*Seattle Post-Intelligencer*

"Bundle up when you read this book because Ann Cook's visual and sensory descriptive writing draws the reader into the frozen north as only someone of the caliber of Annie Dillard can."
—*The State College Centre Times*

"There are so many human interest stories between the covers of *Running North* that it is impossible to cover them all fairly. Although it is a first hand account about a family's trip to Alaska to race in the Yukon Quest, it reads more like a good novel. . . . A great read."
—*Team & Trail*

"A fascinating look at the physical and cultural shift from L. L. Bean–land to one where ratty parkas were held together with duct tape."
—*School Library Journal*

"Fast-paced. . . . Cook knows that she has a terrific story to tell and does so without pretense or embellishment."
—*The Columbus Dispatch*

"A great read for anyone who has ever dreamed of doing something really big."
—*The Volunteer* (New Jersey)

"Full of intriguing characters and insight into the sheer mountain of logistics, culture shock and physical demands of this grueling race."
—*The Everett Herald* (Washington)

"A fast-paced account of culture shock, thin ice, commitment, wolves, family dynamics, a broken-down truck, hallucinations, hot coffee, overcoming obstacles, and more."
—*The Capital City Weekly* (Arkansas)

"An explorer's tale with a feminine slant: Cook tells the story not just as dog lover and race handler, responsible for preparations and assistance, but also as wife and mother."
—*The New York Times Book Review*

Running North

RUNNING NORTH

A Yukon Adventure

ANN MARIAH COOK

ALGONQUIN BOOKS OF CHAPEL HILL 1999

Names of some people and places have been changed
to protect their identities.

Published by
ALGONQUIN BOOKS OF CHAPEL HILL
Post Office Box 2225
Chapel Hill, North Carolina 27515-2225

a division of
Workman Publishing
708 Broadway
New York, New York 10003

Printed in the United States of America.
Published simultaneously in Canada by Thomas Allen & Son Limited.
Design by Anne Winslow.

Library of Congress Cataloging-in-Publication Data
Cook, Ann Mariah, 1955–
    Running north : a Yukon adventure / Ann Mariah Cook.
      p.   cm.
    ISBN 1-56512-213-5 (hardcover)
    1. Cook, Ann Mariah, 1955–   . 2. Cook, George.   3. Yukon Quest
International Sled Dog Race.   4. Sled dog racing—Yukon River Valley
(Yukon and Alaska)   5. Women mushers—New Hampshire—Biography.
6. Mushers—New Hampshire—Biography.   I. Title.
SF440.15.C65   1998
798.8'3'092—dc21
[B]   98-25598
                                                                           CIP

ISBN 1-56512-253-4 paper

10   9   8   7   6   5   4   3   2   1

To Kris K. with love and gratitude

Acknowledgments

I wish to thank the following people, all of whom made our Yukon Quest their quest, too: Don McEwen, Peter and Donna Johnson, John White, Stephen Serafin, Steven Westland, D.V.M., Jill Prince, D.V.M. and the staff of Bristol Veterinary Hospital, Dick Kraybill, the staff of WGAF Radio, G. Whitfield Cook, Phyllis Westberg, and Duncan Murrell.

Therefore I say unto you, Take no thought for your life, what ye shall eat; neither for the body, what ye shall put on.

The life is more than meat, and the body is more than raiment.

Consider the ravens: for they neither sow nor reap; which neither have storehouse nor barn; and God feedeth them: how much more are ye better than the fowls?

Luke 12: 22–24

Eclipse

1

Anyone who has ever been to Alaska remembers the light. There is sometimes too much of it, and sometimes not enough. The land seems to be in a perpetual state of sunrise or sunset. There is always a pink-blue glow in the sky. Trees are silhouetted. Clouds and mountaintops are often rimmed with golden sunbeams. Even after dark, there is magic in the sky.

It is the light that controls the coming and going of Alaskans; not just the human Alaskans, but all living things in the territory. There are long summer days for the gathering of food, and brief winter days for hibernation. The power of nature is strong there: ever-present and overwhelming in the way it supports life and in the way it takes life away.

My husband and I are sled dog drivers, "mushers" in sled dog parlance, and we went to Alaska to train our team to race in the Yukon Quest, a thousand-mile challenge billed as the world's toughest race. We drove nearly five thousand miles from our home in New Hampshire in a truck and trailer that carried us, our three-year-old daughter Kathleen, our handler Sandy, and thirty-two Siberian Huskies. We drove into Alaska at a time when many people drive out. Labor Day had passed, and the snowbirds, as those who go south to escape the cold are called, were headed out in camper trailers, vans, and trucks. On long stretches of the Alaska Highway, ours was the sole vehicle they met. We were traveling into the darkness that they were leaving behind.

Our summer had been spent making preparations for the trip.

We were, in essence, taking a leave of absence from the life we had known for fourteen years. We put jobs on hold, gathered sponsors for our team, made and bought necessary equipment, and said a lot of temporary good-byes. To our friends and relatives, setting off for the Great Land was a huge undertaking fraught with risk. To George and me, it was simply the final step in an adventure we began years ago. We'd been "heading north" in attitude and behavior for a long time.

As small children, George and I both thrilled to stories of pioneers and explorers. George, the only child of older parents, and I, a youngest child who trailed my siblings by a gap of five years, spent long, lone hours wandering lawns, fields, and forests, pretending we were forging off with Lewis and Clark, Admiral Byrd, or Charles Darwin.

We met in boarding school. We were in our early teens when we tried out for the same rowing team. Our instant friendship, which in later years turned to courtship and marriage, was based on a love of athletics, adventure, and teamwork.

In our school community, we were able to act out our dreams of expeditions by organizing real outings for ourselves and our class-mates, and by participating in the modern adventure of traveling with a competing team.

When we worked together we had the effect of pushing each other toward peak performance. If we were bicycling somewhere, we would inevitably exchange a certain glance and start to race. If we were hiking, we'd rush each other up the trail. Underlying all our needling and fun, rivalry and competition, was our admiration for each other's ability to set and achieve goals. In our college years, I rowed in international competition. George became the captain of an intercollegiate lacrosse team.

Graduate school, and later George's job with the State Depart-ment of Environmental Protection, brought us to the outskirts of Hartford, Connecticut. We bought a fixer-upper home and really fixed it. Our goal at the time was to move up in the world enough to move out to the country. We wanted land, animals, and a family.

A bit ahead of schedule, we purchased a rugged, free-spirited Siberian Husky as our pet. We didn't realize at the time that Mocha, as she was named, would be the weaver of the threads of our youthful dreams. In her breed's athleticism and vitality, we discovered a four-footed reflection of ourselves. We began to study her breed, to steep ourselves in the lore of the arctic and investigate the role these dogs played in the settling of distant lands.

This led me to a copy of Jack London's *Call of the Wild*. The book contained vague illustrations of sled dogs in harness, and I had to guess how the tracings were fastened to the dogs. But after toiling over a piece of canvas strapping for several days, I was ready to begin a grand experiment.

Our yard was covered with little more than an inch of slushy Connecticut snow, when I hitched Mocha in her homemade harness to a child's wooden sled. I called Mocha to follow me and she pulled the sled with ease until she realized it was following her. Then she panicked and ran to escape the pursuing monster. The lightweight sled actually began to catch up with her. Within minutes, she gave in to the sled and crouched, trembling, beside it. I rushed to reassure her, and while I was asking her forgiveness, I spied our woodpile. I decided to weigh down the sled with a couple of pieces of cordwood and ask Mocha to try it all again. After some coaxing, she put her back into it. The more excited I became over her little triumph, the more delighted she was to pull the sled.

This wood hauling became a ritual with the two of us. We both enjoyed the outings, and I enjoyed getting some work out of a pet. Spurred on by this activity, I took the whole idea one step further and one day donned cross-country skis and hooked myself to Mocha's tracings. With only the slightest amount of encouragement, Mocha got the idea. We were soon flying over the snow—that is, until I lost my balance and fell. Mocha bounded all around me and pushed at me with her nose. "Get up, get up and try again!" she seemed to say.

That day marked a turning point in my life, and in Mocha's, too.

Mocha and I had used dog power as a means of transportation and we had both loved the experience. We were like two kids with a wonderful secret. I shared the secret with George. He witnessed a few of Mocha's performances and decided that a second Siberian, a dog who could pull him, must be purchased soon.

Our second dog was a massive pup, aptly named Matanuska, after a valley in Alaska where crops grow legendarily large. He was a sweet-tempered fellow and he came from a very reputable kennel. Our first visit to that kennel was a revelation. There, we saw a real dogsled and we also saw a metal cart with wheels that sled dogs pulled in snowless conditions. Our reading led us to believe that dogsledding was a thing of the past, but we learned from Matanuska's breeders that sled dog events were held all over the world, in places where there was snow, and in some places where there was no snow. In Oregon and Australia, sled dogs ran on the sand dunes. In Maryland, they ran on the mud flats. On Long Island, teams of dogs raced through trails in the parks. Races took place everywhere, even in Connecticut.

We quickly joined a little club that held amateur-level races. George, I, and our dogs began to live for rocketing down trails.

When we moved to New Hampshire, it was as much for the dogs, eight Siberians by then, as for ourselves. In New Hampshire, we could race in professional-class events. We also began to travel, often north into Canada, to visit with accomplished racers. Occasionally we were able to buy a dog from their kennels, but excellent sled dogs are seldom available for purchase, so we started breeding dogs for our team. We immersed ourselves in the study of Siberian lineage and breeding stock, and we began to create the sort of dog we needed.

We were particularly lucky when one of our early litters produced a born leader we named Dan. Hard-driving and fast, Dan pulled our team from obscurity to the front of the pack at eastern races.

In twelve years' time, our kennel expanded to house over thirty working Siberians, and each winter, when race announcements arrived in the mail, I read the locations of the races aloud.

"Hey George, want to go to a race in Montana? How about Chicoutimi, Quebec?" At first, I was kidding, but somehow we always managed to be at the starting line in these races. There was something intriguing about having an excuse to travel so far.

Soon we were racing with the mushers who were our mentors. They became our friends. A few of them had run the most difficult races in the world. We admired their accomplishments, but we also saw that they were like us—mortals. Eventually Alaska, the mecca of sled dog racing, did not seem so impossibly far away. We let our dreams take over. We stopped saying someday and started saying next year, next month, next week.

Alaska or bust.

The romantic notion that a family can chuck it all and head for the wilderness is simply untrue. In the movies, haggard businessmen take their families, rush to the station wagon and head out of the city forever. Scene two shows the family happily settled in a lakeside cabin. They somehow have acquired their own floatplane and great chamois shirts from L. L. Bean. There is no explanation offered concerning how they got from here to there. For years, I watched such films and wondered, Did they hire a broker to sell their house? Is that how they managed to afford the floatplane? Did Mom take a course in home-schooling the kids? Is anyone saving for those kids' college educations?

There was no carefree departure for George and me. All summer we worked up lists of what to take with us, then made lists of those lists. We discovered that the "bare necessities" of life just fit into our one-ton truck and a twelve-foot box trailer. The truck was specially outfitted to hold the dogs and all our kennel and racing gear. We affixed collapsible outriggers to the bumpers and connected them to chains so that all the dogs could be tethered to the truck when we stopped. The box trailer held a folding table and chairs, a few pots and pans, four coffee mugs, blankets, air mattresses, sleeping bags, and clothing. Day after day I sifted through our possessions, assessing, deciding exactly which coffee mugs were going and exactly how many towels we'd need. I sorted through drawers, determining which clothes we could live without, all the while thinking that we were going to miss certain comforts and favorite items we'd previously taken for granted. Thanksgiving and Christmas would pass while we were in Alaska, but my silver flatware and serving pieces would be boxed up in a cupboard. My china would remain in a closet. For holiday cheer, I packed only a set of Christmas candlesticks, my daughter's Christmas stocking, and, after some consideration, the ragtag green and red stockings I kept for the dogs' Christmas treats. No tree lights. No damask tablecloths.

The day before we left, George came home from his final day at work. He had taken a seven-month leave of absence from his job. After fifteen years as a professional geologist, he was suddenly a free man. There had been assurances on both sides that George would return to work when our adventure was over and the company would welcome him back, but there was still some sense of being on a tightrope and looking down at an uncertain net. We were giddy knowing that our days were now our own, but worried that those days would become unaffordable on our present savings and sponsorships. Still, we felt we could manage.

My cousin Sandy had worked at our kennel every summer since she was sixteen. She loved our dogs, had learned to drive a team, and over the course of several Christmas vacations she'd even raced in a few short races. In the spring, she'd graduated from college, and I asked her if she wanted to come with us to Alaska. With Kathleen to care for, household chores to do, and my regular magazine columns to write, I couldn't be full-time help for George. He would need someone to help him train the dogs, and I thought Sandy would be perfect for the task. For so long she'd heard us talk of our dream, and in many ways, it seemed impossible to leave her out. When I offered her the job, she jumped at the chance. She even agreed to help me out with a little baby-sitting.

My interest in bringing Sandy along went deeper than just hiring a dog handler. Thin and blond, Sandy had once been a stoop-shouldered, awkward, introverted teen. She was the youngest child of my mother's brother, one of a string of girls who all seemed to be disappointments to their judgmental mother.

After four years of college, Sandy was more self-assured. She was now a wonderful young woman, and I was anxious to protect her from a move home and possible backsliding. I felt it was time for her to go out into the world, and I was pleased to give her this opportunity. Her degree was in photography, and she often focused on the beauty of nature. Alaska seemed like the perfect place for her to ease into both the freedoms and the responsibilities of adult life. The wages we could pay were slim, but Sandy and I agreed the real reward was to be part of the race, to be in the thick of things.

2

The trip west was really a series of good-byes. We stopped in upstate New York, in Ontario, Michigan, and Manitoba, spending each night with friends. All of the friends had sled dogs themselves, and all of them had dreamed of a similar trip to Alaska. The constraints of life, the things that held them back, seemed to be the topic on everyone's lips. I felt lucky, but also nervous.

On our last night in Winnipeg, Manitoba, we visited friends with a young family. Our children played familiar games like hide-and-seek, while the adults chatted about ordinary things: our kennels, our jobs, future plans. All while we talked, I was aware that this was the last in-person conversation we'd have with anyone who knew us. This made the warmth and laughter we shared seem especially sweet.

In the subsequent days of travel, Manitoba and Saskatchewan stretched on and on, flat and motionless except for the occasional twist of the heads of the hawks, who watched from every power line and telephone pole. To escape the monotony and my feelings of uncertainty, I again and again thought of our Winnipeg friends. Eventually memories of that night became scenes, processed and stored in my mind. Not fresh, distinct recollection, but worn thoughts. In that respect, I shared some kinship with the explorers who'd first ventured into this country, and with the immigrants who came to make farms out of its vast grasslands. They must have held pictures in their minds, too, pictures of home, of loved ones, of the eastern shores and of other countries. For those who dreamed of prosperity, the endless rows of wheat and sugar beets, interrupted only by an occasional homestead, were a testament that some dreams come true. For those who wanted civilization, there were railroad tracks that bordered the fields and ran the entire length of the two-lane highway, evidence that cities existed on all edges of the continent. Though it looked almost uninhabited to me, the land was clearly cultivated. Frontier no more.

After three days under bright, empty skies, the Rocky Mountains came into view. At first their peaks looked like high, distant clouds, but soon it was evident that a huge wall of rock jutted up along the western horizon. It took nearly a day to reach the base of the range and begin our climb into the foothills, but then the splendor of Banff and Jasper unfolded. Our cameras came out for the magnificent vistas of river valleys, lakes, and glaciated peaks. At the same time, our truck attracted the attention of tourists, and our sightseeing and dog care activities were interrupted by people who considered us one of the sights.

When we reached British Columbia, our dogs finally quit attracting onlookers, partly because it was now past the tourist season, and partly because dog teams and the trucks in which they travel are not an uncommon sight on the Alaska Highway. We were amazed to discover so many kindred vehicles. Strangers no longer asked us *what* we were doing with our dogs, they asked us *how* we were doing with them.

This was a comfort, albeit a new kind of comfort. Along the Alaska Highway, no motel owner questioned our ability to keep our dogs quiet or to clean up after them. Our routines were familiar to them. This acceptance was nothing short of heavenly.

After passing through northeastern British Columbia, we met other vehicles infrequently, and none were going into Alaska. All were headed south. Every vehicle looked like an enormous pack animal, tied up with tarpaulins, laden with trailers, camper tops, boat haulers, dog boxes, and what-have-you. In one instance, we even saw a small plane being transported in a dump truck. Alaskans, we noted, are quite inventive about moving things from place to place, and they seem to have some unique things to move, so they customize car and truck bodies. Style never seems important in their designs, only function. The results often resemble nineteenth-century peddlers' wagons. Our truck was similarly outfitted. George remarked that he would have felt naked traveling that highway without a trailer and all our exotic paraphernalia.

Towns along the way were commonly fifty miles apart, and I use "town" loosely. We often came to small outposts where only a single building stood to mark that man indeed was there. Each building, referred to as a roadhouse, usually contained a garage, a general store, a restaurant, a bar, and lodging quarters such as cabins or rooms. Some places had entertainment on Saturday nights, and the people, rugged workingmen, would gather from goodness-knows-where to socialize.

In this rough country, there was little reason to dress up. Perhaps not much reason to clean up either. The men had beards and wore wool plaid shirts, jeans, and boots. Their hats ranged from knit toques to broad-brimmed cowboy hats. There never seemed to be many women around, save one or two working behind the counter at the roadhouses.

No newcomer could fail to notice that the men watched any woman with interest. Sandy was unnerved by this and complained that she was repulsed by the appearance of these fellows. She was used to clean-cut college boys and couldn't see that the glances of the locals were prompted by admiration and longing, not ill intent. In fact, these men seemed shy. They opened doors for us and tipped their hats and spoke politely when spoken to. They stared at George with wonder. Some of them seemed to be pondering how a mushing man like him got two women in a country where most men had none! I didn't see the harm of these gentle bears gazing at Sandy's lovely blue eyes. I wasn't insulted when one man working a store counter addressed me as "Miss Red," noting my hair color. Life in these parts seemed based on observation of weather and of nature. Why not of people, too?

It was the Native Americans who unnerved me. They watched us with sullen expressions and took particular interest in our dogs. If we stepped away from the truck while the dogs were out, they would come closer and pat the dogs, but they never risked conversation with us.

My knowledge of sled dog history made me as reticent with the Natives as they were with me. Some of the finest sled dog racers are Athabascans from Alaska and the Yukon, yet most of them can no longer afford to compete in some of the top races. Keeping dogs is expensive, especially in the bush where specialized food and veterinary supplies must be shipped in. Few can field a team without money from sponsors, all of whom later use the musher's name and image to hawk such products as winter clothing, lip balm, and dog food. The sponsors want their products to appeal to the average white consumer. They want the repressed adventurer in that consumer to identify with the musher. Unfortunately, identification runs along racial lines, so few Alaskan Natives are successful at acquiring sponsors, and the privilege falls to white mushers. I often felt like a usurper, someone who took dogsledding—once a way of life for them—made it a sport, and then shut them out of it.

One night in Fort Nelson, we had our first encounter with an Eskimo. He was a Yup'ik man, somehow uprooted from his western Alaskan home. He staggered on elderly legs toward our truck. The dogs were out having their evening meal and the man was delighted to see them. He patted them and clucked at them in a language we did not understand. The dogs happily received him. It looked like a reunion of long-lost friends. The man turned his face to us and we saw that his jaw was twisted from more than one brawl.

"Good dogs, very good dogs!" he exclaimed. "These three!"

He pointed out three he particularly liked, and I had to smile. One was our most prized lead dog, Minnie. The next was her talented sister, Shasta, and finally Shasta's daughter, Patu. He was definitely a man who knew what to look for in a sled dog.

He explained in staccato English that years ago back in his village he'd had a team and our dogs looked very much like his. "Where you get these dogs?" he asked.

"Ontario, mostly," George told him.

"No—bullshit," he replied, certain that George was joking. "These GOOD dogs!" He laughed heartily, gave George a slap on the back, then wandered off.

The border crossing at Port Alcan would give the impression that the United States and Canada do not have friendly relations. The two nations' customs stations are twenty miles apart, separated by a thickly forested buffer zone. The U.S. customs station can be seen for a long way. It is brightly lighted and sits atop a high ridge. Although the actual station is a modern building, I was reminded of the drive up to a Scottish castle. I expected that a moat might surround the place.

The customs official there, a portly, balding fellow in a green uniform, greeted us in an enthusiastic and surprisingly informal manner.

"From New Hampshire?" he exclaimed, glancing at our license plate.

"All the way," George told him.

"What are you going to do out here?"

"Gonna train for the Yukon Quest," George said.

"Is that *right*? That's great! How many dogs in here?"

"Thirty-two."

"All vaccinated?"

"Yessir."

"Okay." He sighed and stood back to look at the full length of our truck and trailer. "I'm from Vermont," he said. "Bet it's pretty back there now."

"Vermont? That's amazing," George said. Neighboring states seem closer together when one is farther from them.

"Well, good luck in the race and welcome back to the U.S.A." He waved us on with a big sweep of his arm.

3

We arrived in Fairbanks, Alaska, on September 16, anxious to get through the city and see our new home. For a year, we had tried to lease a home through newspaper ads or Fairbanks rental agents. Our inquiries had been mostly ignored. Finally, through Joan Buckingham, a friend of a friend, we'd arranged to rent a home in Two Rivers, a little community twenty-five miles east of Fairbanks.

On the day we arrived in Two Rivers, we were unable to contact Joan, so we drove straight to the rental house. We followed Chena Hot Springs Road, a long, bumpy, but paved route that connected the homes and cabins of the community like charms on a bracelet. We passed the only public buildings in town, a small grammar school and a store, and made our way to a dirt driveway. At first, we saw nothing behind the overgrown trees and thicket but a huge pile of refuse. Sandy, George, and I exchanged glances and stepped out of the truck. I released Kathleen from her carseat, but kept a firm hold on her hand while we explored. There was, indeed, a house behind the refuse pile, but it was hard to decide where the refuse ended and the building began.

The house had no particular shape or theme. It was constructed of two mismatched halves of small modular houses, joined by desperate carpentry. The side door was open, so we entered and found ourselves in a dark living room. There were notes hanging from the wall cautioning us that the rug was wet from a recent shampooing. The air smelled of death and propane. A quick inspection of the rest of the house yielded no bodies, but supplied us with much evidence that the roof leaked, not a little but a lot, and that plastic sheeting had, at one time, been stapled up to every window, door, and air leak in the house. Obviously the Alaskan winter often came indoors for a visit.

The kitchen was dirty but functional and led to a tiny dining room, which was taken up entirely by a cheap table and a homely chandelier. There were two small, depressing bedrooms with suspended ceilings that were so out of level that I felt dizzy walking under them. The closet-sized bathroom was musty and the floor tilted so wildly toward the toilet that a false step would have brought one into the customary position for vomiting. A flush of the toilet indicated that the septic system was clogged.

After this look around, George, Sandy, Kathleen, and I all found ourselves outdoors again. None of us wanted to admit that we had been driven out by the smell, even though Kathleen was holding her nose and scowling. Sandy said the fatal words, "Well, we can fix it up. It could be cute." That was when we all realized that the house had no redeeming features.

"Let's look at the trail," George suggested. He gestured toward what appeared to be a vague, unmaintained path. In phone conversations Joan had told us we could access the local sled dog trail system from the yard. Running the Yukon Quest race meant training our team daily for several months, and training a team daily required that we live on a trail. The house was terrible, but if the trail suited our purpose we would have to endure. George was about to go crashing through the bush when we heard a woman's voice, and all of us turned, startled to see a middle-aged woman standing in the yard. She introduced herself as Joan. Her face was framed by long dark hair streaked with gray. She was dressed completely in black, with a flowing scarf, flowing skirt, and high-heeled leather boots. She looked nothing like the able Alaskan woman I had imagined. With a strange simper, she welcomed us.

George took it upon himself to introduce us. When he got to Sandy, Joan asked, "Oh, is this a friend from Fairbanks?"

George was puzzled. "No, this is Sandy. She's our handler."

"Your handler?"

"Yes, you know, someone who helps take care of the dogs."

"She *lives* with you?"

"Yes."

Joan's face became dark with anger. "Well, I don't know," she said. "I didn't agree to rent the house to *her*. My agreement was with you and your wife."

"Well," George said, "we told you on the phone that we had a handler."

"You distinctly DID NOT!" she shouted, stomping one foot like an angry child.

We spent the entire afternoon trying to iron out this case of Joan's word against ours. For our part, I knew we *had* told Joan about Sandy, and I was not at all sure why Joan objected to her living with us. Eventually, it became apparent that Joan was raising the objections so that she could extract more rent from us. She wanted two hundred dollars more a month if Sandy were to stay, and somehow added in an additional fifty dollars a month for damages our dogs might cause. She already had three months' security deposit from us and was charging a rental fee that, given the condition of the place, was absurdly high.

Joan's strange temper came and went in flashes. In between shouts and accusations, she held her face in a girlish smile. It didn't take long for us to realize that there would be no end to her demands. When all possibility of negotiation ended, Joan turned on her heel and called over her shoulder, "Stay the night. Think over my terms. If you decide not to rent, I'll just return your deposit." Since that was the only thing she'd said that sounded even vaguely sensible, we eagerly agreed.

She disappeared into the bush like a sorceress. When I was sure she was no longer near us, I peered through the thicket and saw her enter a beautiful log cabin next door.

Slumlord, I said to myself.

My eyes fell on George. He sat on the stoop of our sad little house, his face in his hands. I walked over and sat down beside him.

"I'm sorry," he mumbled through his palms.

"It's not your fault."

"Yeah it is. I sent the deposit. I set this up. We shouldn't have to live in a place like this."

"Well, maybe we have no choice."

Sandy wandered in circles as George and I talked. Eventually she stopped, kicked at the ground, and said, "Are we expected to put the dog yard in here somewhere?"

"Yes, I guess so, " I told her. "If Her Majesty allows it."

"There's a whole lot of glass here. It's auto glass. I think they must have smashed up some cars here."

"Great!" George groaned. "Just what we need. A team with glass slivers in their pads." He slapped his thigh in anger and stood up.

"Let's find a clear space," he said. "We've gotta drop these dogs somewhere. They've been in the truck too long."

Beyond the junk pile grew a few square feet of safe-looking grass. We all pitched in to feed and exercise the dogs. Though we hugged them and patted them as usual, even they seemed to know something was wrong. We never looked them in the eyes.

As the sun set, we drove off to look for a place to eat. We'd all agreed that there'd be no cooking in that kitchen before it was thoroughly cleaned. We ended up at a very good restaurant near Fairbanks, but I hardly remember the meal. I simply recall that the night went by slowly, and I felt that I was watching my life rather than participating in it. Our Alaskan dream had become a nightmare from which mild shock was mercifully separating me.

When we returned from our supper, we laid our sleeping bags on the dusty floors of the house and stared at the ceilings. Throughout the wee hours, we all had thoughts of giving up and going home. At dawn, I rose and announced, "I don't know where we're going, but we're not staying here!"

Sandy, George, and even Kathleen gave a cheer and leaped out of their sleeping bags. It was time to move on.

George dressed and went off to Joan's house to collect our security deposit, but returned empty-handed.

"She refused to refund the money," he told me angrily. "She said she was keeping it as payment for the anguish *we'd* put *her* through! Then she threw me out of her house."

"What did you do then?" I asked.

"I told her I'd see her in court."

"I'm beginning to think that they don't have courts up here," Sandy grumbled.

We hitched the trailer back up to the truck and drove away from the awful little house.

The general store in Two Rivers housed a café. We ordered coffee there and bought a newspaper to scour the classified ads for information on rental agencies and available homes. After hours of phone calls and no success finding even one lead, I decided to wander around the store and look at the merchandise, just to calm myself. I left the table, bribing Kathleen with a third hot chocolate so she would remain with Sandy.

The first floor of the worn, wood-frame building was one large room. It was neatly sectioned off into the café—a group of folding chairs and plastic-cloaked card tables—a hardware department, a stationery and gifts section, a pet food and sled dog equipment area, and a food market. A small post office window was next to the frozen foods case. Upstairs, on a creaky mezzanine, small appliances and yard goods were stocked. I went upstairs, then down again. I passed the magazine rack and perused the food shelves, but every box of cookies, every jar of peanut butter reminded me that we had no place to go. If I bought a can of soup, I had no shelf to put it on, and no pot to warm it in. For the first time in my life, I was homeless. I thought of our house in New Hampshire, an elegant old Cape buttoned up for the winter, waiting for our return. So very far away.

A heavyset woman strolled into the store and greeted the clerk by her first name. I felt a sudden desire to know someone there, anyone there, by a first name.

The woman said, "Gee, whose dog truck is that out front? That's one I've never seen."

The clerk nodded toward me. She had been eyeing our little group all morning and, as the cashier's counter was located halfway between the café and the pay phone, I think she was aware of our plight. The stout woman turned to me. "That's your truck?" she called cheerily.

"Yes," I told her.

"Oh, well, I have a dog team, too. I live just down the road. You must be new out here. Where do you live?"

It was too much of a question just then. I couldn't hold back the tears. I covered my face with my hands and broke down. A moment later, the woman wrapped comforting arms around me.

"It's okay," she said repeatedly as she led me back to my table.

"It's *not* okay," I blubbered. Sandy, who had hopped up to pull out my chair, hastily explained our situation to the woman.

"She's tired," Sandy justified. "She hasn't had any sleep."

"Don't worry," the woman told her. "This happens to a lot of people when they come here. You'll find a house—everybody does right away." After settling me in my chair, she squatted down and looked into my face. Her blue eyes were brilliant against her weathered skin. Her brown hair, neatly parted in the middle, was arranged in waist-length braids that fell against her red-trimmed anorak. The anorak had seen better days and was belted with what appeared to be a dog leash.

"I'm Laurie Marsden," she said. "I think I can help you. I've got some time this morning, and I'll just stay here and introduce you to everyone who comes through the door. Pretty soon someone will know of a place."

"Really?" I sobbed. As a New Englander, I found the thought of sharing my business with everyone in town *very* disconcerting.

Laurie patted my hand. "Word of mouth is how we do business up here. You'll see. Word of mouth."

I introduced Laurie to George when he returned from the phone. "Any leads?" she asked him, settling right in to our crisis.

"Well, one." He sounded dubious. "Supposed to be a 'musher's paradise' on a road off of this one, a little closer to Fairbanks."

"What's the name of the road?"

"Littleton."

She frowned and fiddled with the leather lace on her knee-length mukluks. "I think there's only one house on that road and it couldn't be that one. I'm sure that one isn't for rent."

"The agent told me it's the second house in."

"Funny . . . ," Laurie said. Then she brightened. "Well, maybe you should take a look."

A tall, thin-faced man in a fur trapper's hat entered the store. Laurie rose when she saw him and hailed him.

"Alan, these people have come all the way from New Hampshire. They're mushers and they're looking for a home."

Alan Parker walked over to us. Laurie rattled off introductions and recounted all the information we'd given her concerning our pathetic twenty-four hours in Two Rivers.

"Who did you rent the house from?" Alan asked.

"Joan Buckingham," Laurie supplied, screwing up her face.

"Figures." Alan nodded, and he turned to George. "So you're mushers. Do you race?"

"Yeah," George said in a voice that sounded small. "I'm entered in this year's Yukon Quest."

"That's great! I've run it a couple of times myself. It's hell, but you'll love it." He looked back at Laurie. "What's Zim Bates doing with his house? It's empty. I bet he'd rent it."

"I bet he would," Laurie agreed.

"Well, I've got an hour or so," Alan said. "Let's go see about it."

George saw three houses that morning, escorted by three total strangers. The houses were either locked up for the winter while the owners were "outside"—that is, somewhere in the lower forty-eight states—or they were for sale, and the economy being what it was, they were not selling.

Alan explained to George that Alaskans are reluctant to leave houses unoccupied during the harsh winter. Cold temperatures cause pipes to freeze. Snow builds up on rooftops, causing beams to shift or crack. Animals take up residence, causing destruction of eaves, walls, foundations, and household contents.

Since demand for rental housing in outlying areas is low and quite a number of homes are not equipped with the comforts a renter might demand, Alaskans often offer an empty house to a house sit-ter—someone who needs temporary quarters and will look after a house simply for the privilege of living in it. Unfortunately, George was not aware that these house-sitting positions existed, or we would have looked for such an arrangement. We were later to find that the phenomenon of house-sitting creates a sort of house gridlock all over Alaska. The effect is that no one seems to live in his own house, and people never write friends' phone numbers in ink, because they are subject to change every few months. In our innocence, George and I were willing to pay rent. For this reason, everyone in Two Rivers was certain a house would become available right away. We were a rare commodity: people with cash.

Friendless and lonesome in the morning, we'd met— thanks to Laurie—most of the population of the village by afternoon. I could put names to the faces of a number of the people who stopped by the café even before Laurie introduced them, because many of them were mushers who'd run the Yukon Quest or the Iditarod. I'd seen them interviewed on telecasts of the races. These people, our he-roes, joined us at our table, talked dogs with us, passed pleasantries, and offered sincere help. I began to feel very much at home.

With five good house leads to work on, we decided to wrap up the day with a look at the musher's paradise the rental agent had told George about. He had explained where the key was hidden and in-structed George to let himself into the place.

A musher named Sten asked if we'd like to stay at his house while we waited for a home to become available, but we declined his offer, thinking it would be a tremendous imposition. After all, he didn't know us and we didn't know him. We figured we'd find a hotel in Fairbanks.

As we drove away from the general store, my eyes remained fixed on its big, flat tombstone facade. I saw the porch, laden with merchandise, and the bulletin board jammed with notices. A long fiberglass greenhouse extended from the left side of the building. From the eaves of the greenhouse hung all manner of potted flowers. The place looked happy, thriving, welcoming. Sure, it was the only place in the village one could buy food or use a public phone, but it was now a point of reference for me, a place where I was known and where people had cared about me. I closed my eyes and prayed that one of the house leads would come through for us. I asked God to help us settle in Two Rivers.

It was nearly dark when we turned onto Littleton Road. Shortly after we passed a nice home, the road ceased to be paved. It deteriorated until it was little more than a raised path, a causeway that crossed a bog. Then it dead-ended abruptly, at what could only be called a high-rise shack. This was apparently musher's paradise, but it looked more like a fire tower.

Wordlessly, George and I approached the bizarre, homemade structure. We found the key under the steps, but discovered that no one had locked the door. In fact, no one had even closed it. We stepped inside.

The first floor was a single room, no bigger than twelve feet square, that contained a few wretched appliances and a rusty woodstove. It took courage to climb the rickety staircase to the second floor, which was another twelve-foot-square room. The third floor was partially open. Fiberglass panels formed a sort of porch. George and I didn't like the look of the floor up there. Some of the boards had come loose, so neither of us chanced ascending another flight. Instead, we returned to the truck, where Sandy and Kathleen waited for word on whether we were desperate enough to declare this our new residence.

"Well," George told Sandy, "you ought to at least look in there to see Alaskan living at its best." We all laughed for a moment, but the laughter quickly faded.

The next two hours were consumed by futile attempts to leave the musher's paradise. We found we hadn't space enough on the small sand pad to turn the truck and trailer all at once. The trailer was too heavy to detach and turn by hand, and it would be too dangerous to retrace our path by backing down the causeway. The roadbed was so narrow and soft that if even one wheel got off the edge, the truck would roll and crush the dogs in their boxes.

George worked the truck two inches forward, two inches back, over and over again, trying to turn it, but it was no use. A horrid stench had filled the air. "Stop it! Now! The clutch is burning," I cried out at last. "We can't—we *can't*—lose this truck! It's all we have."

George turned the key and put his head down on the steering wheel. "We're going to spend the rest of our lives here," he muttered, "in paradise."

"I'm getting help," I said softly. My voice gained force. "It's gonna freeze tonight and we'll all become icicles if we don't get out of this place." I climbed out of the truck.

"Where are you going?" George asked.

"Back to that house we passed. Anyone want to go with me?"

"I will," Sandy volunteered.

Together we started up the road. It was pitch dark by then, on an overcast night, and the road was spooky, but I let my determination overrule my fear.

"I suppose when this gets around Two Rivers we'll be completely branded as helpless easterners," I told Sandy. I tried to see her face, but there was no light at all.

After stumbling along for a half mile, we came to the other house on Littleton Road. "Here goes," said Sandy.

"Here goes," I agreed.

A dog barked as we entered the yard. Then another dog barked, and finally a raucous Husky song began.

"They're mushers!" Sandy and I said to each other with relief.

We knocked on the door and a man yelled, "Come in."

I opened the door slowly and peeked in to see a group of men sitting around a woodstove, sorting dog harnesses. They looked at Sandy and me questioningly, then glanced around at the other men to see if anyone recognized us. When it was obvious no one knew us, one man jumped to his feet. He was tall and wire thin. A long-underwear shirt clung to his upper body, barely making ends meet with the waistline of his jeans. He smiled through an ample blond mustache.

"Come in, come in," he said cheerfully. "What can we do for you?"

"Our truck is stuck down at the end of the road . . . ," I began.

The men looked brightly at one another, and the fellow who was standing asked, "You're driving the dog truck we saw go by?"

"Yes," I said.

"Well, good to meet you. I'm Lou, and this is John, Hans, and Joe. We saw you go down there. That's a big truck! We thought the guy who owned that house had sold it to someone who has even more dogs than we do. You know, retaliation for all the noise around here."

Like an advancing army, the men, Sandy, and I all returned to our truck, led by Lou on his old Ford 9N tractor. Upon introduction, the men bonded with George, a brother in distress, and used teamwork to solve our problem. Lou winched the trailer around with his tractor until the truck could turn and the whole rig could be reunited. They approached the project with such enthusiasm that it took on more the spirit of a barn raising than a rescue mission.

When our truck's headlights were finally pointed in the right direction, a few beers appeared from somewhere. We popped the tops and a sort of social time began, out there in the cold and the dark.

"So you're gonna run the Quest?" John said to George.

George cocked his head to one side. "Gonna try."

John nodded. "I'm a radio operator for the Quest. Now that I know you I'll be watchin' for you." He waved his beer in the air, a little toast to George.

The Northern Lights Motel had only one color of light that I could see: red. Our delay at musher's paradise had kept us until ten o'clock that night. We hurried into Fairbanks and checked into the first motel we could find. We hadn't realized that most visitors at the Northern Lights spent little more than an hour in the rooms.

While George and Sandy dropped and fed the dogs in the parking lot, I stayed in the room and put Kathleen to bed. Wretched homelessness crept back and embraced me. I couldn't seem to think of a cheerful bedtime story to tell Kathleen. Opening a drawer in the bedside table, I found a Gideons' Bible. At least God had not completely forsaken this place. I sat on the bed and held Kathleen in my arms.

"In the beginning God created the heavens and the earth . . . ," I read. Something fell out of the pages of the Bible and landed on the bedspread. It was a tiny white envelope. Can't be, I said to myself.

"What is it, Mommy?" Kathleen asked.

"Oh, I don't . . . really know." I opened one corner of the envelope and saw the white powder.

"Can I have it?" Kathleen asked. Children love all things miniature.

"No honey. It's not what you think. It's . . . garbage." I stood up, marched to the bathroom, and tossed the envelope into the wastebasket. For a moment, I thought about crying, but I changed my mind. Just then the knob turned on the outside door of the room. I startled, but saw it was only George coming in to fill a water bucket for the dogs.

"Look at this," I said retrieving the envelope from the wastebasket. "This was in the Gideons' Bible. I threw it out."

"What did you do *that* for?" George demanded.

"George . . . what do you mean? You wouldn't *use* this, would you?" Perhaps he was more desperate than I thought.

"Of course not! But I'd rather not be arrested for having it, either. For God's sake, flush it down the toilet! The way things are going, it would be just our luck to have a drug charge pinned on us."

I dropped the offending envelope into the toilet and watched it swirl away when I pulled the lever.

George shuffled out of the room and I settled down on the bed, only to be jarred to a standing position again when the phone rang. Who would call us here?

"Hello?"

"Listen honey," a nasty-sounding woman began. "This is the front desk. You got them sled dogs out there and they're makin' too much noise. Our clients can't relax. You know what I mean? Shut 'em up or you're gonna have to leave."

"I'm sorry . . . ," I said weakly, but the woman had hung up on me. For a long moment, I closed my eyes and felt the stinging in my nose, but I still decided not to cry. I'd already had my outburst over this crisis. I figured I'd better save my tears in case some worse situation lay ahead.

The next morning, over breakfast at a Fairbanks greasy spoon, George and I asked Sandy if she thought we should call Sten and ask if his invitation still held. After all, he seemed like a decent man, perhaps in his fifties, cleanly dressed in what I regarded as the Alaskan uniform: turtleneck, heavy wool shirt, jeans, and mukluks. He was even good-looking in a craggy sort of way. I recalled that he squinted, as if to purposely obscure his penetrating brown eyes.

We couldn't stay in that motel, and our dogs had been confined to the truck or the drop chains for so long that it was cruelty. Sandy was quick to decide that someone else's house was better than no house at all.

Sten was gracious, if not also a bit smug, when we phoned him.

"I knew you'd change your minds," he said. "My house is your house. You buy the food. I'll supply the beds."

The week at Sten's house was a classic lesson in Alaskan values. We had come from excellent eastern houses, full of conveniences and fine furniture, and from the rat race of eastern living—high pressure, fast pace. Now we were in Sten's place, a modest house at the edge of the black spruce forest, where the lawn was never mowed and most of the yard was a dog lot. Stakes and chains, dogs and doghouses were everywhere on the property. Inside the house, practicality served as Sten's decorator and clutter was its assistant. What little furniture he had was severely used, but the house did not lack for contents. Shelves, boxes, and piles of books were everywhere. One large poster of the Danish flag brightened the otherwise barren living room walls. The place screamed of bachelorhood and a thorough lack of interest in domestic duties. After two days of life there, Sandy and I conspired to clean the kitchen, vacuum the rugs, and scrub the two bathrooms.

Sten seemed delighted at our participation, but puzzled as to why such actions were necessary. There was, to his way of thinking, more to life than all this sort of fuss. Keeping up appearances was totally foreign to him, as was most organization. Yet Sten seemed to know a lot of important things, like where the training trails led and whom to contact around Two Rivers for any one of a number of things.

His life was interesting, and he shared the details of it freely. Danish by birth, he had followed his merchant seaman father into the trade. World travels had brought him to the United States, where he married an American woman. He had also attended college in the U.S., and there he formed decidedly liberal ideals. Divorce, apparently not one of his choice, caused him to seek Alaska. Though he'd tried twice to reestablish his life in the lower forty-eight, the spirit of the Great Land had drawn him back. During most of his life in the north, he'd been employed by the state as a social worker. He'd lived in some rough Native villages and seen the worst of everyone, it seemed, but that hadn't stemmed his interest in other people. He eagerly observed the foibles of his fellow Alaskans, while carefully withholding any judgments.

Sandy, accustomed to the transience of college living, adapted readily to our temporary quarters, but George and I were haunted by the notion that two adults, parents at that, should not be bumming around the world, stumbling in on anyone who would have them.

Nevertheless, we did not feel *un*comfortable with Sten. He was like no one I'd ever met, yet I felt as at home with him as with an old friend. The effect was dizzying. On the one hand, we had an obligation to find a house of our own. On the other hand, we were being entertained and enlightened by this lively man. I waivered between despair and delight. Nothing in this place was familiar; I had no way of understanding how we were doing. Sometimes I thought we were doing okay. Sometimes I didn't care. I had no scale with which to measure our happiness and our misery.

Days, once crammed with too many activities, now passed at a leisurely pace. We trained the dogs in the morning, following the trail beyond Sten's dog lot. In the afternoon we loafed, read Sten's books, and waited for one of our house leads to come through. At night, when Sten came home from work, I would cook up a storm, and we'd all sit down for dinner and conversation on topics ranging from herbal tea to politics. Often we talked about dogs, the Quest, and Sten's experience in the Quest.

Three or four nights into our stay, he mentioned to us that he had not completed the Quest the one and only year he'd entered. He'd fallen into a creek and had frozen his feet, forcing him to scratch from the competition. Sten's demeanor changed when he told this story. He did not look at any of us. He sat forward, his eyes fixed on some picture in his memory. A chill went through me. Would this be George's fate, too?

A day later, I was searching for some tools with which to fix a dog chain and came across a room full of Sten's Quest gear. Bags marked for the checkpoints, old ganglines, drop cables, and harnesses all lay on the floor. It had been two years since they'd been touched. I had the sensation of stumbling upon a graveyard. Frightening memories lurked here. I backed out of the room and shut the door. Maybe Sten was just too lazy to clean up that mess, I thought, or maybe this was a private museum of sorts. In any case, I was sorry I had seen it.

I was growing accustomed to the very Alaskan notion that if one had food, friends, and a roof over one's head, not much else mattered. On our ninth day with Sten, a man named Sol Martin stopped by Sten's place. He was a shy, woodsy-looking man about our age. Sten had contacted him because he owned the house next door and thought he'd be willing to rent it to us. Sol had wanted to get a look at us before making any decisions. Our appearance must have put him at ease, because he immediately offered to show George the house. George came back with good news: we were moving in!

4

Perhaps it is the fact that many people come to Alaska with the notion that their stay is temporary, or perhaps it is that furniture and things of material value are expensive in a land where everything must be shipped into the state, but our house in Alaska looked no different than other Alaskan houses once we got it organized. Our folding table and chairs seemed right for the kitchen. Our living room ensemble, straight from the Fairbanks Salvation Army store, fit the house nicely. One Hudson's Bay blanket draped over the couch to hide the wear, and a few scenic posters on the walls, and we were settled in.

The large cabin-style home had a kitchen, a living room, a fully equipped bath, and three bedrooms. George and I took the upstairs bedroom. Sandy bunked in the larger downstairs bedroom, and Kathleen had the small downstairs bedroom to herself. After our crowded days in the truck and our homeless days at Sten's, having a place of our own seemed luxurious.

George and I used duct tape to join two air mattresses and that, temporarily, was our bed. There were two porthole windows at one end of our room. At night we were often visited by northern lights. The portholes would glow in shades of pink and green, giving us the sensation that we were watching the world through binoculars.

Training for the Yukon Quest began in earnest, and the knowledge that we were finally working toward our mission calmed all of us. I hung a New Hampshire state flag on the wall in the kitchen. George would carry the flag in his sled bag during the race, in the hope of being the first team from the lower forty-eight to complete the race. Many "outsiders" had tried the Quest, but the challenge had been too much for all of them. We knew it would take more than Yankee ingenuity to conquer that trail. We would have to acquire Alaskan savvy in the months that lay ahead.

Our dogs were as grateful as we were to be living a normal life again. Our yard had an established dog lot, but most of the doghouses had fallen into ruin. We repaired what houses we could, built many more, and drove rebar spikes into the ground near each house. We assembled thirty-two chains, with large rings on one end of each to slip over the rebar. Two swivels, so the chain would not bind up on the dog, and snaps fastened the dog's collar to the other end of the chain. Our dogs were used to being kenneled, but kenneling was impractical at best and dangerous at worst in Alaska, due to the heavy snowfall. Snow could build up in the kennels, allowing the dogs to escape over the fence or causing them to be crushed in their own pens. Chaining dogs on stakes with mobile rings allowed the dogs and chains to adapt to the level of snow. When eventually their houses became buried, the movement of their chains would actually help clear tunnels to their doorways.

We bought an old all-terrain vehicle (ATV) through an ad in the *Fairbanks Daily News-Miner* and used it as a training chassis. It came cheaply, since its automatic starter didn't work. That was no matter to us. We could turn it over when the dogs pulled it up to speed. Sandy and George set to training teams of eight to twelve dogs each day while I watched Kathleen and took care of household chores. Most days, when practice was over and I could leave Kathleen with George or Sandy, I walked the mile to the general store and picked up the mail. There were often letters for George or me, and nearly always something for Sandy from her mother.

Our lives moved at a gentle pace. There was plenty of time for me to neaten our house because it was so much smaller than our place in New Hampshire. Laundry was a snap because we each had brought only the basics of our wardrobes. We had no complicated pots, pans, or kitchen appliances, so fancy cooking was nearly impossible. I took to fixing simple roasts and stews. There was time for everything.

I particularly loved the opportunity to play with the dogs. Since Kathleen was born, I'd given a lot of my dog hours over to mother hours. Though Kathleen was an independent child, she was also very social and well advanced physically and mentally. Just halfway through her third year of life, she could already identify all the letters of the alphabet and recognize many printed words. She required company, conversation, and challenges that ordinarily befit an older child. Since I was keenly aware that some mushers spent more time with their dogs than with their children, I made every effort to show Kathleen that she was not just another puppy. In New Hampshire, that meant some days I had missed out on free time with the dogs. Now there was time for both Kathleen and the dogs.

In this atmosphere, I began to wonder why I'd ever wanted a big house, or a large wardrobe, or a battery of cookware. It all just generated more work and more tension. I wondered if I'd been mistaken about what I wanted out of life.

On clear afternoons Kathleen and I explored our surroundings. A spur of trail led out of our kennel, across a potato field, and onto the Yukon Quest trail. One day we walked to the Quest trail and stood on it. I looked down the trail and back up the trail. I tried to imagine it in winter snow. It didn't feel any different than any other trail. It wasn't at all magic. Not something awesome or fear-inspiring.

I often played little games like this with myself, and for good reason. There are three premier long-distance sled dog races in the world. The Iditarod, which runs from Anchorage to Nome, Alaska, is the longest, with a trail extending 1,150 miles. The Alpirod, which runs in stages through the Italian and Swiss Alps, is the fastest paced. The Yukon Quest is the toughest of all three. In fact, the Quest had been dubbed "a thousand miles of Hell." The principal difference between the Quest and the other epic races is the distance teams must travel in wilderness conditions. All such races have checkpoints, places along the trail where the team must sign in and be accounted for, where medical and veterinary care can be obtained and some sort of shelter can be found. The Iditarod has twenty-six checkpoints between its start and finish line. Teams travel an average of 45 miles and a maximum of 93 miles before reaching successive checkpoints. In the Yukon Quest, drivers have only six checkpoints, spaced 75 to 290 miles apart. There is only one place along the trail where the driver may have any preplanned help, and that is at Dawson City, Yukon Territory, where the team has a mandatory thirty-six-hour stop. During that thirty-six hours, handlers may care for the team. At other checkpoints handlers may offer nothing more than moral support and verbal advice.

That George had chosen the toughest race, the one perhaps hardest for a non-Alaskan to compete in, was a matter of his character and his beliefs about our team. He had a quiet, patient disposition and he enjoyed long hours with the dogs on his team. Our dogs, purebred Siberian Huskies, could surpass many Alaskan dogs in toughness and cold resistance, but most modern racers used hound/Husky crossbred dogs that are speedier than pure arctic breeds. George knew a tough trail might even the odds for our team.

Alaskans breed and keep many, many dogs. This enables them to choose a final team from a large selection of candidates. Zoning laws rarely permit such extensive kennels in the lower forty-eight, even in rural areas. Alaskans also live in a climate that provides them with seven months of snow-covered trails. Ultimate training. A poor easterner is lucky to have three months of full snow cover. Training the dogs to run increasingly longer miles (circuit training) at a constant speed is the key element to maintaining a competitive team. Over seven months' time, an Alaskan team can be brought to peak training in very small increments. In the East, one deals with changing weather and iffy trails, and hopes that the dogs will have enough mileage to stay out ahead of their competitors. Racing in the lower forty-eight is more often a game of chance and natural talent than of strategy.

Despite our team's enormous disadvantages, George and I dreamed of running the Quest with our own dogs. Even among Alaskan mushers, merely finishing the Yukon Quest is considered a great achievement. Winners are viewed as gods. Perhaps the greatest motivation for our dream was the need to know what competitors of that caliber know, to go where they have gone.

Mixed with the excitement of such a great challenge was fear. A specific and personal kind of fear: the fear that we would give the race our best shot and yet would fail. The fear that we would disappoint ourselves and be ridiculed by the people we admired.

That's why I walked to the Quest trail. That's why I examined it. In the warm, golden sunlight of a September afternoon, I decided that the trail was just like any other trail, except longer, tougher. I smiled to myself. Maybe it would be better.

Our neighbors in Two Rivers continued their open interest in us. Daily, teams would pass by our kennel while out on training runs. If any one of us was in the kennel, the driver of the passing team would stop to say hello. Some of the drivers eyed our dogs competitively while they talked. Others paid no mind. In a short time, we'd encountered recreational drivers, drivers who used their dogs for work, and competitive racing drivers including Dave Rummel, the undisputed king of mushing. He lived a short distance from us and had a reputation for being a poor sport, surly with his handlers and intolerant of racing fans. We had met him once when he was a guest speaker at a sports event in the lower forty-eight. He did not live up to his reputation then, and, as I watched him talking quietly with George, he did not seem to be living up to it in Two Rivers, either.

As the days grew shorter, and the northern lights more spectacular, our life settled into a routine. Five days a week, George and Sandy ran teams. One day a week we spent planning for the Quest or doing miscellaneous chores. The highlight of the week was the day we ventured into Fairbanks for groceries and supplies.

Shopping in Fairbanks made me believe, more than ever before, that America is the great melting pot. I often found myself lingering over my shopping list, watching. Scruffy pipeline workers in coveralls reached cracked, peeling fingers toward boxes of frozen pizzas. I saw a tall, strawberry blond Swede select jars of herring from a shelf in the canned meats section. Farther down the aisle, Eskimo women pondered jars of jelly and marmalade. Their winter coats, called parkys, were almost ankle length and made of lush cut velvet, metallic braid, and rickrack. The fur-trimmed hoods formed exquisite mantles on their shoulders. I stared at their beautiful, flat-cheeked faces.

At the fish counter, a clerk waited on a slender Japanese man while a Pakistani couple stood next in line. Under her puffy down parky, the woman wore her traditional draped clothing. The hem of her skirt brushed against lug-soled pak boots.

A hefty man with a full shopping cart pushed by, hailing friends in German. They answered him in English. I turned to look at them. Their knit wool caps and tall, felt-lined boots told me they were fishermen up from the coast. In the produce section, three Athabascan woodsmen looked over the apples while an old Chinese woman muttered to a bin of withered eggplants.

A great number of items were packed to last until the second coming of Christ. These items, such as canned whole chickens, smoked fish, sausage products, and vacuum-canned whipping cream, were available for the many bush families who traveled into Fairbanks only once or twice a year. Bulk sales were the norm in Alaska. Cheese came in five- to ten-pound blocks. Coffee came in eight-pound cans. Alaskans take coffee very seriously we discovered. It is not just a beverage. The Japanese have built rituals around sake, and Alaskans have done the same with coffee.

Any visitor who has braved the cold to bring greetings to another Alaskan receives a fresh, steaming mug of coffee. The roots of this custom go back to the Native people who first populated the land. Teas, brewed from mosses, berries, and other vegetation often had spiritual significance. They welcomed, warmed, and sometimes healed the consumer. Trading brought coffee into the hands of Natives, and sharing this scarce commodity honored both the giver and the receiver. In gold rush times, a pot of coffee was sometimes the only solace for a lonely prospector mining a claim on the Yukon, and for a trapper, coffee is the first pot on the stove when he reaches his cabin on a frozen winter night. Like all rituals, coffee has some rules. We were soon to learn that these rules cannot be overlooked.

On a particularly frosty fall day, George and Sten had gone for a ride on our ATV. George wanted to locate more training trails, and Sten had agreed to show him the area. Our truck was due in Fairbanks for some engine work, and when Sten and George returned home a little late, George bid Sten a hasty thanks and raced off to keep his appointment at the garage.

It had become a custom for Sten to venture over for dinner or just a visit in the evenings. After that day on the trail, we didn't see him for a few days, and I finally phoned him and asked him to join us for a meal. He was uncharacteristically cool to me and declined my invitation. I wondered what had happened.

It was Sandy who finally pried the full story out of Sten. He was hurt that George had not asked him in for coffee after the trail ride. Late or not, that was no cause to overlook a friend, at least not in Alaska.

Fairly certain that Sten had confessed to Sandy in order to give us a second chance, I purchased a good coffeemaker from the general store. The next evening, I called Sten and asked him to come for coffee.

"Why should I?" he said flatly.

"Because," I explained, "we have a new coffeemaker." There was a pause that I knew was a smile.

"I'll be right there!" he said.

Sten's priorities were those of most Alaskans. They place a higher value on human bonds than on appointments or schedules. If someone comes to the door, you don't admit to a prior commitment. Everything stops while the visit takes place.

There is good reason for this. Friends and neighbors—I use the term loosely, for in the bush neighbors may be hundreds of miles away—can easily be the only thing standing between life and death. The newcomer sees Alaskans coming and going apparently at will, unencumbered by permanent jobs, social strata, and restrictive laws. They seem to function independently of their neighbors, but this is not really the case. In a land where nature rules, storms, low temperatures, and isolation put people at risk. People treat others as they hope to be treated. Overlooking a neighbor whose truck has become trapped in spring mud may prompt him to pass your truck when it has stalled in fifty-below temperatures. You don't deny anyone rescue, shelter, or food, because denial is almost certainly a death sentence.

In addition to physical risk, Alaskans recognize a sort of danger that is seldom considered in mainstream America: the danger of descending into madness while living alone in secluded places. As a result, several Alaskan radio stations serve their listeners by broadcasting messages to or from people living in the bush. Each week for an hour or two, the plans and greetings of various people are relayed via programs such as KIAK's *Trapline Chatter*. I heard of children born in the bush: "Congratulations to Mr. and Mrs. John Morris of Fairbanks—you are grandparents! Amanda Kate was born yesterday around two o'clock. Lisa and the baby are both doing fine." I heard of hunters going into the bush: "Party of Martin Swanson of West Bend, Oregon, will meet guide Eric Lowe at the airport east ramp on September twenty-third at four P.M. Expect to hunt September twenty-fourth to October second at Narrow Creek Lodge. Four of us. See you then." And I heard of people coming out of the bush: "Nancy N.: I'll be in Fairbanks October first. Keep a pot on the stove, my love. I'm coming home! Yours, Justin." Though I didn't know anyone sending or receiving messages, I still felt a sense of warmth and belonging.

Blackflies, or some large gnats of boreal origin, took advantage of the relatively mild fall days and descended on our dogs by the thousands late that September. Cold nights seemed to have no effect on lowering their population. I was beginning to think that Alaska had year-round insects. Unable to bring thirty-two dogs into the house or the shed, we watched helplessly as the dogs' ears, eye rims, and lips were bitten raw. One morning, I noticed that our big gray dog Bandit's eyelids were very swollen. His right eye was completely closed. Sticky yellow discharge flowed from the corner of his lid.

"Here, old boy," I called to him. "Let's have a look." I took Bandit's head into my arms and pried his eye open. The dog tensed but stood dutifully still. His eyeball was retracted, a sign of pain and serious injury. A veterinarian would have to be called, but what veterinarian, I wondered. "We'll find you some help," I reassured Bandit.

I returned to the house. George and Sandy were in the kitchen having their morning coffee and planning the day's training session. "We've got trouble," I told them. "Bandit's done something to his eye."

George went to get a look at the dog while Sandy and I scanned the Fairbanks yellow pages for the phone number of a veterinary clinic.

"A few years ago I read an article by an Alaskan veterinarian. It was about improving sled dogs . . . not breeding so many dogs, just better dogs," I told Sandy. "He sounded good. His name was something like Talbot. I only remember that because his brother ran the Quest a while back. You don't suppose he lives around here, do you?"

"Dr. Bill Talbot?" Sandy said, reading the name from a phone listing.

"I think that's it!" I said. "Where is he?"

"Fairbanks. Out by the airport."

"Well, let's give it a try." I dialed the number.

Bill Talbot was indeed the veterinarian whose paper I had read. He was a kind-faced young man with a dark woolly beard. He greeted George, me, and Bandit in the waiting room of the Nesbitt Veterinary Clinic and motioned us into the exam room.

George lifted Bandit onto the steel table. Bandit looked around miserably with his one open eye, while Dr. Talbot glanced at a chart.

"This is Bandit, and we haven't seen him before?" he asked.

"No, we're new here," George said. Dr. Talbot took a quick look at Bandit's eye. "That doesn't look good," he said, almost to himself. Then he turned to George. "You indicated on the chart that this is a working dog. Given his age, almost ten, I'd have to guess he's a leader."

George and I smiled. "Yes, that's right," George said.

"Mmmm," Dr. Talbot said. "Most people don't keep a ten-year-old running unless there's a good reason. He doesn't look ten though, does he?"

"He doesn't run like he's ten, either," I said.

After a brief examination of the Bandit's body, Talbot went back to the dog's eye. He poked and prodded with a light and a few instruments. Bandit stood stoically. Talbot asked us questions about the dog and the circumstances of his injury. Then he asked questions about George and me. George willingly volunteered that we were in Alaska to train for the Quest. That bit of information seemed to hold weight with Dr. Talbot.

Finally he finished the examination. "Well," he said, "Bandit has a bad ulceration of the cornea. Without help, the eye could rupture. I'd like to talk to a canine ophthalmologist in Anchorage, if you don't mind. She might be better able to advise us on our options."

Poor Bandit, I thought. Poor us! We *needed* Bandit for the Quest. He was one of our big boys, a muscle dog. What if we had to do without him? I looked into his big, broad face. He had been lucky before. Could he be lucky again?

In his youth, Bandit had belonged to Ted Thomas, a musher from Ontario. He was born and raised at Ted's farm and grew to be a big, rangy dog who could cover ground easily. Ted hitched Bandit up with Lucy, a smart female who knew her commands well. Lucy's brains and Bandit's brawn proved a winning combination, and Ted enjoyed three victorious seasons with this duo leading his team. Then Ted had a serious accident: his leg was crushed in a tractor roll. His knee was permanently damaged. Unable to balance on a sled, Ted made a pretense of facing reality and sold some of his dogs. Yet he hoped that, in time, he would overcome his handicap, so he kept just a few of his very best racers. Eventually, this group grew too old to be salable, and there they sat, in their dog yard, their glory days behind them.

Ted made a pet of Lucy. He watched the light go out of the eyes of his older team dogs, but Bandit, who was at the prime age of five when Ted had his accident, never adjusted to retirement. He would still whine and look hopefully at Ted whenever Ted passed the kennel. He never forgot what it meant to run.

When Bandit was nearly nine George and I suffered a shocking loss. Dan, our top achiever and lead dog of seven years, developed a rapidly growing brain tumor and died. We were overcome with grief. We had three young leaders coming up the ranks, all offspring of Dan's, but none were old enough to take his place. We had Minnie, Dan's co-leader and mother of the new prospects, but Minnie needed a strong partner. So Ted offered us Bandit.

I was against taking this oldster. After all, we'd lost a fast dog. George differed with me. He thought we should give the dog a try. George was so saddened over Dan that I didn't have the heart to argue with him.

Lack of exercise had greatly expanded Bandit's girth. No musher looking at him would have believed that under that blanket of fur and fat lay the heart of anything other than a house pet. Bandit would have to lose the fat and catch up with the others if he was going to make the team. We weren't at all sure he could do it, and we weren't at all sure it was in his best interest to let him try.

The first day we brought him to our training site, he could scarcely believe his good fortune. He knew from the sights and the sounds that he was going to run again. He barked, leaped, whined, and even foamed at the mouth. He was crazy to get out on the trail. At last his moment came. He was harnessed and brought up next to Minnie. Down the trail he dashed, in lead once again. He ran like a demon for about a mile, and then staggered to a halt, gasping for breath. All the while, his tail was wagging. We had to laugh.

"It's a little more work than you remember, eh Bandit?" George called out.

Despite the rough return from retirement, Bandit quickly reunited his body with his athletic soul. Each day, we increased his mileage, and he soon was back in top form. He never failed to let us know how pleased he was at his second chance. His enthusiasm took on special meaning for us. It eased our grief and longing for Dan, and allowed us to think that some good had come out of the tragedy of Dan's death.

Now, once again, the odds were against Bandit. This eye injury—this senseless injury—would now probably cost him his chance. A long recovery would put him too far behind the others to catch up. Could the eye even be saved?

Dr. Talbot called the morning after he examined Bandit. Dr. Henry, the ophthalmologist he'd consulted, had suggested three options for Bandit: remove the eye surgically, since it would rupture anyway; suture the cornea, which would deprive Bandit of a good portion of his vision but save the eye; or perform a corneal transplant, which could, if successful, restore his vision. In all three cases, an immediate decision was necessary. The most costly treatment, of course, was the transplant, and the latter two types of surgery would have to be performed at Dr. Henry's clinic in Anchorage. In his phone call, Dr. Talbot gave us full particulars on how to arrange everything with Dr. Henry, then brought the conversation to an abrupt end. I had expected him to give us some parting advice, but clearly he felt the decision was ours.

George and I tried to discuss the matter rationally while Sandy hovered. I knew that Sandy hoped we would choose the corneal transplant. Young, idealistic, and not yet independent of her parents' pocketbook, she thought an eight-hundred-dollar veterinary bill was meaningless in the face of the moral issue of whether a dog should be deprived of his vision.

"Bandit is old. Maybe he's had his chance," George said. "We could buy two new pups for what the surgery will cost."

"But we need Bandit *now*," I argued. "We need him this season. It would cost us plenty to buy an adult dog to replace him at this late date, and that is only if there is a dog available." I shook my head. "We got him for free. And we did get one good season out of him last year. Maybe it evens out."

"Yeah, nothing is ever really free," George grumbled.

Ultimately, we decided what I knew we would decide: Bandit would have a corneal transplant. None of us could bear to take anything away from this magnificent Methuselah.

Arrangements were made quickly through Dr. Henry's office. Bandit was booked on Alaska Airlines' afternoon cargo flight to Anchorage. Someone from Dr. Henry's staff would pick him up at the airport. It was all very routine. Animals from all over Alaska commonly flew in to be treated by Dr. Henry.

As we hurried to the Fairbanks airport with Bandit, I told myself that bush families often put their ailing children on medevac flights, sending them off to doctors and hospitals in the city, trusting their lives to strangers, in effect. If they could be that brave, I could certainly cope with sending a dog in, but I felt rushed, frightened.

At the air cargo building, I handed over Bandit's rabies certificate and filled out forms identifying Bandit and releasing the airlines from liability in the event of his death. These forms were also routine, but I hated signing them. They had such an air of finality about them, as if, should the worst happen, I'd have no right to mourn.

George ushered Bandit into his airline crate. Baggage handlers lifted his crate onto a trolley. George reached for my hand, and we stood together, watching until the trolley was out of sight.

There was nothing to do that night but watch the northern lights. None of us could sleep. Finally George and I put on our coats and walked out to the potato field to get a clear view of the sky. The lights were wondrous, glittering all around. Green, pink, and silver, they whirled and flashed in kaleidoscope patterns. The deity seemed quite near. Walking in such heavenly surroundings calmed us.

Dr. Henry called the next afternoon and reported that the transplant had gone very well. Bandit would stay a week in her Anchorage clinic. His environment would have to be dust free while the eye healed and adjusted to the new cornea. He would have to convalesce an additional two weeks after his release, but if there were no complications, he would again be free to run. This was indeed good news.

Bandit's homecoming was such a cause for celebration that all four of the human members of our household went to the airport. The dog greeted us with his big oafish expression and happy swings of his tail.

A few days later, Dr. Talbot called. His voice was even, guarded, as he said, "I was wondering, what did you decide to do about Bandit?"

"Oh, we did the transplant."

"You *did?*" he exclaimed. Evidently he was surprised by our choice. "How did it go?"

"Just fine. He's home and he's doing very well."

"That's . . . *great!*" Talbot seemed to gasp the second word.

It was evident to me that Dr. Talbot was not used to happy endings when it came to dogs like Bandit. Alaska has its harsh realities, and few people would burn a good eight hundred dollars on an old sled dog. In fact, I was fairly certain that Talbot himself thought we were crazy to do so. While he was genuinely interested in the medical facts of the case, a tone of incredulity crept into his voice. "Well, I guess if he's your leader, it's worth it," he said.

I sensed he was mocking me, smiling to himself about sentimental outsiders. We weren't tough Quest mushers after all, but people playing at mushing. When our conversation ended, it ended on a pleasant note, everything upbeat, but as I hung up the receiver, I swallowed hard.

"You think you know us," I told an imaginary Dr. Talbot, "but you don't. You don't know us at all."

"It looks like snow," Sten said, leaning over a cup of coffee. George, Sandy, and I all grinned with anticipation.

The golden light filtering through our kitchen windows was a wintry light, not enough to brighten the room. Looking out, we could see that the clouds were dark with sunset.

"Do you really think snow will come this early?" I asked.

"Hell yes," Sten said, tapping his cup on the counter for emphasis. "We've had snow much earlier than this. It's mid-October. That's rather late, really."

"Well, snow is what we came for," George said.

Sten leaned back in his chair."How's the team going? You getting any speed out of those dogs?" he asked.

"I think so. I think they're training up well," George told him.

"Well, they damn well better because those Questies are tough! Those teams are fast and they'll go by you like freight trains. Zoom!"

He rose and placed his empty cup in the sink. "Well, I gotta go feed my dogs. Thanks for the coffee." He pulled on a dirty blue parky, the sort every Alaskan wore for outdoor chores, and set a rabbit-fur hat on his head. Then he put on his Native-made gloves. The outfit, coupled with his weathered face and thick mustache, made him look fierce. There was no hint that this was a quiet, educated man.

Later that evening, when Sandy and George were out feeding our dogs, the phone rang. I answered it and a friendly voice said, "Hello, Ann. It's Ron." I didn't need a last name. The thick Ontario accent told me it was Ron MacArthur. This was a call we'd been waiting for.

Ron was our main mentor in racing. We'd bought several dogs from him, but more importantly, we'd learned how a true athlete and sportsman conducts himself both on and off the trail. Ron was a gentle and skillful dog trainer, a natural teacher of animals and humans alike. He was a champion of many races. Two years earlier, he'd left his homeland to run the Iditarod. His leader in that race was a bitch named Lightening. Her curiously misspelled name described her—a quick, light-footed creature who took to the snow with ease. Just as legends had grown about Ron, an undeniable master of the sport, legends surrounded Lightening, too. Even then, in the autumn of her career (she was eight), many racers wished to own her.

Just before George and I had departed for Alaska, Ron had asked how were we "fixed for leaders."

"No one can have enough leaders," George had told him.

"Well, now, she's not quite as fast as she used to be . . . she's lost a bit of the edge, but she's a good girl. She obeys commands and has good instincts and she'll get you out of trouble if you happen to get into it," Ron had said, "so I was wondering if you might want to take Lightening along."

We couldn't believe our ears. We instantly agreed to take her. There would be some complications, Ron explained. She'd just had pups and couldn't leave for Alaska as early as we'd planned to go. She'd have to fly up later in the season. Even so, we'd agreed.

By loaning us Lightening, Ron had provided us with a good lead dog, well experienced in the rigors of long-distance racing. A valuable gift in itself. Yet, like the egg-shaped Russian dolls that open to reveal another doll, and then another, Lightening was a gift within a gift. She was a thing from home, a familiar face, and she was a talisman, a lucky charm.

I felt a rush of joy. I threw on my boots and ran to the kennel yard, dashing up to George and Sandy at such a pace that for a moment they thought something was wrong.

"Ron called," I said. "Lightening's coming!"

Snow came that night. Not a howling blizzard, but a quiet, constant sprinkling of snowflakes. We didn't notice that the ground had turned from brown to white until we went out around midnight to check on the dogs. By then, three inches of soft white powder had settled over the land.

In the morning, Sten stopped over for coffee. "See? What'd I tell you? Snow," he said.

Snow meant the end of training with the ATV and the beginning of using what the Almighty intended dogs to pull: sleds. We owned a variety of sleds. Made of strong, flexible wood such as ash and of polyethylene, their mortised joints were lashed together with rawhide or nylon cord. Weighing twenty-five to fifty pounds, some of our models were designed for heavy-duty hauling, while others, light as wicker chairs, were used for short-distance, fast-paced racing.

We needed both types of sleds to condition the dogs for the Quest. Like all distance mushers, we were using a combination of weight training and interval training to produce a team that was both tough and fast.

While the dogs were firming up, George would be getting in better shape, too. In training, the dogs would do most of the work, but during the race, he wouldn't simply ride the runners of the sled. He'd lean, pedal with one foot, run alongside, and generally do whatever was necessary to help the dogs move the sled forward and get around turns. The sensations of riding a dogsled range from something similar to waterskiing to something like pushing a heavy shopping cart up a hill. The weight of the load in the sled and the speed and power of one's dogs create variables. Training with sleds on snow is inherently better for dogs.

A sled dog's foot is designed by nature to travel in snow, so we let our training runs jump from seven or fourteen miles a day to twenty or thirty miles. Once the dogs were running these distances at a good speed, we began dropping two fifty-pound bags of dog food into the basket of the sleds to simulate some of the loads the team would be hauling in the Quest.

To get the most out of our team, George needed to know each dog well. His ability to read our dogs' facial expressions and body language contributed to the success of the team. In general, sled dogs are anxious to run and pull. If any of our dogs failed to display enthusiasm, we knew it was a warning that something was wrong. It could be an injury or illness, physical or emotional. Sometimes several courses of treatment, rest, or retraining were necessary.

The coincidence of Lightening's arrival and the arrival of snow put everyone in our household in a good mood. Everyone, that is, except Minnie. Teamed with Lightening, she was turning in her finest performances over the thirty-mile course, but she was at the same time glum before and after practice. Within a few days, she began to refuse her dinner. At first we worried about her health, but she showed no signs of illness other than lack of appetite. We wondered if the trouble was fatigue. We gave her a day off, but that only seemed to make her more anxious and less hungry.

Finally we decided that, whatever was wrong, it was emotional. Often a cure for this is a night in the house—a little extra attention, some treats and cuddling. So one evening George fetched Minnie from her chain, and as she walked past Lightening, she did something very uncharacteristic. She launched herself at Lightening and picked a fight. Lightening was more than happy to respond with teeth of her own. Jealousy!

Minnie and Lightening were cousins, both out of Ron Mac-Arthur's bloodlines. They looked alike, and were both leaders, but that was where the similarity ended. Even in puppyhood, Minnie had displayed unusual obedience and responsibility. Most young leaders run point, the position right behind the leaders, in their rookie season, but Minnie would have none of that. She spent her first day in harness at point, leaning out of the line, trying to pass the leaders. The next day, and ever after, she ran lead. Her partner was our leader Dan. He was young and fast and full of himself in those days, but not always perfectly responsible. Minnie changed that, encouraging him to stick to the trail and make no errors—intentional or otherwise— at turns. They functioned much like spouses in a good marriage, helping and encouraging each other to succeed. George and I called her "the librarian" because we could envision her glancing up over pince-nez and shushing a noisy visitor. She loved law and order, the straight and narrow path, and she loved being George's second in command. Her greatest pleasure was carrying out his orders to the letter.

When she psyched herself for a race, she watched George, chin lowered and eyes fixed on him. Her ears would flatten back as though she was thinking of speed, and her front feet would knead the ground just slightly as she shifted from paw to paw.

When Dan died, Minnie definitely knew that he was missing. She spent a season leading with her yearling pups, who could not yet match her endurance, or with Bandit, who was too old to match her speed. She was patient with all their shortcomings, a brave widow holding her family together. She was particularly mindful of George, and countered his feelings of loss and frustration with extra effort and enthusiasm. She seemed determined to lighten the burden in his heart. She became his closest confidante, quietly listening to the sad words he could not bring himself to say to any human.

Lightening's reasons for being a leader were very different from Minnie's. Her main goal in life was to have fun. She was an effervescent dog with boundless curiosity, and I think she simply wanted to be the first to see and do everything. She was coquettish, and she batted her eyelashes and waved a front paw to get attention. She quickly surmised that George was the boss and set out to bowl him over with her positive attitude. She was easy to know, easy to love. She was a party girl, and this did not sit well with Minnie.

A few nights of extra affection did much to salvage Minnie's feelings. She began eating again and subsequently demonstrated that although she would never be friends with Lightening, she was far too professional to let personal differences interfere with her work. Lightening let us know that she thought Minnie was a snob, but she, too, stuck to her work.

5

Deepening snow brought a flurry of activity in Two Rivers. With the opening of the winter trail, teams could travel from Fairbanks to Colorado Creek, a distance of more than fifty miles. November training runs became somewhat social, as drivers used the time to practice passing skills.

A bad pass, one in which the dogs on one team stop to investigate, befriend, or quarrel with the dogs on another team, can cost precious time in a race. Worse, it may cause one team's lines to entangle the other team, possibly injuring the dogs. Dogs learn to pass by doing. Each successful pass influences them to ignore oncoming or overtaking teams, so it was common for drivers, even if they were total strangers, to invite other teams to practice passing and repassing when they met on the trail. This was the way George met Jack Patterson. After several days of training together, they identified themselves and a friendship began.

For Jack, I suspect the attraction was linked to business, at least at first. He sold all sorts of sled dog equipment, but since it was mostly equipment we needed to buy, we welcomed his sales pitch. Every few nights George would visit Jack, or vice versa, and the two would spend a few hours trading information.

A round little man with a round face framed in cherubic curls, Jack was quite a contrast to tall, lanky George. Jack was all energy. George was all patience. Like many Alaskans, Jack rarely spoke of his life before he moved to the state, but he appeared to be educated. I assumed he'd been something conventional before he'd become addicted to sled dogs and the north land. A four-time veteran of the Iditarod, he could answer many of George's questions about thousand-mile competitions. In exchange for this information, Jack freely tapped George's superior knowledge of materials science, recognizing that the experience George had gained as a geologist could also be applied to headlamp batteries, runner plastic, and other racing gear.

As the king of barter, Jack thrived on special arrangements. He spoke lovingly of his wife, but admitted that their decision to marry was based on the opportunity to share her health insurance benefits. Another deal Jack enjoyed was the one he'd struck with a musher who stayed on Jack's property during peak training months, and brought with him an exquisite butcher saw that could be used to chunk frozen meats. Jack was kind enough to offer George the use of the saw, too, so one night George and I ventured over to Jack's place with our own boxes of frozen meat.

Jack's small, self-designed house wasn't far from ours. It stood at the end of a narrow, snow-covered road. Its side yard was a sizable dog lot, illuminated by lights that would do a baseball field proud. On a half-finished deck, the butcher saw glowed under its own floodlight, like an icon on an altar. Some sort of bags were piled against the foundation of the house. They were neatly stacked, giving the place a bunker-like quality. I wondered if they were sandbags, put there for insulation. Then I realized they were fifty-pound sacks of ground, frozen meat. Jack was using the great outdoors for a freezer and taking advantage of the weatherproofing the inert blocks could supply. In effect, his dogs were eating their way toward spring, the time when most mushers stop feeding meat and restrict their dogs to kibble to prevent off-season weight gain.

Jack greeted us at a door that opened onto the deck. We stepped inside the house and I was introduced to his wife, Lila. While the men's conversation turned to dog meat and the butcher saw, I spoke with Lila. Tall and pretty, she was decidedly Jack's junior. She began our chat with a rush of words the way someone who is shy grabs at an idea and verbalizes it simply to avoid an awkward silence. She told me she'd been taking piano lessons. I couldn't have been less surprised, for at the moment, we were all shouting over a stereo that was blaring a Beethoven sonata. Further, I noticed that the interior of their tiny house was dominated by a new upright piano. As Lila led me over to a sofa, I realized none of us could walk or sit anywhere without encountering the gleaming black monolith. All furniture, in fact all essentials of living had been relegated to the kneewalls to make room for the instrument.

Carefully I edged my way toward the sofa, trying not to brush the keys with my hip. Lila perched on a chair, leaning somewhat around the piano so she could face me. As she described her adventure into the world of music, I caught glimpses of her and her surroundings. Other than the piano, the place was a template of Alaskan living. The kitchen and living room were merely areas on either side of one long room. Water tanks on the kitchen counter and a cloth skirt below the sink indicated that the place was not equipped with running water. Books, books, and more books were stacked on tables and shelved on the framework of the unfinished walls. Behind a clear plastic drop curtain, there were vague signs that a room was being added to the house. However, I'd been in Alaska long enough to know that unfinished walls and unfinished houses were the rule. If a house kept the cold out, it worked sufficiently. Few people hurried to spend time or money on further improvements.

Lila offered me blueberry tea, and I accepted. The stereo stopped altogether when the sonata ended, and I could better hear Lila's sweet, fluttering voice. Though physically present in her house in Two Rivers, Lila seemed to drift elsewhere in her thoughts. Along with her music, she spoke of her church, her plants, and animals while I wondered how such a delicate rose fared among the scrub willows of Alaska.

As abruptly as the sonata had ended, the butcher saw started up, and I could no longer hear anything Lila said. Jack was showing George his method for cutting the frozen meat into dog snacks. He sliced blocks of ground lamb into inch-wide sheets, then diced the slices. Since hundreds of cubes were needed to fuel a team through a long race, this was the first of several nights Jack and George spent at the saw, and I spent getting to know Lila.

In Fairbanks, there were three dog supermarkets meeting the demand for meat and high-fat, high-protein kibble, which we called "doggy rocket fuel." One carried other animal supplies, but these places mainly provided one-stop shopping for all sled dog needs. No matter how great or small a driver's reputation in the mushing community, he could scarcely avoid a weekly trip to Iceman Feeds. Many champion drivers discussed their needs for their kennels, right there within earshot of other mushers. The friendly folks who ran the shop knew every musher's quirks, wishes, and wants, and tried to fulfill every request. It wasn't unusual for mushers to linger in the crowded shop exchanging ideas on training, equipment, and nutrition. No question was taboo within the confines of these walls. Some mushers even chose the shop as a fitting place to display their trophies. Why hide one's honors out in a cabin when all the world could see them at Iceman?

One dog necessity not carried by Iceman or any other of the doggy supermarkets was fish. In fact, fish for dogs was a controversial subject. Alaskan mushers know that fish is a reasonable source of protein for dogs. Fed raw and frozen during a race, it is also an excellent source of water, a fish-flavored Popsicle that replenishes dogs who have become a little dehydrated from exertion.

Coastal Alaskans catch quantities of whitefish for their dogs. Inland Alaskans load up on the salmon that run up the rivers to spawn. Subsistence fishing permits are granted by the state to Alaskans who use the fish as a source of food for themselves and their families. Some of these subsistence fishermen may use a Native device called a fish wheel that nets many fish at a time. Sport fishermen have complained that the subsistence fishermen are taking too many fish in order to feed dog teams. Further, questions have been raised about the true destination of subsistence fish. Undoubtedly some are sold for profit.

When Alan Parker, one of the men who helped us when we arrived, called one morning to ask us if we needed any salmon for our dogs, George said, "I don't know. Do we?" As New Englanders, George and I didn't realize that bargain fish might be illegal fish. We only knew that Alan was taking our needs for the Quest seriously.

"Well, I used a lot of fish when I ran the Quest," he told George.

This information put us on the road to Circle City, a settlement on the banks of the Yukon River. Alan knew a fisherman up there who was selling whole salmon for ten to twenty-five cents a pound, considerably less than the price of fish trucked to Fairbanks. The two-lane dirt road called the Steese Highway spans most of the distance to the settlement and, as Alan warned us, the road is packed snow in winter and not always passable. Nevertheless, we were happy to make the trip because Circle is a checkpoint on the Yukon Quest and the road to Circle roughly parallels the Quest trail. Along this stretch, Quest mushers negotiate a 3,650-foot peak in the White Mountains, the notorious Eagle Summit, where high winds, storms, and blowing snow whirl unobstructed above treeline. A trip to Circle would also allow us a night at its famous hot springs.

We waited for the weatherman to predict three clear days in our region of the state, and then George, Kathleen, and I departed, leaving Sandy to care for the dogs and socialize with friends.

The trip up the Steese Highway is a trip through the history of Alaska. Roadhouses and gold mining sites, some active, many abandoned, line the road, monuments to the fever that brought so many to this frozen land. The F&E Gold Company that held claims in the territory employed more than miners at the height of the gold rush. In summer, sled dog teams pulled cargo and tailings along the rail tracks at the command of their drivers. The "pupmobiles" they pulled were said to be the invention of the famous Leonhard Seppala, driver of purebred Siberians and winner of every important sled dog race held in Alaska in those early days. After his heroism in the Great Serum Run, when he and several other drivers used dog teams to relay diphtheria antitoxin to the isolated and epidemic-stricken city of Nome, Seppala and his team were invited to tour the lower forty-eight. On tour he met Elizabeth Nansen of Poland Springs, Maine. Virtually all Siberian Huskies descend from dogs that he gave her. Passing a dilapidated roadhouse where Leonhard is said to have lived, we saw some equally dilapidated doghouses peeking up through the snow and wondered if some distant relatives of our dogs had lived there.

The road was full of twists, turns, and ever-steeper climbs. After many hours of travel through open country, we approached Eagle Summit. Once above treeline, the land looked unearthly. Everything, everything, was white. No stone or bush broke through the solid cap of snow. Only pink shadows revealed the contours of the land. The sky was clear, bright indigo blue. The awe I felt was tempered by the notion that I would never want to be marooned there. The temperature outside the truck was minus thirty-five degrees, and there was no shelter at all.

As we rounded the shoulder of the summit, Kathleen informed me that she had to go to the bathroom, and I was suddenly faced with the reality of Alaskan motherhood. We stopped the truck, and while it idled, I removed my outer gloves and fumbled with Kathleen's snowsuit. I unfastened her buckles, snaps, and zippers, preparing to expose the poor child to the ravages of nature. We quickly climbed out onto the roadside to take care of business. To my surprise, Kathleen seemed invigorated by this experience. She was reduced to giggles when a gust of wind swept away all trace of her urine. As we scrambled back into the warmth of the truck, I thought to myself that no one, *no one* leaves any mark on Eagle Summit. The place belongs to nature.

Once in Circle, we were to find the gas station. According to Alan, its proprietor would know who was selling the fish in behalf of the fisherman who apparently lived elsewhere at this time of year. In typical Alaskan form, we'd been given a series of names with no surnames attached. Jeff would know if Billy or Johnny was looking after Sam's fish. We found Jeff at the station. He'd been expecting us since the weather was clear. He called Johnny on the pay phone and told us to drive farther down the road and turn left. Johnny would be there to meet us.

Circle City was no city at all. Its welcome sign indicated that ninety-four people called the place home. Little houses stood on pilings on the riverbank. They looked temporary, ready to be moved at the slightest rise of the Yukon River. In fact, Circle City had boasted a large population in the 1890s. A major shipping port on the Yukon, Circle served as a supply center for the mining camps during the gold rush. Although it was primarily a city of log buildings, Circle's residents saw fit to construct some elegant Victorian structures as well, including a grand opera house. As the gold rush came to a close, Circle's population declined. Later, most of the city was swept away in a series of floods. Now no more than a village, Circle's population was comprised mainly of descendants of its original settlers, Athabascan Indians.

Temperatures had fallen to forty-two below zero, yet as we swung our truck around the left turn and got our first glimpse of Johnny, he seemed unaffected by the cold. He was a small-framed Native man, well advanced in age. He waved us on to a driveway at the very bank of the river. George hopped out of the truck and the two men went almost wordlessly about their work. Johnny opened the doors of a small building that looked to be an abandoned cabin and started piling whole frozen fish into cardboard boxes. The building contained a scale. Each box was weighed and the weight was noted by Johnny, who scratched the numbers in the frost on the wall.

As George and Johnny carried the boxes to our truck, Johnny eyed me, but did not acknowledge me. I suppose he thought I was lazy because I wasn't hauling fish, but I was not leaving Kathleen, even for a moment, on this frozen night, for even with the heater running, the cab of the truck was icy.

When the fish were all loaded, Johnny stood back. With a gloved hand he motioned toward the license plate on our truck. "You from far away," he said.

"Yes," George said, "but we're living in Two Rivers for a while."

Johnny looked directly at George, creating a pause of almost uncomfortable length.

"You buy fish," he said finally. "You need them for dogs. Going to race?"

"Yes," George told him, "in the Yukon Quest."

Johnny smiled, revealing teeth and spaces. "Ah, the crazy race!" he exclaimed. "How will you do?"

"Well, I don't know. I'm kind of at a disadvantage," George said. "I mean, being from New Hampshire—the lower forty-eight—and all."

Johnny's face was immobile again, but his eyes were bright. He nodded, as if to himself, and then said, "Many fine racers come from your home. I raced with them. You know Doctor Lombard? Keith Bryar?"

"Yes, I know them," George said.

Johnny waved George toward his house. It was only when they were inside his little cabin, standing before a warm stove, that Johnny introduced himself by his first and last name. He was a member of an Athabascan family that was known for the quality of the dogs they raised.

Johnny spoke fondly of Lombard and Bryar. He recalled the late 1950s when Roland Lombard, a veterinarian and musher from Massachusetts, stunned the racing community by becoming the first man from outside to win a major Alaskan race. His victory at the North American Championship at Fairbanks began a fierce but gentlemanly rivalry with perennial champion and Alaskan Native George Attla. The rivalry lasted over two decades. Bryar, another top challenger from the lower forty-eight, and Lombard ran teams of registered Siberian Huskies against the Alaskan village dogs.

In those days, the isolation of Alaskan villages was often the reason for their success in sled dog events. Strains of "Indian dogs," descendants of indigenous Malamutes and Siberian dogs left by Russian fur traders, were raised for working animals in many villages. Small groups of dogs were interbred over the years, eventually resulting in inbreeding. In the worst cases, it brought out inherited deficiencies and deformities, but it also created super individuals who inherited all the good traits.

With food supplies limited in villages, lesser dogs were put down. The stronger dogs survived to carry on, building a powerful base for genetic excellence.

Village pride played a role in the organization of these superdogs into superteams. Dog owners in each community banded together to select the dogs for intervillage competitions. The most agile driver was chosen to compete with the team.

Outsiders were slow to understand the power of this pride. More focused on individual achievement, they pitted their ten or twelve dogs against the Native racing machines and frequently lost. But outsiders such as Doc Lombard held a trump card in the game: the understanding of veterinary medicine. In 1962, when Attla defeated Lombard at the Anchorage World Championships, a dog named Nellie led his team. Attla boasted that he was willing to sell Nellie for one thousand dollars. At the time, this was an outrageous price for any dog. Weeks later, when Lombard narrowly defeated Attla at the North American Championships, he used his prize money to purchase Nellie. It was only after he'd paid her price that he discovered that Nellie had suffered a broken foot. He nursed her carefully, and she healed. She later led her new owner's team to an unprecedented string of victories, many over her former owner.

As George and I were soon to learn, today's top Alaskan kennels —Native or otherwise—all practice lending, leasing, borrowing, and swapping of dogs. Good nutrition and good veterinary care are considered a major part of their programs. Easterners, still subscribing to the single-kennel order of things, haven't a prayer of competing with them.

After taking a small walk through history with Johnny, George paid for the fish. I saw the door on the cabin open, and George came out through the light.

He climbed into the truck, anxious to tell me about Johnny. "I hope I didn't give him any ideas," George said after a while. His voice sounded sad. "I hope he doesn't bet on us in the Quest just because of his memories."

The *Fairbanks Daily News-Miner* printed a double paper at the end of each week known as the Friday-Saturday edition. Not merely a bigger copy, this edition was indeed two issues of the newspaper, with two Ann Landers columns, horoscopes for both days, and two sets of comic strips.

One Friday, I perused the current events section and noted that the nearby Church of the Nazarene was holding its monthly Men's Night. The featured activity was a cross-country-ski ptarmigan shoot. Sort of a biathlon with live targets, I supposed. Farther down the page there was an article about a successful whale hunt. "First Whale of the Season" read the headline. Eskimos in a northwestern coastal village had landed the huge creature using traditional hunting methods. The leader of the hunt smiled proudly from a *News-Miner* photo. I couldn't help but pause.

Alaskan life raised many questions for someone with my background. The rules were different here, often for good reasons.

"Gonna need a ruff on that parky," Sten said. He sat on our sofa, enjoying a cup of coffee. I had just come in from examining a dog with a broken toenail. A frosty gust followed me through the door. I stomped off my boots and hung up my parky.

"It's a good parky," Sten said, "but later on you're gonna be sorry if you don't get a ruff. There is just nothing warmer than fur and you've gotta have it when it's really cold here or you *will* frostbite your face."

Sandy sat in one of the side chairs. She looked up at me and raised her eyebrows a bit.

"Oh, c'mon!" Sten exclaimed. "You two aren't some of those anti-fur fanatics, are you?"

"Well, I dunno Sten . . . ," I said.

"I think there is no need to use fur if you can replace it with synthetics," Sandy said with an idealistic lilt. "There are all kinds of excellent products."

"Yeah? I've *been there*," Sten said. "Fur works like *nothing* else."

"Maybe," Sandy sighed.

"You're gonna leave here with some fur products!" Sten grinned. "Wait and see."

I stood aside and let the sparks fly between them. Where I was an agnostic on the subject of banning fur, Sandy was a veritable Catholic. On Sten's part, I think the argument was good-natured needling, but Sandy was a true crusader. Highly sensitive about environmental issues, she had a doomsday attitude about the future of our planet, a black notion that it was too late to salvage much of our former grandeur.

I don't know who won the fur debate. I was busy cooking dinner when it ended, but I know who won the war. As the days of November darkened and George and Sandy ran the teams farther and farther from our doorstep, wool hats failed to keep Sandy's ears warm. One day, as we were shopping at Iceman Feeds, she spied a locally made silver fox trapper's hat. She spent a week and a half's pay on it.

6

I was used to the concept that man must protect nature. I did not have much experience protecting myself or any of my belongings *from* nature. A series of incidents changed that. It began with the wolves.

Sandy and George had discovered the carcass of a moose calf when they were out training one day. They had stopped to examine the carcass and Sandy pointed out evidence that the calf had been the victim of wolves. This was startling news to me. I knew wolves lived north of our area, but hadn't realized they ranged so close to Fairbanks. Still, I didn't fear them, knowing that they were shy creatures who avoided contact with man.

One night, close to midnight, Sten phoned us. "Get a gun and get out in your kennel!" he said excitedly.

"Why?" I asked.

"There's wolves coming through. I saw one of 'em out in my kennel. He's heading your way."

For a second, I wondered if this was a practical joke, but I knew by the tone of Sten's voice that it was not.

I called to George and Sandy. George grabbed his rifle and we all rushed out to our kennel. The dogs were restless, stirring about and staring out toward the trail, but they did not bark. George walked out to the trail. I saw him crouch and shoulder his gun. He turned slowly, following his target. I tried to penetrate the darkness with my eyes. Where was the wolf? I couldn't see it.

"He's coming your way!" George hissed.

"Where?" Sandy squealed.

"Down the driveway."

There was a slight impression. I cannot call it a noise or a movement because it passed so swiftly that it left only the impression that a wolf had been there. Then there was just the stillness of the night. For a few minutes the dogs sniffed the air, and then, content that the intruder was gone, they resumed sleeping. Long after they were settled all three of us remained in the kennel yard. Our sense of alarm receded slowly. Finally, when we were absolutely sure the wolf was gone, we returned to the house.

"Would you have shot it?" I asked George.

"I don't know. I guess it depends on what it did."

The phone rang again. I picked it up. "Hi, Sten," I said on a gamble.

"Everything okay over there?"

"Yeah. George saw him. Do we really need to be afraid?"

"Damn straight!" Sten said. "We got a bunch of wolves in here a couple of years ago and they were picking off dogs from all the kennels around here. Christ, we were all out there sleeping in sleeping bags, camping out in our kennels trying to keep the damn things away. They'll kill your dogs, they will. I think they killed eleven dogs that time."

The next morning, Sol arrived to check on the house. Since our first encounter with Sol, I'd learned that he'd been raised in the bush. His family owned Five Tree, a hunting lodge near Haines, and he was a respected outdoorsman. Although it was difficult to engage Sol in conversation—he was a ghostly landlord, quietly tinkering with the furnace or the well, coming and going with polite monosyllabic salutations—I decided I had to chance things and ask him about wolves.

"Sol," I said, when he was pressed in a corner reading the gauge on our boiler, "the other night Sten warned us that wolves were going though the kennel, and we wondered, is there really any reason to be afraid of them? Will they kill dogs?"

"Yeah," Sol said. "They occasionally kill dogs. But they're shy. They run away from you if they can. They don't like people."

"Sten said a pack of wolves killed eleven dogs here two years ago."

Sol settled down into the corner and smiled. "Every year the story grows. You know how it is. Actually a wolf—not wolves—killed two dogs two years ago. Last year, people recollected that a few wolves killed five dogs. Now it's a pack that killed eleven. But I lived here then and I know it was one wolf and it killed two of Annie Wilmer's dogs, and it ran through a few other dog yards, too, but people knew about it by then. When a pack of wolves is together, they hunt all around and they don't bother people. It's when you see a lone wolf, that's when you have to worry. It's been cut off from the pack for some reason and it doesn't have anyone to hunt with. It gets desperate and starts looking for anything to eat. Certain times of year, the wolves don't necessarily stay together, but this time of year they do, so a lone one this time of year means something's wrong."

I told myself the shadow George had seen moving through our kennel may not have been a wolf, but after Sol left, I walked to the outer edge of the dog yard, and I saw the most enormous tracks. They were unmistakably, unforgettably wolf tracks left by only one wolf.

For several nights, the slightest stir from the kennel yard awakened me, and by day I searched the trail for more wolf tracks, but our unwelcome visitor had fled. Things did not remain peaceful, however.

Jack Patterson stopped by one evening full of news about a moose encounter. Fortunately, no one had been injured. A musher named Rick Thomas had been traveling with his team on a nearby trail known as the Refrigerator Loop (a discarded refrigerator lay on the side of the circular trail) when a cow moose emerged from behind the refrigerator and cut across Thomas's path. The moose fled, and the team pursued. Thomas could not stop the team, so he capsized the sled and used his body to drag the dogs to a halt. This was a common but chancy maneuver, for what the driver gains in team-slowing friction he loses in control. Eventually, the moose was out of sight and Thomas was left, heart pounding, to recover from the close call.

By nature, moose will take the path of least resistance. When snow deepens or woods become thick, moose gravitate to trails or any area where the walking is easy. Their eyesight is poor. Their demeanor is stubborn. These two traits combine to make them regard anything that approaches as an adversary. Sled dogs are more than happy to give chase to wild animals. They will dart toward a moose, anxious to investigate. Invariably, the moose will respond as if it were being attacked by a wolf pack. It may initially stand its ground, then kick, butt, and leap fiercely if the attackers get underfoot. A team of dogs may accidentally ensnare the moose in their tracings. The animals become hopelessly intertwined and the moose may stomp and drag the dogs to death.

"Yeah," Jack said, tipping back in one of our living room chairs, "snow's getting deep and the moose are coming in, so be careful. We have a time around here—sunset—when the moose get active. We call it Moose Happy Hour. You oughta carry guns. I wouldn't train without one."

Two days later, we were alarmed to see three moose—a cow, a calf, and a bull—crossing the potato field. We'd had a few exciting moments with New Hampshire moose, but we'd never seen moose as large as these three. Alaskan moose, we discovered, are a subspecies of *Alces alces,* so classified because of their grander size. Our three moose took up residency, yarding up in a small clearing in the spruce trees at the far edge of the field. It behooved us to watch their comings and goings. We noted that they would get on the trail at first light and then wander somewhere away from the area during the day. We did not realize at first that they were returning in the evenings.

At the mushers' club meeting George asked if anyone knew a way to move the moose away from our trail. "Put a bale of hay in Dave Rummel's driveway," was the wry response. "Let it go eat at his house."

Daily we heard more neighborhood rumblings about close calls with moose. Then one evening, George was returning from a practice run. Two moose leaped into his path. Both moose jumped over his lead dogs, one kicking up his hind legs so far that George could see the underside of his hooves. Minnie and Lightening were startled and bolted forward. Both moose tried to head for the woods, but they were pinned against an old fence that ran along the trail's edge. The moose panicked, turned back, and galloped along next to the team, inches from the dogs. George gripped the sled, thinking that at any moment the moose would collide with the team and he'd see his precious dogs dashed to bits before his eyes, but a break in the fence came just in time and the moose veered off into the spruce trees.

I was waiting in the field when he returned that evening. It was just getting dark when he arrived. The beacon of his headlamp highlighted his face. He wore a dazed expression.

"What's the matter?" I asked.

He looked down at the team and tied them off. Slowly he walked to the front of the team, dropped down on his knees in the snow, and hugged Minnie and Lightening. "Moose," he said.

"Oh, no!" I cried. "Are you okay?"

"Ann . . . it could have been over, all over, *just like that*. No dogs, no Quest."

The temperature was well below freezing, but he rubbed sweat and melting snow from his face. Suddenly his eyes widened. "Did Sandy see them?" he asked.

"Sandy's not in yet," I told him.

"She's not? She left before me! She was running the shorter course."

"Oh, no!"

George sprang to his feet, then stopped. We could hear Sandy's voice in the distance calling to her leaders to take the last turn on the trail. When her team pulled up, we both ran toward her.

"Are you okay?" we shouted.

She was covered with snow, evidence that she had been dragged behind her team. "News travels fast," she said with disgust. She removed her outer gloves and fumbled to tie her team off.

"Did your dogs chase the moose?" George asked.

She wrinkled up her face. "Moose? What moose?"

"You mean you didn't see them?"

"No," she said. "Did you?"

"Yeah. Now what are *you* talking about?"

Sandy started to laugh. "Now I feel kinda lucky. I thought *my* run was bad! I stopped halfway through the practice and hooked down to check feet and see if anyone needed booties, and Abe chewed through the gangline! He let the front six dogs loose, and there I was with just him and the other wheel dog. I took off after the loose dogs and grabbed for their gangline, and I got it, but then I was dragging along behind them on my belly, yelling for them to stop. Who should pass me but Dave Rummel, and right then and there our teams did a head-on pass, a perfect one, except that I'm dragging along. He says to me, 'It's a lot easier to mush *with* a sled.' Then I look, and here comes Abe, Comet, and my sled down the trail behind me. They pulled so hard they popped the hook and followed me. So Dave stopped and held my leaders while I strung the line together with an extra neckline. I prayed all the way home it wouldn't come apart on me."

We all laughed with relief.

Sandy's mishap was not unusual. Sled dogs are easily capable of pulling twice their body weight. A team in harness functions much like any dog pack. Their excitement is infectious. When a team is being hooked up to the sled, the sled must be tied to some stationary object to keep the dogs from running off before they are all on the line. Once the line is released and the dogs are running, they quiet down instantly and get to work moving down the trail. If a driver wishes to stop along a trail, he slows the team by voice command and by dragging the sled brake. When fully stopped, the driver holds the team with a metal claw or hook that he stomps into the snow. The snowhook may hold the team for several minutes, but a team that is anxious to go will eventually pull the hook loose. Many an ill-prepared dog driver has been left behind while his team raced off into the distance.

To George's chagrin, Sandy viewed the moose as harmless friends. She tracked them and photographed them. She spoke fondly of their doings way too often for George's taste. Then one afternoon just before Thanksgiving, her feelings were radically changed.

I saw her team come in from a training run. She hooked the dogs off and did not unhitch them or offer them water, but instead headed directly for the back door. She staggered into the kitchen and slumped in a chair.

"What's wrong?" I asked. She couldn't speak, but her shoulders were shaking. Her eyes filled with tears. Her mouth made the shape of the word "moose." I knelt down and clasped her arms with my hands. "Are you hurt?" I asked. She shook her head.

"Any of the dogs hurt?"

"No," she sobbed. She was finally able to gulp in enough air to cry aloud. While she cried, I removed her hat, gloves, and boots. I watched her carefully to be sure she wasn't injured and simply too shocked to be aware of it. I was worried that the dogs might have been injured, too. I wanted to see them, but I needed to comfort Sandy. My thoughts raced.

Eventually Sandy took a deep breath. "I was coming down the trail," she gasped. "The bull moose came right onto the trail and right at my lead dogs. He stomped right over the team! It all happened so fast! The dogs crouched and stopped, and then they started forward and I was thrown into the moose. My forehead hit its belly. Ann, he was so big, so big!" She began to cry again.

I heard the dogs in the kennel yard barking, a sign that George's team was back. I rushed to the door and saw George hooking down his dogs.

"Are you okay?" I called to him.

"Yes," he shouted.

"Sandy's had moose trouble. Will you check over her team?"

There were no injuries, but later we realized that, simply by coincidence, Sandy had been driving a team of eight dogs, all of whom represented a single bloodline in our kennel. We decided, as a precaution, to mix teams in the future rather than risk wiping out a whole family.

Before Sandy or George trained again, we took another precaution. We went down to the shooting range and polished up on our marksmanship. Sandy, who had previously been opposed to carrying a firearm, proved a deadeye with a 12-gauge shotgun. For the rest of the winter, we carried guns when out with the teams or in the back country.

"It's the only sensible thing to do," Jack Patterson assured us.

Still, one can be too cautious. One night not long after Sandy's moose encounter, I was awakened by noise from the kennel. The dogs were barking. I thought perhaps one of the dogs was loose, so I headed downstairs and peered out the living room window. The moon was bright and full. At first I thought the shadows it created were spooking the dogs. Then I saw eight huge legs walking among the dogs. I could not see anything above the legs because of the low branches of the spruce trees in the kennel yard. I had heard of this: moose wandering through a kennel yard and stomping dogs. The dogs, tied to their posts, were defenseless in this situation.

"Moose!" I yelled. "George, Sandy, get up! Moose in the kennel yard!" My cries awakened everyone in the house. I grabbed my parky and threw it on over my flannel nightgown. I slid my feet into my boots and rushed out to save our dogs from destruction. Picking up a heavy snow shovel that was resting against the barn door, I headed for a face-off with our intruders. Sandy was right behind me in her nightgown and parky. She waved a broom. George was the only intelligent one among us. He brought his rifle. Kathleen toddled to the door and called to us. We shouted to her to stay back.

I don't know what I thought I was going to do with that shovel. I just knew I couldn't bear to have any one of our dogs crushed to death. As I approached the offending legs, I looked up and realized that they belonged not to moose, but to two horses.

When the horses saw me, they walked right up to me, as if greeting a friend. I lowered my shovel. Sandy and George stopped short behind me, and we all burst out laughing. The horses had been enjoying the straw lining our dogs' houses. We surmised that they'd escaped from a stable that was a little farther down the trail, so George drove them back to their barnyard while Sandy and I returned to the house.

       To say that sled dogs change a person's life is an understatement. Aside from the hands-on things one learns about dogs, dog care, dog gear, racing strategy, and the like, there is also a body of knowledge that comes to the musher secondhand, by-products of the life dogs have caused the musher to lead. If I didn't have sled dogs, I wouldn't have been lured to Alaska. If I hadn't lived in Alaska I would never have understood saunas.

       Behind our house, there was a quaint little log cabin that Sol had called a sauna. It stood about eight feet high at the roof peak, had a footprint of about ten feet by ten feet, and had just one little vent window and a solid wood door. When I first inspected this building, I wondered what we'd use it for. It was too elegant to turn into a communal doghouse, too devoid of windows to be a playhouse for Kathleen. I thought of using it for storage, but there was already a sizable shed on the property that was more convenient to the kennel yard.

       Eventually, I decided that we should use the building for its original purpose and have a sauna just so the building would not go completely to waste. I had never been fond of saunas, but I thought I might get used to one if I had one. I have never seen the joy in sweating. I like my body clean and dry, and excessive heat gives me a headache. Yet I found myself asking for a barrel stove kit for my birthday. Not jewelry or perfume, but a black cast iron stove kit so we could fire up the sauna.

       It was no problem locating a free barrel to go with the stove kit. Alaskans never throw anything out. They have elevated recycling to an art. For instance, late-model cars and trucks are not common. People run their vehicles forever. In fact, any motorized machine still capable of service is powering a sawmill, washing machine, homemade heater, or dog food mixer, regardless of whether it began life as a Cadillac or a plane engine. Alaskans are similarly fond of containers. They hoard everything from drywall compound buckets to food jars. Finding a steel oil drum was simple: we just dug around in the snow behind the shed until we uncovered one.

The barrel we selected was already stripped of paint and contained no remnants of hazardous waste that we could see. In just two hours' time, George and I had the barrel stove constructed and in place in the sauna. A copper stovepipe, also gleaned from the yard, ran from the top of the stove up through the thimble in the roof. We were ready to explore the true mysteries of the sauna.

I laid a small fire of dry spruce logs and plywood scraps left over from doghouse construction. I struck a match and stood back. In just a few minutes, the building began to heat up.

I was lulling myself into the notion that this would be a warm haven from Alaska's cold, dark days when red steam began to rise from the surface of the barrel. The sauna filled with smoke, and I hurried to the door, choking. Whatever burned off that barrel probably took ten years off my life and lungs. For a while, I stood outside in the cold, watching various colors of smoke emerge from the door and the chimney. I felt a bit like I was waiting to choose a pope. When the smoke was just plain white again, I went in. By opening the vent window, I cleared out the remaining smoke, but it was too late for my clothes and my hair—I smelled like a smoked salmon. I threw some fresh spruce boughs on the fire in an effort to sweeten the air and returned to the house for some real reinforcements.

In our kitchen, I grabbed a pinch of most of the spices in the cabinet, stirred them up in water in a tin cup, and brought them out to the sauna. I placed the spice cup on the stove and the air was instantly fragrant. I let the fire, the spices, and the sauna sit until after we ran our dogs that day.

The return to the sauna was glorious. George, Kathleen, Sandy, and I went for a wild run in the frozen air, then stripped down to almost nothing in the dry, spice-scented building. It was an incredible experience. After baking in the sauna for an hour or so, we could step out into the snow and not even feel the cold. After days of wearing heavy parkys, snow pants, pac boots, and hats, the freedom of being warm while attired in less than your long underwear is indescribable.

"I think the dogs have become exercise junkies," George told me one evening after he'd returned from a training run. "The longer and harder I work them, the more they seem to love it."

It was true. We were training them five days a week in frigid temperatures, running them twenty to fifty miles per session, and they were racing along like demons. On days when they did not get their exercise fix, they were restless. Sometimes they howled in concert, and if a human came to hush them, they looked up expectantly, trying to force an unscheduled hookup. Harnesses had to be tucked away in the barn, or they would be gnawed to pieces. At times I felt that we were raising a group of errant goats. They chewed their houses, the branches of nearby spruce trees, even their own feet in an effort to expend energy. They astounded us.

The dogs' exercise-induced high was inspirational to us, their human counterparts. Life seemed to tick along at an enjoyable pace. Some days Sandy watched Kathleen so I could ride with George and help him analyze the individual performances of each dog. Practices became synonymous with accomplishment. Our team was performing better than ever before, climbing to speeds that would have won races for us in the lower forty-eight, and would at least keep us in the running in world-class competition.

"I think," George told me with a hint of surprise in his voice, "that maybe we *do* have a team worthy of the Quest. For the first time, I really have faith that we can hold our own. I just want to finish. That's all I care. If I can just finish that race, I will have squeezed every bit of potential out of our little guys. They are doing their very best. I know I'm not a Dave Rummel and they aren't Dave Rummel's superdogs, but they aren't lousy dogs either. We can hang in there."

The words were music to my ears. A confident dog team and a confident driver are a formidable combination.

Darkness

7

Most evenings, after the dogs were fed, George and I spent time with Kathleen and Sandy went out to visit friends. I can't quite recall how she met Jeffry, but the two began to spend a lot of time together. They had much in common. Both were in their twenties and had come to Alaska to work as hired handlers. Both claimed a passion for sled dogs and the wild country and both dreamed of owning a great team someday. Jeffry was a little ahead of Sandy. He was no longer a handler, but had a job working in a Fairbanks market. He had graduated to owning his own cabin and a team of six dogs. The dogs were mostly other drivers' discards and a few promising pups, but they were a team, nevertheless.

Jeffry quickly became a fixture around our house. His interest in Sandy surpassed friendship and moved to romance early on. George and I found Jeffry a likable young man. He was pleasant, entertaining, polite, and helpful, and he made a special effort to include Kathleen in activities.

"I'm one of six children," he told me one day. "I'm used to kids!"

Jeffry was raised in Florida. His family was of African-American and Hispanic descent. His friends thought he'd gone crazy when, after watching a telecast of the Iditarod, he struck out for Alaska.

"I just felt that sled dog racing was the neatest sport I'd ever seen," he told Sandy and me over coffee one morning. "I didn't know how you got into it, but I'd seen Dave Rummel on the TV and so I got his phone number, called him up, and volunteered to work for him. He told me he'd already hired a handler for the season, so there weren't any openings. So I asked him"—Jeffry shook his head and laughed, remembering his boldness—"no, I *begged* him to let me visit him. I wanted to see his dogs. So he said, 'Okay, c'mon.' He wasn't very happy about it. I went over to his place and met all the dogs. He never really warmed up to me, but he answered my questions and I think he could see that I really loved dogs."

Dave asked Jeffry if he wanted to take out a team. "Of course I said yes," Jeffry said. "Right then he hooked up fourteen dogs. They were all screaming to go. I didn't know what I was in for."

Dave pulled the snubline and Jeffry was off and running. He fell and got dragged. He bounced off trees. He got lost on the trail.

"Thank God the trail went around in a loop and ended in Dave's yard. When Dave saw me coming in, he came out of his tack shed. He got the team tied off and then he went back in the shed without a word. I stood there shivering, dying, really. Then he returned with a heavy parky, a big pair of mitts, and some pac boots. 'Okay,' he said to me, 'You did a pretty good job out there. Take these clothes and come back tomorrow. You've got the job. You're gonna be my handler.' I was in heaven! I was frozen, but I was in heaven."

Jeffry sat back in his chair and thought for a minute. "Yeah," he said. "Dave is a perfectionist. There's a good reason why he's a champion. He's not an easy guy to work for, but I learned an awful lot from him. It turned out okay for both of us, I guess."

The general store sponsored an early season sprint race just before Thanksgiving. Sprint teams and distance teams alike entered this event as a shakedown for their dogs, a chance to see how their teams reacted in actual competition. The trail extended six miles for limited-class teams, and ten miles for unlimited teams. Sprint teams would be using the event to peak their dogs to a fast pace. Distance drivers, whose dogs generally move at a trot, would not be competitive against the sprint teams, but would measure their speed against other teams of their type. Sandy expressed an interest in running this race, so we offered to stack her team with Orah and Kirk, two of George's fast young leaders.

The afternoon before the race, Sandy and I were passing time the Alaskan way, over coffee at the store café. Sten wandered in and checked his mailbox. It was empty. He noticed us and strolled over to our table.

"I see you've entered the race!" he called out to Sandy. I motioned to him to sit down at our table. He flopped into a chair and crossed one leg over the other knee. "Those teams are gonna *fly* by you!" he continued. "You won't know what hit you! They'll blast your Siberians right off the course, they will!"

Neither Sandy nor I needed to hear Sten's thoughts on this subject. We'd heard it all before, not only from him, but also from other mushers who felt that Siberians were has-beens in our sport. In the lower forty-eight George had often had the satisfaction of defeating mushers who taunted us for our choice of breed. Here, we knew it would be a different story. No one could beat Alaska's special crossbreds, so we had little choice but to put up with Sten's diatribes.

"Do you know who Buster Mason is?" Sten asked. Sandy nodded. He was only the top sprint musher in the world.

"Well, he showed up at this race the first year I ran it ..."

"Buster Mason?" Sandy paled. "Buster Mason at a tiny little race like this?"

Sten bobbed his head emphatically. "Darned straight! Just about anybody might show up here tomorrow. That's the thing about Alaska. There are so many good racers, you never know who's going to show up where. Anyway, there I was getting ready for my first Alaskan race and he comes up to me, watches me for a few minutes, looks over my dogs, and says to me, 'I like to pass on the right. So when I catch you, just pull a little left if you don't mind.' You've gotta stay out of their way, because I tell you, these guys are serious."

Sandy stared into the bottom of her coffee cup, trying to block out Sten's words. With a nervous hand, she picked up a spoon and stirred a quarter-inch of coffee. I could see that her race had been ruined before she even got to the starting line.

"Sandy, don't listen to him," I said right in front of Sten. "You just go out there and have fun and do your best."

"Well, don't say I didn't warn you," Sten said darkly. He rose from the table and, in a more jovial tone, added, "I've gotta go. See you tomorrow at the start."

Sandy didn't sleep that night, and as a consequence, neither did I. I heard her get up and get some water, then I heard her making tea. In the morning, she looked ashen, but she said nothing and set to preparing her gear for the race. George and I helped her rig her sled and load her dogs into the truck. We all drove down to the starting line together. It was 10:00 A.M. The sun was just rising in a pink and gray sky. Dog trucks jammed the parking area at the store. Attached to the bumpers of each truck were several sled dogs. They were all barking wildly, enjoying the din and the excitement. Mushers were tending to the dogs, harnessing them up, giving them meat juice and water. Race officials were setting up the sponsors' banners over the starting chute.

Jeffry hailed us from across the parking lot. We found a place to park, and while George and Jeffry helped Sandy get her sled down and her lines organized, Kathleen and I surveyed the other teams. Dave Rummel was there, but no sign of Buster Mason. Nevertheless, there were a few excellent sprint mushers present, and also a fellow I thought I recognized from somewhere else, somewhere else like home. Couldn't be, I thought. Perhaps he just looked like someone I knew, but his eyes, his salt-and-pepper beard were familiar.

I returned to the truck and reported the results of my survey to Sandy. "I think these are all okay teams," I told her. "Some are faster than you, and maybe some aren't. Just do your best."

"That's what I told her," Jeffry said. "It ain't over till it's over."

"So, are you all set? Going to need some help to the line?" someone said to our little circle. It was Sten.

"Yes, Sten," Sandy sighed, "I need some help to the line."

At the starting line, Kirk and Orah leaned into their harnesses, ready to blast out of the gate on the starter's count of zero. Soon Sandy's team was barreling down the trail. The next team to the line was Dave Rummel. Jeffry greeted him as Dave rode the runners into the starting chute. After Dave was away, Jeffry introduced me to Dave's current handlers, Susan and Morse Lessert.

I was amazed to see that Susan was carrying a newborn baby in a chest-style baby carrier. Handling could be rough at times. I doubt I would have taken such a chance with Kathleen. When I remarked about the baby, Susan shrugged. "The pack leaves my hands free so I can scoop dog poop!" she laughed.

Dave Rummel did not win the race. A sprint team did. The driver was an older lady with gray hair drawn up in a neat little bun. I figured her to be somebody's grandmother, and essentially she was, but she had dogs that looked and ran like antelopes while she hung on for the ride.

Sandy finished low in the standings, as expected, but her overall time compared well to other distance drivers, so Sten couldn't say much in the way of I-told-you-so's. The outcome of the race was positive for me, too. I struck up a friendship with Susan that day, and we made plans to visit each other.

After the race, I overheard Sten inviting Sandy to lunch at what I knew was a very nice restaurant in Fairbanks. She declined, stating that she'd made plans with Jeffry. After she walked away, I heard Sten snort, "Jeffry!" and I suddenly realized that Jeffry wasn't the only man in Two Rivers who was interested in Sandy.

I saw the man again a few days later, the racer I thought I recognized from home. He was buying some groceries at the store. He turned to me and said, "Mrs. Cook?"

"Yes?" I said.

"I'm Walter Therriault. I raced against your husband some years ago in Ontario."

"Oh, that's where I've seen you!" I exclaimed. "When I saw you at the race the other day, I knew you looked familiar. Are you living here now?"

"Yes, I'm handling for Henry Sanders." Sanders was a sometimes Quest musher with a reputation for toughness.

"Do you have your own team, too?" I asked.

"Yes, those were my dogs at the race. New dogs. I used to run Siberians back in Ontario."

"Well, we're still running Siberians," I said with a smile.

"They won't do you any good up here," Therriault said bluntly.

I paused. Not you, too, I thought. "I know their drawbacks, Mr. Therriault," I finally said. "But we like our dogs. That's the breed we started with, and we're going to see it through to the Quest."

"I liked my Siberians, too," Therriault continued. "I thought they were wonderful, but I brought them up here and I showed them to Henry and I asked him what he thought. He didn't tell me at first."

It was obvious by the way Therriault said "Henry" that he revered the man. *Henry*'s opinion was very important.

"He said to me"—Therriault was practically whispering now, as if giving away a secret in a crowded room—"that I should shoot my dogs. That they were no good, they had no speed, and they were all shooters." I looked away from Therriault. "So I shot them, every one," he said, "and I got some new dogs from Henry and now I'm going much faster. You should think about this."

"I try not to," I said flatly. I turned toward the door. "I have to go now, Mr. Therriault."

He winked at me. "Nice to see you," he said.

I left the store without the gallon of milk I'd gone there to buy. Although it was only 3:00 P.M., the sun had set. I walked home in the darkness, alternately trying to forget Walter Therriault and trying to imagine what series of thoughts or emotions could lead someone to kill his own sled dogs, dogs that he had patted, fed, trained. Dogs who had trusted him, worked for him. How could he pull the trigger once, and again, and again? Wouldn't the experience haunt a person forever? Wouldn't he see the eyes of those dogs in his nightmares?

The Big Dipper was huge in the sky above me. Vague fingers of northern lights shimmered in the sky, hints of a more brilliant display that would come later in the night. The beauty of Alaska was always visible, always breathtaking. But now I knew an ugly thing about this place too, and even a view of the bright, clear sky could not chase it from my thoughts.

Thanksgiving came and went and felt like Christmas because of the darkness and the snow. Jeffry singled out an excellent turkey for us at the market and agreed to be our guest for the meal. Our little kitchen couldn't hold all the provisions for the feast, so we hung the turkey and other freezable items in the sauna and refrained from heating it up before the holiday. On Thanksgiving Day, Sandy and I dressed in the only skirts we'd brought to Alaska. Since both skirts were basic black, we made sure to wear very different sweaters. I wore the only heels I'd brought, which were also basic black. They felt tighter than usual, and I realized that my feet had stretched out after three months in nothing but pac boots or slippers.

I dressed Kathleen in a chintz and lace dress, and I curled her hair. She was delighted with the pink ribbon I placed in her hair, and she danced around the kitchen, making her patent leather shoes click on the floor. I remembered doing that with my dress shoes when I was her age, and as I watched her, I wondered if I was being fair to her. She was always bundled up in polar fleece and goose down. She wore clodhoppers and pac boots and blue jeans. She'd asked for snowshoes for Christmas, not dolls. Perhaps in her three and a half years with her dogsledding parents, there hadn't been enough ribbons and dresses.

"Mommy, watch me!" she said, making the hem of her dress swirl.

"Very pretty," I told her. Not just the dress, I thought, but the whole package. She had beautiful skin and bright brown eyes and a strong, healthy-looking body.

I recalled that her first word, other than "Momma" and "Daddy," was "self." Fists curled in anger, she would shout this word to anyone who tried to button her buttons, or zip zippers on her clothing, or do anything she wanted to do *herself*.

Right or wrong, I had encouraged and capitalized on this independent streak because it allowed me to continue my own active life. Kathleen was a willing traveler, a junior socialite who greeted new places and new people with enthusiasm. Her positive outlook on life was even expressed by her behavior at mealtime. She loved fish, strong cheese, spicy foods, and a host of items not generally enjoyed by small children. Even on her worst days, she was simply stubborn, but I took this as just another manifestation of her excellent determination.

I watched her wander off to the living room and thought that surely a child with this personality would let me know if she wanted something, anything we hadn't provided for her. But she *was* only three. She could recognize most of the dogs in our kennel. She often asked me to help her write lists of their names, arranging them in teams as she had seen her father do. Her fantasy world was a complete imitation of George's and my life. I hoped that this was because she was like us, and not because I hadn't given her a choice.

"Our house is for sale," I told Sandy as she came in from training her team one December afternoon.

"*This* house?" she asked.

"Yes. Sol stopped by today. I guess he and his wife are putting the house on the market."

"We should buy it."

"I know. I thought of that." We locked glances and giggled wickedly.

"What if we just never went back?" Sandy said.

"We can't do that. Or, I can't. What about our families? Your parents and our parents?"

"Well, I'm coming back *someday*," Sandy said.

"George and I have thought about that, too. We like it here."

I made tea for both of us. We sat in the living room and studied the house with new eyes, discussing improvements we would make if we owned it. We figured out how to add a second bathroom. Eventually, we fell silent. Staying there was just a dream. Or was it?

"Our lease is secure," I said after a while. "Even if they find a buyer, they won't close on the place until spring."

"Why are they selling it?" Sandy asked.

"I guess because Sol and his wife are never going to live here again."

"Did they split up?"

"No, not really. I think it's just an Alaskan marriage, if you know what I mean."

Sandy shook her head. "It's a shame," she said.

We were becoming used to Alaskan marriages, but I don't think we understood them.

Sol was a bush pilot for his family's lodge. He met his wife when she came from the lower forty-eight to study at the University of Alaska. After the birth of their two sons, she moved with her children to San Diego to follow her career. She and Sol visited each other as time and money allowed. They never mentioned divorce, and they seemed to envision some perfect time when they would be reunited, but I had my doubts.

We knew several women in Two Rivers who lived apart from their husbands most of the year. They raised their kids while their husbands fished on commercial vessels or worked on "the slope"— the oilfields of Prudhoe Bay. We also met mushers whose wives were perpetually "outside." While the trails were snow-covered, these mushers remained in Alaska. In summers, they'd return to the lower forty-eight to summer with their wives.

As Sandy and I further explored the pros and cons of staying in the state, buying Sol's house, and learning to call Two Rivers home, I wondered if I could get used to a life of such loose ends. For the moment, the freedom of being away from my extended family and personal commitments was relaxing, but too much independence can take its toll on the heart, too.

The first showing of our house happened just a few days after Sol informed me that it was on the market. A man named Max Regan stopped by and introduced himself as the listing agent. He gave me several of his business cards and insisted on bringing a prospective buyer there that same evening at 6:00 P.M.

In recent weeks Sandy's team had continued to run twenty miles per practice, while George's team had increased its mileage to longer runs. Dogs showing more ability were moved up to George's team. Those with less ability were demoted to Sandy's team. As a result of this divergence in training plans, Sandy often trained on a nearby section of trail while George took his team to more outlying areas. It was necessary to expose potential Quest dogs to a variety of terrain so that they felt confident in all conditions. George sought out flat trails as well as hilly ones, and forest trails as well as those in open country. Most of his new-trail investigations took place in the dark, as the sun was now rising after ten o'clock in the morning and setting before three in the afternoon. He used a headlamp to light his way.

Jack Patterson had described a forest trail that could be accessed from the potato field behind our house. It looped around toward Fairbanks. At a certain point, a narrow path linked that trail to the mail trail, some ten miles from our house. A team could negotiate the narrow path at slow speed.

George chose to investigate the trail that evening. He planned to take the narrow path, but missed the one Jack had described and ended up on another cut-across to the mail trail. The cut-across was brushy and rough. Realizing that he was lost, George hooked his team down and flashed his headlamp down the trail. It looked open enough. He pulled the hook and stood up. The team lurched forward. A low branch, the sort mushers call a sweeper, hung over the trail. George hit it almost before he saw it. His headlamp crumpled against his face. Miraculously, he was not swept off his sled. He felt a warm rush over his eye. The pain of the impact made him feel dizzy and disoriented, but in a few moments he saw that he was on the mail trail, so he hung on to the sled, hoping to make it home before losing consciousness.

I greeted Max Regan and a middle-aged couple at our front door. They were stepping into the living room as George stumbled in through the back door. They saw him before I did, and I heard them gasp.

"Ann, you'd better come here," I heard Sandy say in a tense voice. I looked around the corner into the kitchen. George stood there expressionless. There was blood frozen in strands all over his face, on the front of his parky, and on his gloves. He looked like a ghoul from a horror show. He teetered by the refrigerator for a moment, then sat down hard on the floor. I rushed over to him.

"What happened?" I cried. It seemed like lately I was always asking that.

"I hit a sweeper," he said, and closed his eyes.

I don't exactly recall what happened to Max Regan and his clients. I know I never heard them leave.

I laid George out on the kitchen floor and sent Sandy to check on his team. I examined his face closely with a flashlight and discovered that all the blood was flowing from a two-inch gash over his brow bone. I got a wet cloth and cleaned the wound, then grabbed a handful of snow from the front porch and pressed it on his face. I made sure the edges of the wound were forced together. "Do you feel dizzy?" I asked him.

"Yes, a bit," he said.

"Nauseous?"

"No."

"Any pain or numbness in your neck or back?"

"No."

"Can you move your jaw?"

He wiggled his jaw. "Yes," he said. I looked at his pupils. They looked normal. The eyelid below the wound was puffing up despite the snow pack.

"Can you remember which dogs ran lead tonight?" I asked.

"Orah and Kirk."

No concussion, I said to myself.

After ten minutes, the bleeding had slowed, but it had not yet stopped, and I could distinctly see muscle where George's skin was split. Sandy came in through the back door.

"I unhitched the team and gave them water," she said. "Everybody's okay."

"Thanks. I think this needs a few stitches, but I'm not sure, so I'm gonna call Sten."

Sandy leaned over George's wound and then looked away quickly. "Yeah, better call Sten," she said.

Outlying villages do not have hospitals. A few have health centers. Most rely on emergency medical technichians like Sten who volunteer their time to their community. Sten waded through a gathering snowstorm when I summoned him. He arrived in his better brown parky, the one emblazoned with yellow lettering that read TWO RIVERS EMERGENCY SQUAD. He carried a medical kit.

"Holy mo-lee!" Sten said when he saw George's wound. "I wouldn't take directions from Patterson again!" He bent over and examined George more closely, asking him the same series of questions I'd asked. "Well," he said, stepping back, "I think he's okay, but that cut does need some stitches."

The timer on the oven buzzed as if to emphasize Sten's words. Dinner was ready. A pot of sausage stew simmered on the stove. Instinctively, I'd put on the coffee when I'd called Sten.

George, who had been silent for some time, said, "I'm hungry." He sat up slowly and looked around the kitchen. "The table's set," he continued. "It's at least an hour's drive to Fairbanks with this snow coming down. Then another hour at the hospital, and I don't want to go. I'm hungry."

"He speaks sense," Sten said.

It was cozy in our house. The food smelled good. We were just calming down, relieved that George's injuries were not worse.

"I could put a couple of butterflys on it and see if it stops bleeding," I told Sten.

Sten shrugged. "You could. Then if it's still bleeding after dinner, you could still go into town."

"Sounds good," George said.

So it was agreed. I lined up the edges of George's wound, joined it with butterfly bandages, and all of us, including Sten, sat down to eat. By the time dessert was on the table, the wound was no longer saturating bandages, so we decided to let well enough alone.

Alan Parker's wife, Karen, knew how to make exceptional sourdough bread. When she offered to give me a couple of cups of the yeasty starter mixture, I accepted. When she offered to teach me her secrets of bread dough success, I knew we were friends. Her son was Kathleen's age, and her daughter was just a year younger. We spent long peaceful days together while our husbands trained dogs and our children played. She was a veteran of all that I aspired to. Alan had run the Quest twice and the Iditarod, and she had been there to support him. She'd packed the meals. She'd sent messages to the checkpoints. She'd been there at the finish. A statuesque woman with green eyes and thick chestnut hair, she exuded strength and a kind of woodsy femininity that cast a spell over men and women alike. She was genuine, easy to trust, easy to admire.

One afternoon, while a new variety of sourdough bread was rising, Karen and I sat in her kitchen and caught up on the events of the last few weeks. I mentioned that Sandy had been seeing Jeffry and that we liked him.

"I don't know," Karen said. She flashed her eyes at me, then looked quickly away.

"Don't know about what?" I asked.

"Well, I hear he's pretty cruel to his dogs."

"Jeffry?" I was amazed. "Really?"

"I don't know him, but the Mortons live next door to him. He used to visit with them, get advice on his team and so forth, but they say he had a temper and he strikes out at the dogs. Mortons won't have anything to do with him anymore."

I was stunned. Jeffry spoke so highly of his dogs. He seemed so caring.

"Karen, it couldn't be . . . ?"

"Couldn't be what?

"Prejudice. He's black. Are people just talking?"

"No, I don't think the Mortons are like that, and anyway I heard from someone else that he was beating one of the dogs on his team in front of the store one day. People were going to call the SPCA."

"Really? Gosh, I've never seen any indication of that. I wonder if I should tell Sandy. I wonder if it's fair to repeat this to her. But Karen, he's even nice to Kathleen. He takes time to be kind to children."

Karen leaned over her coffee cup. "I've wondered whether I should tell you about this," she said. "I've seen Sandy with him and I know she wouldn't agree with mistreatment of dogs. But you know how it is when people get into racing—sometimes they don't understand that brute force is not the way to teach a dog anything. Jeffry is new to the sport. He might not realize what he's doing."

"But he used to handle for Dave Rummel. I'd think Dave is good to his dogs."

"Yeah, Dave's okay in that respect," Karen said.

I took a sip of my coffee and sat back in my chair. Poor Sandy if this news was true! Poor Jeffry if it wasn't true. I supposed I would tell Sandy the allegations, but I wasn't sure I believed them.

There is a saying among mushers that goes "No foot, no dog." This means that no dog can be expected to perform if his feet are hurting him. When selecting future team dogs from a litter, a musher looks for pups with thick pad leather and strong, well-arched, and closely spaced toes. He chooses dogs whose feet do not toe in or turn too sharply out, and he sees that the pasterns above the feet are flexible but not weak.

Even such careful selection for proper feet does not prevent all foot injuries. The musher must also use dog booties—small polar fleece socks—to cover his dogs' feet when trail conditions may cause pad abrasion. Booties protect dogs from "snowballing"—collecting snow or ice between their toes. They also place a cushion between sharp rocks or rough surfaces and the dogs' tender nail beds.

There is a knack to fastening these booties in place. The cuff should not be too tight or too loose. Too tight could cause circulatory problems and freezing. Too loose and the booties fall off. In any case, some booties work their way off during every run. While an average bootie wears through after just one or two runs, any lost booties that are still serviceable are worth retrieving, since they cost between sixty and eighty-five cents apiece. Mushers do not stop their teams to chase after lost booties. That would be an interruption of the training process. They do, however, scoop up whatever booties they can catch on the fly. Jack Patterson always referred to his training runs as "gainers" or "losers" depending on how many booties he'd found or lost in a single practice.

Since booties are made by a variety of outfitters and stitchers, many variations in design exist. In the flourishing sled dog community of Two Rivers, an enterprising collector of lost booties had an opportunity to try out all of these variations and decide for himself what sort suited his team. Identifying the owners of the booties was sort of a Cinderella-and-the-glass-slipper task. If one successfully located an owner, one could then order a quantity of the desired booties for one's own team.

While George bought booties from one of the very few suppliers in the lower forty-eight, he too participated in the bootie collect-and-try game. He was surprised when, several days in a row, he found his own lost booties not on the trail, but posted on a fence that ran alongside the trail. Whoever recovered the booties apparently did not want them, but in true Alaskan waste-not-want-not fashion left the booties out for someone who did.

A few days later, George was buying some supplies at Iceman

Feeds when a musher approached the counter and asked the clerk if he could have a little advice on booties. At the clerk's nod, the musher reached into his parky pocket and pulled out a handful of used booties. He laid them on the counter and spread them out.

"I've been pickin' up these booties," he said. "I've tried 'em all, except one, and I like some of 'em. Wondered if you could identify 'em so I could get some more."

The clerk glanced at the jumble of colorful fleece. He singled out a green bootie.

"Well, that's a Dave Rummel," he said. "This one's from Hoffman's. She's a stitcher in Salcha. This one's from Jeff Robbins and these are from FrigiDesign. This one's from Patterson's wife. She makes them. And this one"—he held up a gray bootie—"this one, I don't know."

"Yeah, I don't know either," said the musher, "but I didn't use that one."

George recognized the bootie and was about to state that it was his.

"Never saw anything like this," the clerk said, holding up the bootie. " I wouldn't use it, though. Got a tall cuff."

"Yeah, that's what I thought," the musher added. "Tall cuff lets the snow pack in around the pastern. Bad as hell for the dogs. Forms a bracelet of ice that scrapes the hair and the skin right off the legs."

The clerk shook his head. "Whoever made these must never go out in snow deeper than a couple inches. Maybe it's some recreational musher. Do you mind?" He dangled the bootie over a wastebasket.

"Naw, go ahead. It's these others I'm lookin' at," the musher said.

A new snowfall gave us the chance to run the team in fresh conditions, but we were disappointed in the time it took to complete the run. The power they'd exhibited in earlier practices just wasn't there. We finally admitted to ourselves that the team was in some kind of slump. Dogs, like human athletes, reach training plateaus. Patience and extra effort is required to move beyond these plateaus. Push too hard and the dogs go sour. They become injured or sore, or simply bored with running. They start to act up. Go too easy, and the dogs never properly toughen, either mentally or physically, to meet the challenge of competition.

At the end of a week of slow practices, George returned to our kennel yard early. When I saw his headlamp flash by the kitchen window, I pulled on my heavy gear and went out to help him unhitch the team.

"You're early," I called out. "Something wrong?"

He didn't answer me. I watched him fumble with the dogs' traces, while the team stood still. I had never seen them look so sad. Not a one of them wagged or looked pleased with himself. Not a one of them met my eyes. Looking down the pairs of dogs, I spotted Pete. He held up a front paw. Boomer, his running mate, hobbled on his front as well.

"Pete and Boomer are hurt," I said, almost to myself.

"I know," George snapped. "I don't know what it is. I can't get this team to go! Pete and Boomer are the only two who are even working hard, and *now* look at them!"

We finished unharnessing the dogs and in silence we fed and watered them. I examined Pete and Boomer. For Boomer, it was his shoulder that was troubling him. I couldn't determine what was wrong with Pete.

Later in the evening I tried to talk to George about the slump. "Maybe we need to talk to Ron, Jack, or someone we trust about this slump. Someone who has trained seven hundred miles and knows what to expect."

"I don't know," George pouted.

"Well, we *are* rookies. We can't know everything. Can it hurt to ask? We're easterners. We know about slush and glare ice. We don't know about deep snow and breaking trail. Maybe they've got a method for getting them through this."

George shrugged and walked away.

We gave the team two days off, and gave Pete and Boomer a mild analgesic with their meals. Both dogs were free from pain and on all fours when we harnessed them on the third day. Boomer completed the practice without reinjury. Pete came home limping.

I watched George patiently unhitch the team and water them. Then he walked behind the shed and threw his gloves down in disgust. Another dismal day on the runners.

This was not our only problem. We were finding out from Sten and other mushers that the sled George had purchased for the Quest was too big and too long. Each day we discovered that more and more of our plans regarding the Quest were infeasible, or not the accepted method. We were like an Olympic delegation whose country had sent them to the Games for the first time. Our "country" seemed a tiny, underprivileged place that no one had heard of. We had arrived at the Games only to be drowned in technological advances that completely impaired our already tenuous ability to compete.

Pete's lameness continued. It was frustrating. We would rest him. He would seem to recover. He would run well in practice, but an hour after practice, he'd be lame again. We owned few other dogs of Pete's ability. I tried to convince myself that a well dog working at full potential, even if that potential was less than Pete's, was a better bet for the Quest than Pete, who from the looks of things would have to be nursed through the race or, failing that, be dropped from the team. Nevertheless, my heart cried out for Pete. I wanted him whole again. He was the dog we wanted. He was what we'd had. Now the doubt was agonizing.

Tension traveled from the kennel to the house. Little annoyances started to bother George, Sandy, and me in a big way. No one could stand anyone else's taste in radio stations. If dinner wasn't perfect, everyone felt cheated. Sandy and I disagreed about which soap powder to use in the washing machine. Then we both backed down, feeling foolish and recognizing that soap had nothing to do with our troubles.

Susan came over for a visit and a sauna. "We've been through competitions before," I told her as we warmed ourselves in the little log house. "I've been through pre-race jitters, but it has never been so intense because the stakes have never been so high. I'm just worried. There's a constant fear of having our dogs wiped out by an act of nature, or the fear that George might be injured during training. We've had too many close calls. I guess I'm worried because these are things over which I have no control. Christ, the other day George fell in a parking lot in Fairbanks while he was whisking snow off the windshield of our truck. All I could think was, Please don't let him break an elbow or a wrist! All because of the Quest!"

The candle lantern that provided light in the sauna shone down on Susan's face. In the deep shadows she looked like an earth mother, her long brown hair flowing over her shoulders. She smiled.

"Don't worry. It's push time."

"Push time?"

"Yeah. Like when push comes to shove. Haven't you noticed that everyone in Two Rivers is out of sorts? It happens every year. This is the time to toughen the dogs. Time to see if all that training effort is paying off. My husband is up to his ears in sleds to repair. Every merchant who supplies mushers is going crazy trying to fill orders for dog food, equipment, you name it."

"So what do you do to unwind?"

"Me? I go home."

"Home?"

"Yeah, to Pennsylvania. I get out of my husband's way, I take my kids, and I go to my folks' house as soon as Christmas is over. I can't cope with the fever pitch of this community. No one can."

"Well," I said wistfully, "I'm going to have to. I'm needed here."

I was needed all right. To balance, prepare, package, and freeze some forty-eight meals and two dozen snacks for George to eat during the Quest. I had twelve dog coats to sew: little polar fleece blankets with belly bands and a windproof shell that the dogs would wear when resting in subzero weather on the trail. I had gear to organize, equipment to customize, headlamp batteries to wrap: a seemingly endless list of chores to do and things to pack for

George's adventure. I had been working diligently, crossing each chore off a list when it was completed, but as our slump continued, I found it harder and harder to concentrate on these tasks. Everything seemed to be on hold. My private thoughts were depressive and frightening.

What if Pete didn't recover? I wondered. How would we replace him at this late date? I felt suddenly jealous of the Dave Rummels of the world who kept 150 dogs. They could discard a Pete or a Boomer as weak and move on to the twenty other Petes and Boomers they owned. Our kennel was hanging on by a thread. We had narrowed our field to seventeen candidates for the team. Seventeen from which to choose twelve. The margin for error was too slim.

At night, I couldn't sleep. I wandered through the house and spent time staring out at the northern lights. Negative thoughts lowered me down slowly. I explored each layer of hopelessness, trying it on, checking to see if I could bear it, because the one thing I could not bear was the ultimate disappointment of not finishing the Quest. That would be all the layers all at once. One night, I tried on the idea of withdrawing from the Quest. It was a possibility, I decided.

After practice the next day, I tried the idea out on George. Sandy was off for the afternoon. Kathleen was asleep in her room, so George and I were alone. I thought it might be a good time to talk.

"How was practice?" I asked when he came through the door.

"Just okay. I'm getting used to going slow," he said. His voice sounded weary.

I took a deep breath. "George," I started, "I love you and I know, given the right team, you are the man to run the Quest. I love our dogs, too, but I can separate my emotions for them as pets from their performance as sled dogs. We are trying to race in a whole different league. Maybe we can't succeed. Don't you think you ought to withdraw from the Quest?"

I will never forget the look on George's face. He was stricken. He was a man of nearly endless tolerance, endless gentleness, but this time he lost his temper.

"*This* is the support I get?" he shouted. "This is what I get for going out there every day and freezing my ass to train this team?"

I felt as if a tidal wave had hit me. Then suddenly there was silence. George left the room. The wave subsided.

I stood in the kitchen with my face in my hands.

Speaking of withdrawing from the race had punished George in a way I hadn't planned. Still, I had learned something from his reaction. He was more determined than I had realized, and as determined as I'd hoped. All at once I felt calm. I had needed to ask my question and I had needed George's vehement response. It gave me a reason to continue and to believe.

I stepped into the living room. George sat on the couch, staring into space.

We looked into each other's eyes, and agreed. There would be a Yukon Quest.

8

The solstice was near. A long dawn began after 11:00 A.M. The sky was pink. The trees were backlit. Full sun came just at noon. Kathleen and I bundled up in our warmest clothing and went out to catch the daylight. Gray jays, or "camp robbers," as the locals called them, chattered in the trees, warning us away from spilled bits of dog food they had claimed for themselves. In the potato field there were moose tracks, fox tracks, and the brush-like prints of ravens' wings, left by the birds as they touched down for a bite to eat.

It was hard to ignore the ravens. They cackled and laughed and plotted. They strafed the dogs, surveying the kennel yard for strips of meat or fat. It was not unusual for them to approach our dogs at feeding time. They strutted dangerously close, tempting the dogs to stalk them, yet they never got caught. They seemed to know the exact measure of each dog's tether.

The Natives believe that Raven is the creator. He is a fickle god, a clever and daring figure who often plays the trickster. Even seen through the eyes of white men, the raven is no ordinary bird. It loves absurdity and chance. It remains boldly black in a season when other animals camouflage themselves in white plumage or fur. It is pompous and bossy. It insinuates itself into all Alaskan activities, witnessing and commenting on the daily lives of animals and man.

It is fair to say that, like the Christian deity, Raven is always watching us, even when we are not aware of him. Thus the lines of knowledge and superstition are easily crossed when it comes to Raven. Natives have their rituals and taboos, while whites grudgingly respect the bird with an uneasy sense that the Natives may be right.

It was a particularly noisy raven that led me into the kennel one day. Sandy and George were out on a practice run and only the puppies, the dogs who had been cut from the team, and the old dogs remained in the yard. I liked to make times like this their special time to be loved and patted. Kathleen toddled along behind me, hugging the gentle oldsters and fending off the slurpy affections of the pups.

When I looked around the yard, I felt something akin to the joy a grandmother feels when she surveys three generations of her family. I could not look at a pup without seeing features of his dam, his sire, or his grandsire. It was this sense of ongoing life that pleased me. I loved the pups for their potential, the team dogs for their pride, and for the oldsters, I felt not only love, but also deep respect. They had given us their whole lives.

At the moment, there were four dogs who'd been cut from the team. All but one of them got to run at least some of the time, as they were rotated through Sandy's team. The one who never ran was Firebird, a dark red husky whose features and shape reminded me of Bette Midler. Firebird was affected with hip dysplasia, a malformation of the hip sockets. The affliction is inherited through a complex and recessive set of genes. Like many young dogs with this malady, Firebird did not show any sign of disease. Her body was a time bomb; sooner or later her condition would deteriorate and she would become arthritic and crippled. Sooner or later she would have to be euthanized to free her from the pain.

As a yearling, she'd run well. We'd had high hopes for her. A season later, she had trouble running distances of more than fifteen miles. Her tugline would go slack. Her ears would twitch. We knew something was wrong. The wear and tear of running in a team was pounding her pelvis apart.

Though her body was hardly racing material, Firebird possessed the pedigree, mind, and soul of a sled dog. She longed to run and could not understand why we'd retired her at the age of two. She languished in our kennel, and all the attention we gave her could not fill the emptiness she seemed to feel.

Bred to pull, sled dogs take enormous pleasure in running with a team, but age or accident may steal that pleasure away. They lose their speed. Like human athletes, old sports injuries come back to haunt them, causing soreness in their joints. Nevertheless, many sled dogs resist retirement. They strive to remain useful to their team and their master. When at last the team leaves the yard without them, some become hysterical. Day after day, this sort refuses to adjust. Their misery is so great that they may have to be euthanized. Some oldsters drift off into retirement more easily, but if ever their master comes to them with harness in hand, they will struggle on arthritic legs to ready themselves for the trail. There may be pain in their backs, but there is always hope in their eyes.

Common sense calls for the culling of dogs that cannot be placed and are no longer working. In Alaska, where survival of the fittest is a rule instead of a theory, and usefulness is more valuable than sentiment, culling takes place. George and I knew about culling. We'd practiced it. Not the vicious, wholesale culling of a Walter Therriault, but a sensible sort of culling. If a new pup had no chance of a healthy life, or an old dog suffered in pain, we'd had the vet euthanize it, but we had never put down an adult simply because it failed to make our team. We'd worked at retraining such dogs and then looked diligently for new homes where they could live out their lives as house pets.

For kennels in the lower forty-eight, this is a good solution, but in Alaska, there are more discard dogs than homes available and this creates a dilemma for many mushers. Having watched Firebird linger in an unhappy limbo between sled dog and pet, knowing she equated her forced separation from running with punishment, I could not judge what I would do if I'd been faced with seven or ten Firebirds in my kennel yard. Since there was just one I'd let her remain.

Giving Firebird away meant foisting her on someone who would have to suffer through her eventual crippling. I did not want her getting into the hands of someone who might breed her. So many people breed inferior dogs out of sentiment or greed, ignoring the trouble they pass along to the offspring. Spaying Firebird was the only guarantee that she could not reproduce. In the process of diagnosing her dysplasia we had discovered she was allergic to anesthesia, so I could not spay her without risking her life. I would have to keep her in order to keep her safe.

As Kathleen and I continued our kennel rounds that day, we approached Firebird. She pawed and howled and greeted us with joy. Her face looked bright. Her coat was as red as a fox and thick. In fact, it wasn't only her coat that was thick. Her belly looked suspiciously low. No tuck up. She had *the glow*. I don't know how I had missed it before, because I had seen it in so many other pregnant dogs, not to mention pregnant women. It was that healthy, contented look. I stood back. Kathleen hugged Firebird's neck.

"Oh gosh, Kathleen," was all I managed to say.

"What, Mommy?" Kathleen asked.

"Nothing. Keep patting Firebird." I couldn't explain this predicament to a three-year-old.

I glanced around the kennel yard. Firebird's nearest neighbor was Alex, a seven-month-old pup. Untried in harness, Alex didn't have much of a drawing card as a stud dog. There was no guarantee he was the sire of Firebird's litter, but no males had been loose during Firebird's breedable time, and Alex's tie-out chain looked a little long. He might have been able to reach her if he'd really stretched.

Tears burned in my eyes. Despite all of my plans and convictions, nature had taken its course.

I broke the news of Firebird's situation to George and Sandy when they returned from practice. George was dismayed. I could tell from the look on his face that I wasn't going to get any help from him on this one.

Sandy was strangely hopeful. "Couldn't we just let her have this one litter?" she asked. She was too new to kennel life to understand the heartache of raising a genetically doomed litter. When I tried to tell her we simply could not have these pups, she sulked away.

"Drown 'em," Sten said when he stopped by later that night. "Let her have 'em and just drown 'em when they're newborn. That's what I did."

Sandy's jaw dropped. "You *drowned* puppies?"

"I sure did," Sten said. "One of my females got caught by one of my males. I didn't think he was good enough to raise up pups from, really. So, when the litter was born, I picked out the biggest one, hoping she'd turn out to be something, and I dunked the rest of 'em. The one I saved, that's the one I call Neva."

"Sten, that's *awful*," Sandy said.

"Yeah, well . . ." For a moment Sten looked introspective. "What are you gonna do? You can't keep 'em all."

Jack Patterson was even less consoling when I mentioned Firebird's circumstances to him a day later.

"If the mother is useless, why go through the trouble of having a litter? Put her down before the pups are born," he said.

Over the next few days I tried desperately to decide what to do.

"Have the puppies. Have unwanted puppies," I said one night to my reflection in the kitchen window. I felt a wave of sadness. An arriving litter had always been a cause of celebration in our house. Every previous litter had been planned. A cozy whelping box was prepared, towels were washed and set out with a birthing kit days in advance. We lavished attention on the mother-to-be. We fed her the best of foods. We dreamed about the new pups, speculated on their appearance and their talent. Through no fault of her own, nothing had been made ready for Firebird and no one looked forward to her pups.

A pregnant spay was an option. Canine uterine structure is too complex to permit abortion. The only possibility is to remove the uterus, thereby spaying the animal and removing the fetuses within. The fetuses do not suffer. They are asleep, having absorbed the anesthesia the mother has been given to facilitate the operation. Because of her allergy, such an operation could prove fatal for Firebird. Maybe it was better to expect nothing, to go ahead and end her life and not try to put her through recovery.

Put down her pups? No. I couldn't do that. I couldn't end new life. At least Firebird had her puppyhood and her yearling year to look back on. Not a bad life, however brief.

I knew that some people culled their own dogs. I had heard that a single bullet to the brain was quick and painless if the killer knew where to place the shot. This was the Alaskan way. Self-sufficient. No need for costly veterinary intervention. But this would not do for Firebird. I decided she would die in my arms in Dr. Bill Talbot's office. Injections, after all, can't miss.

I called Dr. Talbot in the morning and briefly explained that I had a pregnant, dysplastic dog whose life I wished to end. "She's not a sled dog anymore," I told him. "She's more of a pet."

"You could let her have the pups and then euthanize them," he said flatly.

"No," I said, "I can't do that. I'm not comfortable with that. She'll wonder where they went. I don't want to torture her."

Dr. Talbot offered no comment, and the silence was awkward.

"She's allergic to anesthesia," I continued after a while. "She reacted when her hips were X-rayed, so I don't think she will survive a spay."

Still no comment.

Did the silence mean approval? Disapproval? This man was part of a sled dog dynasty. He'd seen it all. Culling certainly wasn't new to him. He probably practiced it himself.

"A pregnant spay would be very expensive," I reasoned into the silence, "and, you know, risky." There was not so much as a sigh on the other end of the phone. "Maybe I'm not doing the right thing," I said. "Do you think I'm doing the right thing?"

With no expression whatsoever in his voice, he said, "Ann, you are asking me a moral question, not a medical question."

Now it was my turn to be silent. Firebird was a living, breathing creature, given into my care by the miracle of creation. Since when had I decided that turning my back on her was an acceptable thing?

In the Alaskan mushing community, there was subtle pressure to be unsentimental about "bad" dogs. One could wax poetic about a good leader or a powerful team dog, but let a dog be or become uncompetitive and one was to sell it, part with it, or do away with it in an unwavering fashion. A musher who failed to take action against such "bad" dogs was considered weak and foolish, unworthy of his competitors' respect. Sten, Jack, and others like them adhered to this notion and advanced its cause by coldly advising other mushers to rid themselves of "bad" dogs. Nevertheless, I'd seen a few useless dogs in both of their kennels. Their advice was cheap, given out as proof that they were *real* mushers, tough enough to make the grade. It was a bluff. They repeated the common stories, saying that Dave Rummel shot whole teams when they did not live up to his high and precise standards. I had lived virtually next door to Dave Rummel for three months and I'd never heard so much as a single pop from any weapon. I'd never heard a dog cry out in pain, and common sense told me that Dave would hardly shoot dogs that he could sell for good money. After all, his discards were welcome on the legions of teams that could not compete with him.

Some mushers, after their initial hellish baptism of putting down their first victim, awakened to the realization that they could keep bad dogs. Once in a while, a monster was created, when the pressure got to an insecure person, anxious to "measure up" to his fellow mushers. This was how the Walter Therriaults were created. Strangely enough, such monsters not only failed to receive the validation they sought, they were actually shunned by other mushers. Madmen were, after all, not to be trusted.

If I took the step to euthanize Firebird, it would have been that first step toward madness. As I spoke with Dr. Talbot, I suddenly recognized that I was, indeed, sacrificing Firebird on the altar of validation. I was considering something that, prior to my indoctrination in Alaskan values, would have been out of the question. I decided that this was one initiation ritual in which I would not partake. I was not, and never would be, *that* Alaskan.

For Talbot's part, he risked losing his membership among the tough mushers if he advised me to save Firebird. Nevertheless, his clear definition of moral versus medical issues was, I think, designed to guide me through a fog of mixed values. Perhaps, after all, he did know me, know us, and perhaps he was not smiling at us behind our backs.

The phone line, open for long seconds, hummed in my ear.

"Is there any chance you can get Firebird through a spay?" I asked quietly.

"We can use gas and watch her carefully. That's all I can tell you," Talbot replied.

I made the choice for surgery and hoped with all my heart that Firebird wouldn't die.

Firebird came home with a shaved, empty belly. She was delighted to see us when we picked her up at the veterinary hospital. Kathleen rushed up to her and hugged her. As I watched them, I tried to push aside my guilt over how differently the day might have turned out.

Later in the day, Firebird snored on our living room rug. Sten and Jack dropped by our house.

"You spayed her," Jack commented, looking at Firebird's bald expanse. I had expected his comment to be an indictment of my need to keep the useless alive, but it was just a comment, spoken in a tone that quietly acknowledged Firebird had some value, however hidden from a musher's eyes.

Sten was less understanding. "I *knew* you'd keep her," he said.

"Don't start with me on that macho dog-culling thing," I told him testily. "If that's what it takes to be in the club around here, George and I aren't joining."

"Hold on," Sten said. "Nobody *likes* to cull. We just defend the right to make that choice for our dogs."

"Well, I don't see either of you out there waving a gun around your kennel. You encourage people to do things you wouldn't do yourselves."

Sten and Jack smiled at each other.

"What's so funny?" I demanded.

"Remember Doris?" Jack asked Sten.

I looked from one man to the other. "Who the hell is Doris? Some fool with a heart, I suppose."

"She was a lead dog," Sten said.

"I sold her to Sten," Jack explained, "and I got her from Glenn Frame, who got her from Dave Rummel. I didn't know who bred her. Glenn said he wasn't sure how old she was. He thought about five or six years. She was a great leader. Took every command like that." He snapped his fingers. "At one point, she was getting a little stiff in the joints. I was starting to see signs that she was going deaf, but I hated to put her down because she was still a dependable leader. So Sten needed a leader and I sold her to him. I told him she was maybe seven or eight."

Sten took up the story. "She led real well, but after a while I though maybe she was getting a little deaf. I hated to put her down, because she was still"—Sten laughed—"dependable. So I sold her to Myra Robbins over in Salcha. I told her I thought Doris was maybe as old as nine years and getting a little stiff in the joints. One day, three years later, Myra was at a race, still running Doris up front, though Myra couldn't figure out how the dog was managing to take her commands, because she was stone deaf. Who walks by the truck but Astrid Armistead—you know, she's a real good sprint musher from the Anchorage area—and Astrid stops in her tracks. 'Doris?' she says. 'I can't believe she's still alive!' So Myra says, 'Well, she's not very fast anymore but she's dependable. I don't know how she takes her commands, because she's deaf.' 'I never knew how she did that either,' says Astrid. 'She was born deaf but she was so good that I hated to put her down so I sold her to Glenn Frame.'

"'Born deaf?' says Myra. 'You bred her? How old is she?' Astrid thinks a minute and says, 'About fifteen.' Myra couldn't believe it. If Astrid was right, that darn dog raced for fifteen years. Myra retired her after she found out how old she was. I heard Doris died a natural death the next year."

Sten and Jack continued laughing, but their smiles faded when they saw that culling was still on my mind.

"You know," Sten said thoughtfully, "you never know what you do when you cull. That Neva is the best dog I've ever had." He shook his head as if to dismiss the memory.

If culling working animals by means of instant death is not necessarily frowned upon, cruelty to a living creature is considered quite a different matter.

One afternoon Sandy and I tried to sew dog coats. It had been a frustrating day. Both of our sewing machines were balking at stitching the heavy materials. Eventually her machine jammed completely and I ended up taking it apart, hoping I could rebuild it. We found that an essential thread guide had broken off inside the machine arm. I called a sewing shop in Fairbanks to ask if they could replace the guide. They were noncommittal.

"That machine is old," a man at the shop told me gruffly. "We'd at least have to send to Seattle for the part."

"How long would that take?" I asked.

I heard a sigh of exasperation. "Does anyone ever know how long it will take to get parts from Seattle?"

Later I called Laurie Marsden. She did a good deal of commercial sewing for the sled dog industry.

"Don't go to that guy in Fairbanks," she advised me. "He'll take your machine and keep it for years. He'll never get you the parts. Mail your machine to the shop in Soldotna. They perform miracles there."

Soldotna was over five hundred miles from Fairbanks.

"How long will it take to get it back from Soldotna?"

"Two or three weeks, maybe. Sometimes a month."

"But I haven't got two or three weeks," I said, "and certainly not a month."

I returned to the ailing machine and set to work trying to fabricate a guide.

There was a familiar knock at the door. Sten. Sandy and I exchanged glances. We didn't need company at the moment.

"Come in!" I shouted from the kitchen. There was some rustling in the living room as Sten took off his parky. He sauntered into the kitchen.

"How are ya?" he asked.

"We're upset. We're fighting with sewing machines," I told him.

"Oh yeah? Making dog coats, are you?"

"Well," Sandy said, "we're trying to, but the machines aren't in the mood."

"Maybe this will cheer you up." He reached into his vest pocket and pulled out two chocolate Santa Claus figurines. He put one down in front of Sandy and one in front of me. "I got a Santa lollipop for Kathleen too," he said. "Where is she?"

"Out back sledding with George," I said. I picked up my Santa. "Thanks. I could use a lift. But you know, it reminds me that Christmas is coming and I haven't even thought about it."

"Yeah," Sten said dreamily. He wasn't even listening to me. He was looking at Sandy. She mumbled a thanks to him and started pinning fabric together. Though the gifts had been for all three women in our household, it was clear that Sten's focus was on Sandy.

"I had my annual physical today," Sten announced.

"Are you going to live?" I asked.

"Forever!" Sten exclaimed. "But my doctor said I should find a girlfriend."

Sandy hunched over her work. She pretended not to hear Sten. His intentions had become obvious lately. He acted like a boy in the throes of a first crush. He had already convinced himself that Sandy would never care for him, but he couldn't conceal his interest in her. Rather than taking the role of a suave older man, he drifted about like an adolescent, a lost puppy. He made no attempt to court her.

"I miss having a girlfriend," Sten continued. "I used to date a Native woman. She taught me how to mush. It's hard to find a woman who wants to mush. And just think, anyone who moved in with me would have an instant team. I've got enough dogs for both of us."

No one responded to Sten's musings, so he finally said, "Yeah, I guess I have too many dogs. I really ought to sell a few of them."

Sandy looked up. "Jeffry's looking to buy a couple of dogs," she said.

Sten winced. Then he said in a low growl, "Jeffry, huh? Well, I wouldn't sell a dog to *Jeffry* if he was the last musher in Alaska."

"Why not?" Sandy asked defensively.

"You oughta know—all you do-gooders from the lower forty-eight who don't want to kill anything for fur and wouldn't cull a dog if it had three legs and one eye. Your Jeffry is about the cruelest bastard I ever met. He was hammering on that little black and white leader of his with an ax handle one day right in front of the store. I thought to Christ he was going to kill her! So that's your Jeffry."

Sandy and I were speechless.

"I'm outta control," Sten said, "and I'm outta here." He stormed out of the room, tossed on his parky, and left the house.

Sandy stared at her lap. She looked dazed.

"I guess it's true," she said, "everything you told me you've heard."

"What should we do?" I asked.

"I don't know. I don't want to confront Jeffry. I don't want to ask him about this because if Sten isn't telling the truth, Jeffry will be so hurt."

"If Sten isn't telling the truth, maybe Jeffry better know what people are saying about him," I told her.

9

Like magic, our team picked up. The slump was over before we figured out why it had happened. No longer limping, Pete rejoined the team, and they turned in a strong, fast thirty-five miles. My heart jumped when I saw that George had scrawled "back on track!" in our training log.

With no hours of full daylight, we spent our days working by the glow of our headlamps. Temperatures, even at noon, were very cold. When the mercury dipped to forty below, we suspended training, because snow that thoroughly frozen is very abrasive to dogs' feet. We reasoned that missing a training run or two might cause the team to lag, but skinning the dogs' footpads would put them out of commission altogether.

Several times a day, I visited the old dogs to make sure they were not freezing in their doghouses. If their bellies were warm and they were not shivering or listless, they were okay. Any dogs who looked questionable were moved to the shed, where a woodstove kept the temperatures above freezing.

George tried out various combinations of specialized arctic clothing and made decisions about what to wear in the Quest. He experimented with his trail cooker, a type of camp stove that runs on methanol and is designed to melt large amounts of snow efficiently. Whole teams of dogs can be watered each time it is fired up.

Sandy did not welcome the cold as George did, and dragged her heels about training in the frigid weather. She never said she didn't want to take her team out, but she found a few excuses not to run.

She mentioned that she needed more time for her photography, though I didn't see her with a camera. I wondered if she was discouraged by having fewer and fewer of our best dogs on her team, but I said nothing to her about this because it couldn't be changed. We figured she would get over this personal slump of hers when the weather got warmer.

Sure enough, before the cold snap ended, she returned to her regularly scheduled workouts. On a thirty-five below afternoon, she traveled off down the trail with nine dogs hitched. About two hours later, I heard someone pounding on the back door. When I opened it, Sandy came running in.

"I can't feel my hands!" she screamed. "I couldn't turn the doorknob!" She raced toward the woodstove in the living room, pulling her heavy mitts off with her teeth. I watched in horror as she placed her palms less than an inch from the scalding surface of the stove.

"Sandy, let me see your hands," I said.

"I just want to keep them here," she moaned.

"You can't, Sandy. I know you're cold, but you're going to burn yourself."

"No! No! I want to get warm!" she cried. "Leave me alone!"

I grabbed her wrists and pulled her hands away from the stove. She struggled with me. She was completely hysterical.

"Let me warm them!" I told her. I put my hands over hers. If she was frostbitten, the skin on her hands would suffer less damage if warmed slowly.

"Can't you see I'm freezing!" she shouted, trying to break free.

"All right, it's all right." I wouldn't let go of her wrists. I tried to think of some way to calm her. "Hold your hands up here," I said. I steered her hands over the woodstove, but so high off its surface that she couldn't be burned. That brought about a tenuous truce and gave me a chance to look over her fingers. Her index and middle fingers were white on the ends. The rest of each hand was bright red. There was nothing to fear. At worst, the white areas would peel. She might loose a fingernail or two, but they would grow back.

"They're just red," I told her. "They're okay."

She glanced at her hands as if she was afraid to look. Then she relaxed. I could feel the tension go out of her and I let go of her wrists. We both stood quietly in front of the stove for a moment.

"I'm sorry," I said. I felt awkward. I had overpowered her.

"No," she said, "it's okay. I got pretty upset there. It's pretty scary."

When I was certain she was going to be okay, I went out to unhitch her team. It was slow work getting the snaps released and the harnesses off. Everything was stiff with ice. I'd remove one harness then curl my hands up inside my gloves to warm them before going on to the next harness. As I worked, I talked to the dogs. They were resting on the snow, their muzzles and whiskers frosted over from their breath. They were undaunted. This was their element. A run that could have cost Sandy her hands was business as usual for them. I wondered, as I passed hot water and treats to all of them, how man can consider himself superior to animals.

In early December, George and I sent Christmas packages home to our families. It was easy to shop for gifts, because there were so many out-of-the-ordinary things for sale in Fairbanks. We packed up smoked salmon, halibut, Native-made dolls, cranberry candies, caribou mittens, moosehide slippers, rosehip tea, and mailed it all from the post office at the store. After that, the holiday seemed to evaporate. With none of the familiar reminders of Christmas around, there was little to trigger thoughts of past celebrations.

Three weeks later, when packages addressed to us began to arrive at the post office, I felt a sudden rush of holiday spirit, as if Christmas had returned.

One morning, Tom, the postman, called our house. "I've got six big boxes down here for you," he told me. "They're taking up the whole mailroom. You'd better come get them."

Hastily I hitched a team and headed for the store. On the way I sang "Sleigh Ride" and convinced myself that the dogs were running to the tune. When we pulled up to the entrance of the store, I viewed a perfect holiday scene. Snow drifted against the rustic building. Light from the windows looked deep yellow against the darkened facade. A string of Christmas lights traced the eaves of the porch, and a wreath hung on the door.

I tied off the team and went inside. The shop smelled of rich coffee, cooking from the café, and the spices that were kept in big jars on shelves behind the counter. I took a deep breath.

"Hi, Tom is looking for you," Marion, the cashier, called out to me.

"I know. He phoned us."

"I hear it's going to be a good Christmas in your household!" she said. I laughed and headed for the mailroom.

A small, glorified storage closet located at one end of the store, the mailroom had a half door with a tray affixed to it that served as the transaction counter. Above the door, a homemade sign warned POSTMASTER WILL NOT RETRIEVE MAIL FROM BOXES. PLEASE REMEMBER YOUR BOX KEY. Forty-odd postal boxes were installed in the hallway to the right of the room. They were filled from the front by means of a passkey.

As I approached, I saw Tom at the counter. He was pressed between the door and a wall of boxes. Apparently, excess mail was not something Two Rivers ever planned on.

"Am I glad to see you!" Tom exclaimed. "Guess the whole East Coast misses you." He pushed open the door and started moving boxes out into the room. I glanced at the addresses on them. They were from my parents, my sister, and George's father.

Taking up three boxes at a time, I teetered through the store and out to my team. My sled filled up quickly. Other customers watched me, helped me with the door, and commented on the happy predicament of having so many presents. A strange feeling of pride came over me. Though I enjoyed the life in Two Rivers, and though the people had been kind to me, George and I were still in many ways the newcomers, the people from the East who thought they could run the Yukon Quest. Here, in the packages, was proof that we were not new-

comers somewhere in the world. Somewhere people loved us and believed in us and wanted us to come home again. I tied the boxes into
my sled and drove my team home singing a joyous rendition of "Jin-
gle Bells."

That afternoon, George and Sandy spent some of their training
trip selecting a spruce tree from the forest. They agreed on a particular one, cut it, and brought it home in George's sled. We had no
Christmas tree stand, so George retrieved an old metal bucket from
the shed and grabbed a bag of sand that was originally intended for
the driveway. He brought the tree into the living room, hoisted it into
the bucket, and filled the bucket with the sand. We had no ornaments
to decorate the tree, but Karen had loaned us a string of lights and I'd
bought some colored paper and foil. Sandy, Kathleen, and I set to
work making ornaments while George popped popcorn and threaded
the kernels together to make chains.

Later in the day, I brought out Kathleen's Christmas stocking and
the ones for the dogs, and hung them on a low beam near the woodstove. Finally, I set the brass candlesticks I'd brought from home on
the kitchen table. Their delicate forms, that of a stag and a doe,
looked out of place in the modern, heartily built Alaskan house. The
deer seemed to gaze at me reproachfully. I was not missing home, nor
my family, nor my old friends. I hadn't been homesick, not even a
minute, since we'd found our house and begun to live in Alaska.
When would the homesickness kick in, I wondered. Here it was, a
holiday, and I was not reflecting on the past at all. I didn't miss taking out the china, polishing the silver, giving parties, and going to
parties. I was far from the structure and tradition of countless New
England Christmases, a structure and tradition that, as a staunch
Yankee, I'd upheld, believed in, and enjoyed. The antiques I'd studied
and collected, the material trappings of a lifetime seemed unimpor-
tant to me now, the time I'd spent seeking them, dusting them, polishing them, a waste. Freedom seemed the only precious thing, and
it could not be collected, quantified, or dusted; it could only be
celebrated.

We interspersed Quest work with Christmas baking and present wrapping. On Christmas Eve, I cooked wild goose and made an old New England dessert called syllabub. Our dinner guests were Jeffry and Robin Peters, a graduate student and recreational musher who had befriended us early that fall. Just before Jeffry and Robin arrived, I dressed for dinner. Glancing in the mirror, I finally felt a great swell of homesickness.

I was wearing my only skirt and a jeweled sweater. I didn't look half bad, but it didn't matter. There was nobody to see me. Nobody to know that my hair had come out right and my makeup was on evenly. There was George, but he loved me in flannels as well as in lace. There was Sandy. What did she care? She was a grown-up tomboy like me. There was Kathleen, who was too young to notice. Then there were two strangers. I was spending my Christmas with strangers.

I could envision my family. They would be gathering at my sister's house about then. The relatives would all be arriving. As they swept through the front door, the cold fresh air would mix with the warm air in the foyer. There'd be laughter and chatter, the smell of good wool coats, perfume, and fire from the fireplace. There'd be so many packages under the tree. Home-baked goodies would pile up on the table.

The sound of Kathleen's footsteps on the stairs ended my daydream. She was fresh out of her bath, running around in tights and a slip. She believed Santa was coming to Alaska tonight, just as surely as she'd believed he'd come to New Hampshire the year before. I figured I'd better get her into her dress before he, or any of our other guests, arrived.

Later, as we all sat down to dinner, George led us in prayer. "Heavenly father," he began, "we thank you for indoor plumbing." Everybody laughed. "And for the company of friends and the food we eat. Also for plenty of snow and for strong dogs." More laughter. "Help us to always be kind and understanding, both of our fellow humans and of our dogs. Amen."

I noticed that Sandy's glance had immediately traveled to Jeffry when George spoke his last line. The doubt that I saw in her eyes told me that Jeffry was a passing fancy. Rather than confront him, she was going to scrap the entire relationship. I wasn't sure that this was just, but I, too, could not face knowing that such an evil might exist in him.

Christmas morning brought emotional ups and downs. Each present we unwrapped bore a silent message from our families and friends: Come home. There were gifts of maple syrup, Quebec-style pancakes, and New York deli items, all the things we couldn't hope to obtain in Alaska. There were sweaters and warm clothes sent by people who presumed we were desperately cold. There was love in every package, the sort of familiar love we'd gotten used to living without. Fortunately, our melancholy was overshadowed by Kathleen's enthusiasm. She approved of everything that Santa had brought.

Alaskans take clothing seriously. They think about it, discuss it, and admire it openly. A woman sporting a quality pair of western boots can expect compliments on her footwear from men at the roadhouse on a Saturday night. A person wearing a warm-looking pair of pac boots will be stopped on the street by strangers who want to know if the wearer is satisfied with the boots and, if so, where a pair can be purchased.

In Fairbanks, several custom stitching firms create outerwear to meet the needs and tastes of Alaskans. On any given day at any one of these firms, burly blue-jeaned customers can be found picking apart the clothing like expert tailors from London's finest haberdasheries. Despite an eye for economy, they will pay good money for well-constructed, long-wearing garments. Because they must work outdoors in beastly temperatures, they want the latest in lightweight, cold-resistant materials. They want clothing that contours to the body to keep wind out. They want clothing that is comfortable. They don't want to waste time dealing with frozen zippers or stiff, unyielding gloves at subzero temperatures.

One firm named FrigiDesign made all sorts of specialized sporting goods. They produced dog booties in lots. There was a "bootie board" hanging over the sales counter. This chalkboard listed the names of mushers who'd ordered from the firm. As orders were filled, a check mark would appear next to the musher's name, but the name would not be crossed out. I suspected that this was a subtle form of advertising. It let people know that the tough guys shopped here. It was certain that many unknown mushers shopped there as well. I doubt their names ever made it onto the bootie board, so we were surprised to see George's name up there with the gods of our sport. Apparently, the *News-Miner's* recently published official list of Quest entrants had thrown us into the limelight. George and I exchanged a smile as Mary Ann, FrigiDesign's top designer, assured us that our booties would be ready early the next week.

The pursuit of good clothing led us to Martha Pavik. George admired a pair of mukluks Martha had made for Robin Peters, so Robin brought George to visit Martha. An Inupiaq Eskimo from a tiny village in the Brooks Range, Martha now lived in a rundown housing project in Fairbanks. She had charge of her three young grandchildren and supplemented her welfare check working in the only trade she knew: skin sewing.

In her cramped apartment, slippers, boots, gloves, mittens, parkas, and fur blankets adorned the worn-out sofa and chairs. This was Martha's display counter. This was where she did business. George was impressed with her excellent beadwork and extraordinary embroidery. He had seen moccasins and other Native work for sale in the tourist shops, but it couldn't compare to what he saw there. This was Alaskan Native work for Native people and for friends. Martha was strict about her customers. She wanted to know who was wearing her clothing, as if a part of her spirit went off with every garment she sold.

George eagerly ordered a pair of mukluks and a set of beaver mitts. Only a week later, Martha called to say both items were done. She arranged for George to pick them up the next evening and invited him to dinner.

George arrived at the apartment with a little flowering plant. Martha made a fuss over it and then proudly showed George his mitts and mukluks, how she'd matched the trim on them and used the scraps from the beaver pelts to decorate the mukluks. She'd used every bit of fur, no waste. George was very pleased with both items. When he told her so, she beamed, and he saw the space where her front teeth should have been.

"I show you my village," she said suddenly and waddled off to the kitchen. She returned with a few dog-eared photographs. The first two pictured meadows. "Very good berries in my village!" Martha exclaimed. "Every field, berries and berries." The next picture was of a dilapidated modular home. "My son live here," she said. "Good hunting all around!"

The last two pictures showed racks of salmon drying by a riverbank. "This our fish camp," she told George. "In summer, my family stay here. Fishing very good most times." Her grin faded to a wistful expression. "I miss my village," she said quietly. She returned the photos to the kitchen.

"Do you visit there now?" George asked.

"When I can. I have arthritis." She held out gnarled fingers for George to see. "The Public Health Service sent a doctor. He says I have to live where there is heat all the time. I was in pain, so I go. I leave my husband, my family. A year later, I get my grandchildren."

"Were they sick too?" George asked.

"No." She shook her head. "Alcohol. It's very bad, right?"

George nodded.

"My daughter-in-law was killed. A man with a gun had too much to drink. He started a fight with another man one night. My daughter-in-law was in the way. Shot."

"Oh, I'm sorry," George said.

"Alcohol did this," she said and pointed to her missing teeth. "It took away my parents. I was raised by my grandparents, so I know the old ways. My grandmother taught me to sew."

"Your work is beautiful."

"Yes, the old way," she said with a smile. "Children should learn this but they don't anymore. If children learned the old ways they would be healed. I teach my granddaughter, and here at least, I have the church. That where my grandchildren are tonight. At church group. I want them to grow up—no alcohol."

Martha made a delicious dinner of potatoes, sautéed vegetables, and caribou steaks. She coated the steaks with crushed gingersnaps before cooking them. This is an old-fashioned way to prepare large game in Alaska. The gingersnaps lend a spicy flavor to the meat and create a sort of gravy. The taste was intriguing.

Throughout dinner, George and Martha talked of Alaska, travels around the state, his plans for the Quest, and her plans to return to her village. The conversation was light and pleasant. Martha was forthright about her troubles, but she also seemed to find merriment in her daily life. She loved her grandchildren and she felt hopeful about their future, even if that hope was tempered by poverty and a sad history. George got the impression that Martha had never considered giving in to her difficult circumstances.

Before leaving that evening, George asked Martha about a very ornate pair of mukluks he saw on the display sofa.

"Oh, those dancing boots," she told him. "For very fancy, dress-up!"

"I wonder if you'd make a pair for my wife."

"Very expensive," she said, as if concerned he'd gotten in over his head. She thought for a moment. "Tell no one else. I make them for you only—a hundred and twenty-five dollars."

"That sounds fine," George said, "and then you can teach my wife how to dance."

Martha threw back her head and laughed.

In two weeks, the beautiful rabbit fur and embroidered moosehide boots were done. Martha called and spoke to George. "Better come quick," she told him. "Others offer me more money for the boots, but I say they are for you."

This was Inupiaq bargaining. A small bonus might need to be paid for holding off other customers.

"Don't worry, Martha, I'll come pick them up today," George said.

"Oh, today! Okay!" Martha agreed. Then in a teasing tone she added, "When you come to get, bring your wife. I want to see the woman that a man would spend so much money on. I want to meet who will dance in my boots!"

Susan called to say good-bye. Her bags were packed, her kids were ready to go. She was leaving for Pennsylvania in the morning. She'd be back in time to see us off in the Quest.

"I'll miss you," I told her.

"No you won't," she laughed. "Believe me, you won't have time."

"Oh sure I will. Sandy and I only have five hundred and seventy-six dog meals to pack."

"Did you get the dog coats done yet?"

"No, but I fixed the sewing machine without sending it to Seattle."

"Really?"

"Yeah, I used a paper clip and some Super Glue. Hope it holds."

"So what are George and Sandy up to today?"

"Oh, they're out on the trails. Sandy should be back soon. She took her team up to Nordale Road and George heard that the winter trail is open all the way to Angel Creek now, so he's headed up there."

"Oh, no!" Susan gasped. "He's not going *all* the way up there, is he?"

"He plans to. Why? What's wrong?"

"Oh, Ann, the ice up there isn't safe! Patty Rummel took a team up there yesterday and she went out on the river. The ice is snow-covered so it looks safe, but she broke through and her team went in the water. One of her dogs drowned!"

"What should I do?" I said almost to myself. "Even if I hitch a team, I'll never catch George. He's been gone for two hours and there aren't any fast dogs left in the kennel."

"You could use your ATV," Susan suggested.

"It doesn't start."

"Dave took his up to the store or I'd ask him."

"Jack Patterson's got one. He's probably out training, but it's worth a try."

"Yeah. Give him a call. Call me back if you need me."

We said a hasty good-bye, then I dialed Jack. No answer. I thought of Sten, but he wasn't home from work yet. It was useless anyway: George was probably all the way to the river by now.

The first twenty miles of trail intersected Chena Hot Springs Road twice. I could drive down the road and hope that he hadn't crossed through both intersections. If he had stopped the team and rested, there was a slim chance he hadn't gone through the second intersection. A very slim chance.

I wondered if there was another road crossing farther down the trail. I recalled that George had taken out a map that morning to check the trail route. I ran up to our bedroom and searched through the Alaskan topo maps he kept in a pile near our bed, but I didn't find the map of Angel Creek. He had taken it with him, I supposed.

Maybe this is not an emergency, I told myself. George was an experienced outdoorsman. He knew enough not to venture out onto thin ice. But he was not familiar with the trail and it was dark. I remembered Sten describing a trail to George, saying something about, "You come out of the trees and down a drop-off, and you're on the river before you know it." Was it this river he was talking about, or was it the Chena River? I didn't know. I hadn't been paying attention. I had become so confident in George's abilities that I hadn't even asked much about his plans. Now he might be in trouble, serious trouble, and I didn't even know where to find him.

I grabbed the keys to the truck and headed out the door. Once in the truck, I traveled down the snow-covered roads at a speed that just barely prevented skidding. It took an eternity to get to the first road crossing. I stopped, checked the trail, and noted the tracks of sleds and dogs. At best, three teams had crossed there recently. One probably was George's. I hoped the other two were ahead of him. They would surely stop him before he came to the river.

At the next road crossing there were two sets of tracks heading toward Two Rivers and one set heading to Angel Creek. No one lived beyond Two Rivers on this trail, so I gathered that two teams had turned around! I knew that if George was determined to go to Angel Creek, neither of those two teams would be his. He was on the trail alone!

I waited, desperately staring down the trail, hoping for any sign of a headlamp. Twenty minutes passed. The woods looked eerie and black. There was nobody out there. Not a soul. No one would know if our team went into the river. Chilled and scared, I returned to the truck. Reluctantly, I started the engine and drove back toward Two Rivers.

While I was driving, a vision of Minnie kept forcing its way into my mind. Minnie caught in her traces, taken by the current, dragged down by her harness. Panicking, drowning—drowning like Patty Rummel's dog.

"God, no!" I said aloud. I felt like screaming but couldn't even give myself that comfort. I'd been foolish. I'd let George go alone on an unfamiliar trail. I hadn't paid attention. *I hadn't paid attention.*

Another vision came. George slipping under the ice, hammering to break the surface. Sinking in his heavy clothes. I gripped the steering wheel tightly.

Not far from the store, the winter trail turned out of the woods and paralleled the road. I saw a light on the trail. As I drew closer, I could see it was a musher's headlamp. A team was passing by. I couldn't identify the driver because a thin row of spruce trees stood between the trail and the road, obscuring the view. This team must have been one of those that turned back, I thought. Perhaps the driver had seen George!

I stopped the truck and rolled down the window. I could hear a jingling sound—the sound of dog tags striking against metal collar rings. Our team made that sound, because back in New Hampshire, rabies tags were mandatory. In Alaska, few dogs wore tags.

"Hey, musher!" I yelled. "What team are you?"

"George Cook," came the reply. I leaped out of the truck. "Ann, is that you?" George called out. He stopped the team.

"Yes. What are you doing here?" I asked.

"What are *you* doing here?" he said, peering at me through the spruces.

"I was worried about you. I tried to catch you before you got to the river. I thought you were going to Angel Creek."

"I turned back. The ice isn't safe."

"I know. Susan called and said Patty fell in yesterday."

"I met Patty on the trail today. She warned me about that. It's a good thing, too. You can't see the river until you come out of the woods. Then it's too late."

The dogs were yapping, anxious to get going again.

"I can't hold these guys," George said. "I'll see you back at the house." He pulled his snow hook and was gone.

I climbed into the truck and headed for home. I passed the store, turned onto the road that led to our house, pulled into our driveway, and then I cried big tears of relief until I was all cried out.

10

The scientists who tell us that dogs are simple creatures have never owned sled dog teams. They have never tried to organize twelve canine minds and forty-eight canine legs into a unit that moves forward with conviction. The physical differences in dogs are sometimes the least of the musher's worries when matching up a team. He must consider the dogs' personality quirks and varying degrees of dedication. When a well-trained team glides quietly down the trail, spectators may think the sport looks easy, but I guarantee that the driver of that team has put in his time.

In January, George scrutinized his seventeen Quest candidates. There were certain dogs who were going to make the team: Minnie, for one. She was a little soldier of a dog, so much of a soldier she was nerve-wracking. She seemed to pride herself on immediate response. Lately, when approaching a turn in the trail, George had to be careful not to give the command too soon or Minnie would veer off in whichever direction she was told at exactly the moment she was told, whether or not she had approached the crosstrail. I believe she would have sprouted wings and flown if George had asked her to.

Lightening, Minnie's archrival, was also going to make the team. Her Iditarod experience would be important if the weather turned bad, for once a dog realizes it can go on through a storm, it will do so without fear or fatigue time after time. Lightening's cool-headedness and lightheartedness were definitely an asset to the team.

Minnie's young son, Kirk, would be on the team, too. He had matured that season and had good muscle on his frame. He could still be a little goofy at times, and occasionally inattentive, but for the most part he was a worker.

Taro would unquestionably be holding one of the wheel positions, the spots right in front of the sled where the most powerful dogs run. Born and raised in Quebec, he was known around our house as the "crazy Frenchman." Like a stereotypical Frenchman, he was passionate about food and affection. He ate with gusto, barking and squealing delightedly between bites. He didn't just accept patting from his loved ones. He rubbed his body all over us, drowning himself in our scents and vice versa. There was a wild streak in him, an untamed part that none of us could really reach. However, I often sensed that an emotional war was going on inside him. He wanted to fight the other dogs to dominate, but he desperately needed to win our praise as well, so he vented his aggressions through his work, pulling with unbelievable strength.

For the first six years of his life, Scamp had belonged to Ron MacArthur and had contributed to Ron's wins at most of the major mid- and long-distance championships in the eastern United States and Canada. George and I had purchased Scamp two years ago and were very pleased with him. A big gray wolf of a dog, with a quiet, hard-working demeanor, Scamp made the perfect running partner for Taro.

Moose would be running somewhere in the middle of the team. Like Orah and Kirk, he was part of the special litter that Minnie and Dan had produced shortly before Dan died. Unlike his siblings, he had inherited none of his parents' leader skills. He was, essentially, the dim-witted brother in an otherwise brilliant family, but he was an honest dog and never gave us any trouble.

Boomer was much like Moose, but with an edge. He did his work, ate his food, and minded his own business. Teamed with Pete, he could move mountains; these two were well matched in power and stride.

Shasta, Minnie's sister, would run at point. A mere thirty-eight pounds, she was our smallest female, but she was fast and stronger than she looked. She kept the pressure on the leaders by running close behind them, as if to say "I could have your job if you slack up."

Had the Fates not conspired against her, Shasta could well have been a leader herself. Unfortunately, she had a tangle with a skunk in the first year of her life and suffered the loss of one eye. We knew that she managed very well if her running partner was placed on her blind side, leaving her single eye to view the trail. When hooked to the line, she would crane her head around to see her partner. As soon as she was sure she was teamed with a dog she trusted, she would turn her head back and concentrate on running.

With the inclusion of Shasta, nine dogs were as good as chosen for the Quest. Reviewing our trail log, we compared notes on the performance of the other dogs and decided to cut three more of them from the list of available candidates. Five dogs remained in consideration for three open positions.

We had celebrated Bandit's tenth birthday on the second of the month. He got an extra dollop of meat on his dinner and an after-dinner bone. He was pleased with the treats but unaware of their meaning. In his mind, he was still a young fellow, and his mind seemed to have complete control over his body. He had come through his fall surgery without complications, trained hard for four and a half months, and showed no sign of giving out. Could a ten-year-old dog run the Quest? "I guess we're going to find out," George told me.

In mid-January, a stumble on the Angel Creek trail put Pete back on the injured list. He went lame on the same front foot he had favored a month ago, so George took him to see Dr. Talbot.

X-rays revealed a small shadow on Pete's metacarpal ligament. At some point, probably before we owned him, he suffered a hairline fracture in a bone or a tear in his soft tissue, and now, though healed, the wound site was becoming arthritic. That explained why, when warmed up and exercising, Pete seemed fine. It was only after a work-out that the foot stiffened and lameness set in.

"There are several medications that can help him, but not many are legal in the Quest," Dr. Talbot told George.

Of course, George knew this all too well. No steroid-based anti-inflammatories and no analgesics, not even aspirins, are allowed in dog racing because they can mask pain. To recover, Pete might need banned medications. The Quest was in four and a half weeks. If the medications worked quickly, we could stop treatment in time to clear his bloodstream. He would then pass the drug screening test prior to the race. If they did not work quickly, he would have to be dropped from the team. The alternative was to use less effective, but permissible, medications and hope they worked. George decided on the latter route. Carefully, he and Dr. Talbot worked out a plan that included a week's rest for Pete.

The prescribed rest proved to be torture for Pete and for all of us. Each day as George went out to hitch the team, Pete would come to attention. He'd stand on his sore leg, wag his tail, and wait for George to bring his harness. George would walk by him as he tended to the other dogs. Pete would seem puzzled. He would watch the other dogs get suited up. Still no harness was brought out for him. He'd stand, stretch, and pad around in a circle trying to get George's attention. After a while, he'd lie down and try to ignore the other dogs who, by then, were all jumping and barking. George would pass again and Pete would leap to his feet, thinking there might still be a chance. Then he'd lie down again, then he'd get up.

When the team finally left, Pete would watch them until they were out of sight. He'd put his nose in the air and let out a deep, haunting howl. Eventually, he'd curl up with his disappointment and close his eyes.

While Pete waited out practices, Abe excelled. Impossible as it may seem, I believe there was some correlation between these two happenings. Abe was an extraordinary dog. He had the tough, serious, opportunistic nature of a Wall Street stockbroker.

Though he was not an aggressive dog, there were few people he liked. He didn't care to be bothered with humans who doubted him or could not further his career. He liked me especially. I suppose we shared a certain hard-headedness, and he knew I admired him. He depended on me to plead his case with George, whom he liked a little less well, only because he knew George appreciated him less than I did. As for Sandy, he tolerated her. He knew she had no say in any matters that concerned him, but she fed him sometimes and brought him water in the morning, so he conceded that she could be useful to him.

Abe's strength was impressive. We called him the "Iron Man" behind his back. He had a thick, steel gray coat and piercing blue eyes and he was every inch an athlete. The only problem was that the inches didn't add up. He was a small dog, barely taller than our mid-sized females.

Abe had to stretch his body to the limit to keep up with the first-string dogs when they were moving at top speed. But when the team settled, Abe came into his element. We could actually feel the difference his strength made as he put his back into the job and pulled. Since races of a thousand miles are run almost entirely at a settled speed, we wondered if Abe's size was truly a limiting factor. Still, we reasoned that a bigger dog would cover ground more effortlessly and, therefore, not tire as easily. In drifting snow and bad conditions, the smaller dog would simply have a harder time of it.

Whatever our thoughts on choosing a bigger dog might have been, Abe did not agree with us. In fact, he had a five-year history of disputing this point and winning the debate. Abe had always managed to make the first string one way or another. He replaced and outdid injured dogs. He outlasted younger dogs. He even learned to respond to directional commands, though we never trained him to be a leader. It seemed he kept track of whatever positions were open on the team and honed his talents to fit where he'd be needed. We were sure he understood every word we said. If George had the slightest complaint about him after a practice, the very next day Abe would take deliberate steps to improve that aspect of his performance. It was uncanny.

In recent weeks, Abe's attitude had gone from hopeful to exasperated. He was spending all of his time searching for a sign that he would make the team. He scrutinized us, watched our body language, and tried to make eye contact. His vigilance put pressure on all of us. It is hard to live under the gaze of a dog who thinks his owners are fools.

I devised a series of tests: knotting tuglines and putting bungy cords in tuglines to prove to George that Abe was a worthy puller. Abe tightened the knots, stretched all the cords, passed all the tests, but still George hesitated.

When Pete came up lame, I almost believed that Abe had wished Pete out of the picture. He was the only candidate left who could match Pete in strength.

George's own physical limitations gave him an idea. A survivor of bilateral knee surgery, he knew well the pain of arthritis. He knew that heat and massage helped. He decided to try this out on Pete. For several consecutive nights, he applied warm liniment to Pete's metacarpals and wrapped the area carefully in a medicine boot. After a half hour, he'd remove the boot and massage Pete's foot. As George massaged, Pete blinked his eyes sleepily. Obviously, this felt good.

By the end of the week, Pete was running again. After each practice, George gave Pete his massage therapy. The lameness didn't return. We hoped it was gone for good.

Two positions remained open on the team, three if Pete had any more troubles. Abe, Gilbert, Orah, and Essie were left to evaluate.

The runners of the sled made a whirring sound as they rode over the snow. George drove the team and I sat in the sled basket bundled in my heaviest parky. Gilbert? He had been one of our best mid-distance dogs. He was four years old and in his prime, but he had gotten off to a bad start that season. He'd been lazy in a few practices and George had lost some faith in him, even though lately he was running well. Gilbert had a giddy, enthusiastic personality, sometimes so giddy that he couldn't concentrate. George didn't identify with Gilbert's highs and lows. He wanted steady work out of a dog.

Orah or Essie? For several practice sessions, I'd watched Orah and Essie put in flawless performances. We could not find a reason to cut either one of them, but a decision had to be made. Like all Quest decisions, logic, not emotion, had to guide our choice. I glanced at Orah, then Essie. They moved along like machines, stride for stride, perfectly matched. If George decided to take both of them, then Abe wouldn't be on the team. I didn't like that idea. Neither Essie nor Orah was as strong as Abe, even if they were more fluid. I was certain George would need Abe's strength and determination during the race's summit climbs. That was the logic talking. Then there was the voice from my heart: Abe had worked hard, far beyond all expectations, to win a spot on the team. He deserved to race.

I watched a ptarmigan pop up from the snow and throw itself into flight. The team sped up for a few moments, pursuing the fat white bird. Then they settled, obeying George's command of "On by," a signal to ignore this distraction. My eyes returned to Orah and Essie.

Essie's father was our oldest dog, Matanuska, who had sired her at an age when most dogs have forgotten about sex. Essie had Matanuska's vitality and good sense. Through her mother, a Dan daughter, she had inherited speed. Her body was flexible and strong like Dan's had been.

She was a cheerful dog and a solid, honest worker. She almost never needed correction because she was eager to conform and to please. She put her trust in George and did not tire herself questioning the wisdom or direction of whatever mission he chose for her.

For all her strengths, Essie was young. A two-and-a-half-year-old, she had run only two sixty-mile races. Both races were with our second-string team because physically she'd been too immature to make the first string. This year, she had grown up. We were pretty sure she now had the body to run the Quest, but her mental capabilities had not been tested. Rookie dogs sometimes give up under the sustained pressure of a long race, yet Essie's general behavior on the trail seemed reason enough to gamble on her.

Though built much like Essie, Orah was a different dog entirely. A daughter of Minnie and Dan, she was a lively lady with a lot of personal ambition. She was a full month younger than Essie, but she'd been quick to mature both physically and mentally and had won a spot on last year's first string. Orah was a capable dog and she knew it, but coupled with her self-confidence was a measure of mischievous independence. She worked only for herself, pleased only herself, and so George could never be sure what she would do when the pressure was on. Nevertheless, she was calculating enough to see the advantages in behaving well. Her way was almost always George's way, so there was seldom a conflict. I couldn't help but think she was much like a woman who, insulted by taking orders, makes a poor soldier in peacetime, but then in battle displays the bravery, creativity, and cool-headedness that saves an entire platoon from destruction. In short, Orah had "guts."

So Orah or Essie, I wondered. Another day had passed and we'd made no decision. At George's command, the team took the last turn and we swung onto the trail to our house. "Going home!" George called out to the leaders, and they sped up, knowing they could sprint toward their cozy houses. As we pulled up to the kennel yard, I felt the sense of mystery that I always felt when I saw sled dogs run. It amazed me that they worked this happily and this hard for food, shelter, and human affection. Each day was an adventure to them, each practice a new challenge. What secret, held deep inside them, made them *want* to do this work? They were admirable creatures, beautiful to look at, breathtaking to watch. How lucky I felt that they were willing to pull me through the Alaskan woods and take me places I otherwise could never go. They were magnificent and they chose to love George and me. What human could ask for more?

Sandy seemed restless. She was turning down invitations from friends and spending more and more time alone in her room. If she opened a book to read, she quickly closed it. If she turned on the radio, she couldn't decide on a station. She took the truck into town on her days off and returned in the evening with little to say about how she'd passed her day. In fact, she shunned my casual questions of "Did you have a nice time?" as if I were asking about deeply personal things.

On several occasions, I asked her if she was unhappy about

something, but she shrugged off my concern. I spoke to George about her moodiness and he questioned her about it, too, but she insisted everything was going fine. I was torn between wanting to believe Sandy and knowing that she couldn't be telling the truth. She seemed to want more and more time off, often just to sleep the day away. She expressed a desire to cook, but when I turned the kitchen over to her, she was overwhelmed by the task of making dinner for the four of us. Doing her own laundry seemed too much. Babysitting for Kathleen seemed too much.

Since she would not communicate directly with me, I began to question others about her depression. Through Robin Peters she'd met a number of people her own age. She had enjoyed their company in the fall but now avoided them. Had something unpleasant happened within their group? Robin said no.

Sten heard a rumor that Sandy was having trouble controlling her team on the trails. Without mentioning this to her, I suggested that she practice with smaller teams if the dogs were getting too powerful. She continued to train nine or ten dogs at a time.

Determined to lift her spirits, I declared a holiday for both of us and offered to treat her to a day at a bush resort that Karen had told me about. Sandy, Kathleen, and I all rose early and drove to the resort. We spent the day swimming in the pool. We tried out the hot tubs and splashed around playing water games. At one point, the pool attendant struck up a conversation with us. He was a skinny young man with a horsy face and a few tattoos. The tattoos appeared to be gang war symbols. As he spoke with us, I couldn't help but notice that the nails on his ring and little finger were long. Cocaine user, I assumed, though he looked clean. I quickly decided we had little in common with this fellow, but he continued talking with us and I could think of no polite way to escape from him.

Eventually, he introduced himself as Richard, and said he had recently moved up from White Plains, New York. He asked which one of us was Kathleen's mother. When I said I was her mother, he focused his conversation on Sandy. I swam away with Kathleen, but Sandy lingered for a while. I could hear her chatting with him about the differences between life in Alaska and life back east. Later, Sandy, Kathleen, and I left the pool and said a polite good-bye to Richard.

In the changing room, I remarked about Richard's tattoos and nails to Sandy. "He seems pretty weird!" I laughed.

Sandy was distant. "Oh, I don't know," she said. I wasn't sure she was listening to me.

That evening we returned home to find George reading in the living room.

"I've made the decision," he told us with a smile. "Orah's on the team."

"Really?" Sandy cried. She sounded excited for the first time in weeks. "What made you decide?"

"She just showed me something in practice today," George said. "She led with Lightening and she was . . . I don't know . . . strong in every way. I *know* she'll be good."

"It's a sound decision," I said. Then I thought about Essie and Gilbert and Abe. One position left on the team. Essie probably wouldn't make it, but she was young. There'd be other races. I decided not to think about Abe and Gilbert, poor souls. They were trying as hard as Orah, but Orah had that way about her. She made everything look easy. She was a natural.

George grabbed some beer from the refrigerator and a juice box for Kathleen. We all toasted to Orah.

Late that night, when Kathleen was asleep and George and I were dozing off in our bedroom, I heard Sandy dialing the phone.

"Hello, Richard?" I heard her say. I could hardly believe my ears. She hadn't seemed interested in him at all. I closed my eyes and drew my pillow around my head to avoid hearing their conversation.

As Orah became a permanent member of our team, Richard became the man in Sandy's life. Though George and I respected Sandy's right to date whomever she pleased, we could not warm up to Richard. We felt he was self-absorbed and condescending. Alaskans, the environment, even the wine we poured him one night were targets for his criticism. He did not seem to make Sandy any happier. Rather, they seemed to mope around together in a state of mutual discontent. George and I believed that our best course of action was to avoid much contact with Richard, but the more we tried to run from him, the more our lives became entwined.

He lived at the resort. He had no transportation and no money and, it seemed, little ambition to acquire either of these things. While that in itself was no sin, Richard's motivation to use others so that he needn't acquire these things became an annoyance to us.

At every chance, Sandy began to borrow our truck to drive to the resort. On days when Richard could hitch a ride into Fairbanks, he came to visit Sandy. He'd stay until midnight and then expect her to drive the sixty-mile round trip to drop him back at the resort. George and I worried about Sandy driving on that rough, desolate road. Temperatures were often thirty to forty below at night, the truck was ailing, and moose frequently crossed the road. If the truck were to break down, or Sandy were to have an accident, no one would come upon her for hours. Since we all shared the truck, and it was our sole vehicle, George and I had no way of searching for her.

I tried to explain my concerns to Sandy, but she reacted like a teenager. I suggested that she call us if she were going to be late, so we wouldn't worry, but she would make no agreements.

George and I began to endure her 3:00 A.M. arrivals, her habit of leaving the gas tanks empty, and the large phone bills that resulted from Sandy contacting Richard by radiophone relay. Of course, Richard never called Sandy. Having no credit, he could not initiate a call from the relay.

I had known Sandy as a responsible young friend and family member. The twelve years' difference in our ages had never much mattered, but suddenly we were polarized, acting more like a mother and a rebellious child. I wasn't sure why this was happening, and I tried to dodge a full-scale confrontation. I did not want conflict in my house while I was busy with the race. My life was jammed with the final month's errands and preparations. Every time Sandy made another request on Richard's behalf, I felt I would explode.

11

On a very cold day late in January, Shasta injured her feet. Neither George nor I were certain how the injury happened, but snow or ice made its way into her booties and rubbed the tops of her toes raw.

Over the next week, I cleaned, disinfected, and pampered Shasta's toes, but the wounds actually became larger and more angry looking.

I took her to see Dr. Talbot.

"She's not a good candidate for the Quest," Talbot said. "Even if you get these feet healed up, they're bound to open again. They'll just be trouble all the way."

She didn't deserve this, I thought. She'd been a shoe-in for the team. A *shoe-in*.

Sten brought Merle Hoskins by the house and introduced him as "the most organized man ever to run the Yukon Quest."

"I thought you might like to talk with him," Sten said, and he winked at George. "He might part with a few secrets."

Merle was tall, lanky, and soft-spoken. He looked down when he talked as if he were examining his shoes, but he was worth straining to hear. He'd been through the race three times and, though he'd never won it, he'd placed higher each year. It was easy to see that someday he'd be in the winner's circle.

"I'm not running the race this year. I've got a new young team and they aren't ready yet," Merle told George, "so I'd be happy to answer any questions you have about running it. Just fire away."

George was full of questions, so I kept the coffeepot warm while the men talked.

When he spoke about the race, Merle was calm. He recalled precise details. There was none of the bravado of Sten's Quest stories and, consequently, none of the sense of panic. To Merle, the race was not a demon, but simply a challenge: If a driver kept his wits about him, he'd finish. Merle's methodical approach to race preparation mirrored George's approach, so the two saw eye to eye immediately.

For the entire afternoon, Merle and George pored over topographic maps of the trail. Merle pointed out hazardous areas and good camping spots. He showed George where cabins were located. He discussed proper gear and looked over George's sled. Much to George's relief, Merle felt that the ten-foot sled was not really a detriment. He said an eight-foot sled was not a must, nor would George be the only driver in the race with such a long sled.

"It's a matter of preference," Merle told George. "You and I are tall, we need a longer sled to stretch out on when we rest."

Merle gave George a list of items he'd packed in his checkpoint bags. This gave us a better idea of how much food, clothing, and other supplies we should send to each checkpoint.

As the afternoon drew to a close, George asked Merle how he had gotten into racing. The question seemed to surprise him and, for a moment, I wondered if it was a question that shouldn't have been asked.

"Well," said Merle to his toes, "I started out with six big Eskimo dogs. Used them to run my trap line when I lived in a little village way up north of here. To tell you the truth, I didn't think much of those dogs. They didn't work very hard. They were slow and they loved to fight. They'd fight over anything—food, females in season, the shady spot in the dog yard—just anything. There were only a few people in the village, a couple of families and few single men like myself. One guy didn't get along with anyone and, when the winter closed in and there was no way to avoid him, everybody would get pretty annoyed with him. The last winter I was there, he was driving everybody crazy, stealing anything he pleased, teasing people about personal things, threatening to butcher a kid's dog. We all wished he would die. We even talked about it openly.

"Then the darnedest thing happened. A friend of mine, a peaceful guy that we all liked, kinda snapped one night and shot the troublemaker dead. We all witnessed the shooting, but we just couldn't believe our eyes. He was the last person you'd ever think would kill someone." Merle gazed into space, reliving the scene.

"The authorities came and took my friend off to Fairbanks. While he was awaiting trial, there was nobody to care for his house or his dogs, so I volunteered. I went out to his place and hitched up his team and drove them back to my place. I wasn't out with that team a minute when I realized I was having a great time! They were some fine racing dogs. They were fast and they didn't fight. They were terrific.

"Sad to say, the guy got convicted of murder. He gave me his team and I sold my Eskimo dogs as quick as I could. So all my dogs are pups out of that racing team. Three generations of them now."

Merle tapped his finger on the checkpoint list he'd made. "Good planning has a lot to do with the outcome of things," he said, "but, you know, a little luck doesn't hurt sometimes, too." He smiled and looked up just enough to meet George's eyes.

Merle Hoskins wasn't all that Sten brought over in January. As Sandy and I prepared George's checkpoint bags, Sten popped over with one helpful item after another. First he brought a few small stuff sacks for dog booties, then a foam-rubber liner for the sled. One day he arrived with a set of stencils that bore the names of Quest checkpoints. I had already labeled our bags, but I took the stencils anyway. I couldn't refuse him.

The truth was, I didn't want any of Sten's things, for though he offered them freely, they came with emotional baggage. They came from his room, *that room* in his house that was a Yukon Quest graveyard. I sensed that as he resurrected each item, he relived his failure. Imprisoned by fear and disappointment, he had lost too much faith in himself to race again. He gave his things to George in desperate hope that *they* would cross the finish line. In this symbolic way, he could become a finisher and perhaps this would set him free.

Sten's need to give away the contents of his room was as strong as my need to prevent George from taking it. I was no better than Sten when it came to superstition. I believed those things could bring about our doom. They were haunted.

George had always kidded me about my superstitions. Sandy had, too, but I couldn't escape my Irish background. I knew there weren't any little people or banshees, but whenever I declared that this was all foolishness, a voice within me would quickly whisper an apology to the spirit world for doubting their existence.

One night, as I sat staring at Sten's latest gift, a waterproof matchbox, George looked up from the *News-Miner* and said, "Don't worry. I'm not going to use it."

"Use what?" I asked, but the casual tone I tried to affect didn't quite come off.

"The matchbox—or any of Sten's other things. I'll avoid them."

"Oh, you don't have to avoid them," I said. "It's just superstition on my part. You don't have to go along with my feelings. I just can't help myself, that's all."

George folded the paper and put it aside. Leaning forward in his chair, he reached out and took hold of my hands.

"It's all right," he told me. "I've had the same reaction to Sten's stuff. I just didn't tell you. I know carrying a matchbox can't logically affect the outcome of the Quest, but I don't want to carry it, just in case."

Sandy walked into the room. "Are you talking about the things that Sten brought over?" she asked.

"Yeah," I said.

"I wouldn't use them. I think they're bad luck. I don't know why. I don't usually worry about things like that."

"Oh, gosh," I laughed, "instead of you two curing me of my superstitions, I've infected both of you!"

"I think you have," Sandy said. "The other day I was in the kennel yard and I said something about not finishing the Quest. I had to drop everything I was doing and run into the shed so I could knock on wood!"

"I almost died when Kathleen opened that umbrella in the house last night!" George confessed. "I couldn't take it from her quickly enough."

"The poor kid is going to develop a complex," I said. "I stomp on every comb she drops and yesterday I shrieked at her when she put her little shoes on the table."

"What does putting shoes on a table have to do with it?" Sandy asked.

"Oh," I waved my hand in the air, "it's another old Irish superstition. It's supposed to be bad luck to put your shoes on the table."

"Well, don't tell me about any more superstitions." Sandy said. "I've got enough to deal with now. I'm already crossing my fingers and throwing salt over my shoulder.

"I know," George laughed. "By the time this race is over, we'll all be a little nuts from following these weird rituals." He made a crazy face and Sandy and I giggled.

My fears weren't absent for long, though. They returned in the early hours of the morning when I awoke and glanced at the digital clock on my desk. Through sleepy eyes, I saw that the face read 999. A sense of panic came over me. Numerology claims that 333 is the sign of God, of the Trinity; 666 is the sign of the devil. What significance was 999? I wondered. *What could it mean?* It was the very addition of good and evil forces!

A thought struck me and I laughed. Perhaps 999 meant we were going to hell and back and—I hoped—in that order. I let that thought fade and then realized a clock *can't* say 999. There are only sixty minutes to the hour. I looked again and realized that the clock had actually read 9:59.

"I'm not going to bother to analyze *that* number," I grumbled to myself as I lay back down on my pillow.

The furs arrived in the nick of time. I called a neighbor back east and asked her to pull all the mink stoles and fox collars out of our attic, box them up, and send them out to us. For years, the furs had hung on a pole under the eaves. They'd belonged to George's mother. When she died, George's father gave them to me. I'd never had an occasion to wear them and I knew I never would, but they were going to be useful to us in Alaska. George's mother wouldn't be around to see what I did with them.

Carefully I cut them up and used them to line overmitts and hats. I used a particularly lush stole to line George's best mushing hat. The fur helped keep cold air from leaking in under the cheek flaps. For fun, I saved the label of the snooty Beverly Hills furrier who made the stole and attached it to the inside of the brim.

I knew that for all her finery, George's mother had preferred a good hike through the woods to the fancy parties her husband's career had often forced her to attend. Perhaps she might not have minded what happened to her furs. If she knew they were protecting her son from frostbite, she might have agreed to my plan.

After the fur projects were completed, I sewed reflective tape to the front and back of George's parky to make him more visible to passing teams and snowmobiles. As I worked, we kidded about locating his frozen body by means of the tape. I guess this was something akin to warding off evil spirits by mentioning their names.

There was a friendly spirit with us, but not in the house. It was in the kennel. It was Dan. I saw him at every turn and I knew George did, too. When we ran his children and grandchildren, he was with us. I sometimes grieved over him and longed to see him again, but then I went out to the kennel and saw his personality in Kirk and his eyes in Orah. He'd been a one-in-a-million dog. When George and I had dreamed of running the Quest, he'd been included in that dream. We didn't know back then that he would not be running it as one dog, but as several. His strength and speed were with us. Maybe this was how he'd intended it. I talked to his spirit when I was alone. I'd even overheard George talking to him. It was possible that we were just talking to ourselves, but we hoped not. We hoped Dan could hear us.

When I slept, I often dreamed of Dan. He came back to me in an amazingly realistic image. I felt his soft coat and patted his big, bony head. One night, I saw him standing over George and me as we lay in bed. He was backlit by the aurora. He looked beautiful and somewhat frightening. Then I woke and everything was just as it had been in the dream, except Dan was gone. I couldn't go back to sleep. I gazed at the foot of the bed for hours and wondered if this dream was truly some form of spirit visitation. It had been so real! Were I an Athabascan, I would have accepted this dream as a source of information. Its meaning would not have eluded me. Whether or not I imagined Dan's presence would not even have been an issue.

Curled in flannel sheets, Hudson Bay blankets up to my chin, I smiled to myself. Believing in spirits was easier than banishing them. If Dan was hanging around, he was more than welcome. Since he had been no ordinary dog, who was to say he was not an extraordinary spirit?

12

Two weeks prior to the start of the Yukon Quest, entrants must deliver their completed checkpoint bags to a shipping depot in Fairbanks. The bags are then distributed to checkpoints along the race trail by Yukon Quest trail workers. Because the bags may be carried by truck, snowmobile, or plane, they must be sturdy. Rules state that bags must be made of burlap. No bag may weigh over sixty pounds, although multiple bags may be sent to each checkpoint. Identifying tags must be attached to both the inside and outside of each bag before it is sewn shut. The tags are color-coded to indicate the intended destinations. Since some bags will cross the U.S./Canadian border, detailed customs forms declaring the contents are filled out in triplicate. Entrants are warned that they must comply with both countries' regulations concerning the importation of animal products. This can be tricky where game meats, skins, or fur of endangered species are involved, since the countries do not necessarily protect the same species.

Along with the constraints of rules and regulations, Quest entrants must carefully consider how the food, fuel, and other supplies in the bags will fare in subzero temperatures. Bags are kept frozen during distribution and stored in unheated caches at checkpoints.

To prepare George's bags, we transformed our kitchen and boiler room into a factory of sorts. First, I posted all the literature that the Quest officials had sent us, taping the twenty or so sheets of regulations and reminders to the side of our refrigerator. These sheets included information on allowable foods, medications, equipment, race rules, customs information, as well as announcements of mandatory prerace meetings, such as the draw for starting positions. On the front of the refrigerator, I taped a six-page master list I'd drawn up. It listed everything that was to go into the checkpoint bags.

Then I posted signs in various corners of the kitchen and living room. On each sign I wrote the name of a Quest checkpoint. Items destined for a particular checkpoint were piled under the correct sign. As items were added to the piles, they were checked off the master list.

George filled small metal bottles with the methanol he would use to fuel his cookstove and distributed the bottles to each one of our paper checkpoints. He counted out lithium batteries for his headlamp and figured how many he'd need for resupply at each stop. Sandy and I wrapped the batteries in pipe insulation, as lithium cells can be unstable if they strike one another in transit. I doled out medications, packing three kinds of foot ointment into small rubber containers, and stocked basic first-aid kits for each location. Sandy prepackaged 576 dog meals and divided them up. I dropped pairs of George's socks, extra mittens, extra underwear, rubber gloves, and boot liners in various piles.

In the evenings, we turned dog booties. They arrived from Frigi-Design as they would from any maker—inside out. Turning them right side out in advance of the race saves time for the musher, whose dogs will use eight hundred to twelve hundred booties in the course of a thousand-mile trail. When the booties were all turned, we packaged them in small bags according to size and number needed at each checkpoint.

Sandy mixed a batter of ground meat, animal fat, and vitamin powder in big buckets, then rolled it out on plastic sheets and cut it into big cookies with a cookie cutter. We froze the cookies and packaged them by the dozen. The cookies would be nutritious snacks for the dogs.

George portioned out his sawed-up squares of frozen turkey

skins, lamb, and salmon. These would also be used as dog snacks, so they were put in bags in multiples of twelve.

We marked the total numbers of booties, snacks, or anything packaged in small bags on the outside of the bags so that George would know at a glance when he located the right amount of whatever he wanted. There would be no time to count out such things on the trail.

While we worked, Kathleen played amid the piles. She got out her stuffed animals and put some discarded booties on them. She placed her little backpack in her "sled"—a cardboard box—and used a jump rope to link her animals to the box. She asked me to fashion her a headlamp, and I made a facsimile out of tape, a large strip of elastic, and a spool of thread. She pushed the box around the kitchen, calling out commands to her team of bunnies, dogs, and bears.

"Well, she's warped," Sandy said, "but no worse than the rest of us."

I prepared fifty-four meals and two dozen snacks for George, enough to sustain him for eighteen days on the trail. I was almost certain the race would take him fewer days, but we planned some extra meals in case injury or bad weather delayed him.

A musher must consider the weight of every item he will be carrying on his sled. The wise musher cuts corners by carrying dehydrated and calorie-dense foods instead of less food.

Dehydrated foods can be rehydrated and frozen foods defrosted using a trail cooker. This cooker is a portable campstove with a two- to three-gallon chamber designed to hold water. Snow placed in the hot chamber melts, and when the resulting water boils a musher can use it to drink, feed his dogs, fill his trail thermos, and thaw prepared, vacuum-sealed frozen meals.

We cooked, sorted, packed, and labeled all of George's Quest meals in our kitchen. We'd worked out a chart that estimated where George would be after each day on the trail and, based on that, I determined how many meals should be included in each checkpoint bag. The task was frustrating because, on the one hand, I had to be sure I was not saddling the team with excess weight. I could not put in a lot of extras. On the other hand, the chart could not reflect the unknown. When would storms take place? When would the dogs be tired? We had a clear idea about how our team would perform in the first 250 miles of the race. We had experience with those distances. After that, it was all extrapolation: the speed of the team, the number of days the race would take, the number of meals needed. All theory. I was haunted by the fact that George could not eat theories; any miscalculation on my part could have far-reaching consequences.

George had started a pocket-sized logbook for the Quest. On the pages, he recorded the location and contents of his bags so he wouldn't have to search for his supplies when he arrived at a checkpoint.

Long-distance teams follow a pattern of approximately six hours of running, then four or six hours of rest. The pattern may vary somewhat due to trail conditions, competition, and spacing of checkpoints, but basically a team must rest almost as much as it runs. When a musher begins a rest cycle, he boils water, feeds his dogs, removes their booties, and checks each dog for injury or illness. If he is at a checkpoint, race veterinarians examine the dogs. If it is very cold, the musher beds the dogs down in straw when it is available or blankets them in dog coats. After the dogs are settled, he feeds himself and sees to his own medical needs. He changes any clothes that may have gotten wet and dries out his wet clothes over a campfire or, if he has reached a cabin, over a woodstove. He repairs any damage to his sled or to the dogs' harnesses or lines, then plans for the trip ahead, resupplying and repacking his sled. If there is time left over, he tries to get some sleep, either by lying on his sled bag or huddling in a checkpoint cabin. Before he leaves, he must rouse his dogs and replace their booties—a forty-five-minute task if the driver is very efficient. He may give the dogs a snack.

While the team has been stopped, the dogs have relaxed for four hours and have probably slept for at least three of the hours. The team will average eight hours of sleep in a twenty-four-hour period.

The musher may sleep only two or three hours in each twenty-four-hour period. He may gain a little more sleep if he spends a minimum of time cooking, cleaning, and searching through his checkpoint bags. This is why his prerace preparation is so important. It can buy him sleep on the trail by saving time.

At the end of our food preparation day, I labeled the last bag AFTER CARMACKS and laid it out on the porch to freeze. I felt a sense of accomplishment. That pack of food would carry George to Whitehorse. Symbolically, I was *in* Whitehorse! I had crossed the finish line. I would no longer have to ask myself "Fruit now?" or "Breakfast bars later?" Everything was organized. In all, I had used three boxes of tea (caffeinated or decaffeinated depending on when it would be used), a box of instant oatmeal, a box of instant farina, powdered milk, two large jars of Tang, two boxes of Jell-O powder, three pounds of powdered Gatorade, a dozen dehydrated noodle soups, five pounds of dried fruit, frozen orange sections, several Snickers bars, one tray of shortbread with almonds, one tray of brownies, two boxes of granola bars, eight individual-size fruit pies, eight Polish sausages, several sticks of salmon jerky, a few bread and butter sandwiches, several stacks of peanut butter and cracker sandwiches, four small bags of unsalted peanuts, dehydrated pasta, frozen potato puffs, one can of beef stew, six corn muffins, one small frozen lasagna, fifteen servings of boil-in-bag vegetables, and two or three servings each of steaks, hamburger patties, fried chicken, lamb steak, and boneless pork chops.

"This would be a great idea for a diet," George said as he stood on the porch surveying the frozen food packs. "When you see all the food you're going to consume laid out like this, meal after meal, you think twice about eating all of it." He picked up one of the packs and examined it. "It sure feels funny to know exactly what I'm going to be eating a month from now."

We stacked the completed checkpoint bags on our porch forty-eight hours before they were due in Fairbanks. The night before we left, we stitched the bags closed and loaded them into our truck. There were twenty-six bags in all. Each one weighed thirty-five to sixty pounds and each one carried a colored, reflective marker so that George would find them easily regardless of the hour he arrived at the checkpoints.

We affixed the sign that bore our sponsors' names to the back of our truck. I had carefully painted the letters and logos in bright red and blue paint. YUKON QUEST 92 read the sign, and on the next line GEORGE COOK, ALKASIBER KENNELS. It looked very professional, very real. George and I stood behind the truck, reading the sign again and again. Then we hugged each other. It was really happening. The sign said we were running the Quest—and we were.

In the morning, George sat at the kitchen table drinking a cup of coffee and reading a day-old *News-Miner*. I poured some cereal for Kathleen and helped her into a chair. Sandy wandered in sleepily.

"Want some coffee?" I asked her.

She yawned. "Yeah, sure."

I filled two cups and handed one to her. We joined the others at the table.

"Look at this!" George laughed. He laid the paper on the table and pointed to a headline.

"Rummel Loses Team at Angel Creek," I read. The article told how Dave Rummel's team had dashed away from him on the winter trail. Off-duty sports writers from the *News-Miner* had been enjoying a few beers at a nearby lodge and had spotted the driverless team as it went by. Recognizing the emergency, they had tracked the team and recovered it.

"I tell you, I don't think I'd want to be Dave Rummel," George said. "If he even burps in the wrong direction, it's in the paper!"

"Yeah," Sandy agreed. "They ought to give him a break. Anyone can lose a team."

"But it's news if you're the world's top musher!" I added.

"Being a nobody in mushing has its benefits, I guess," George said. He tipped his head and smiled. "If I lose my team, no one cares!"

There was a knock on the door. I scowled at George and Sandy. "Someone here this early?" I asked.

"It's . . . uh, Richard," Sandy said demurely. "I told him we'd give him a ride to Fairbanks today." She hopped up to answer the door. George batted his eyelashes at me and I laughed.

The four of us, and Richard, headed into Fairbanks when breakfast was over. Since the checkpoint bags would soon be out of our hands, we were all in a mood to celebrate. Twenty miles short of our destination at the freight depot, the truck made a strange noise.

"What was that?" Sandy and I said in unison.

"I don't know," George said. Suddenly there was an ear-splitting bang. George steered the truck over to the shoulder of the road and leaped out. Richard and I followed him. Steam filled the air. Oil was pouring out of the underside of the engine.

All three of us cried, "Oh shit!"

"What happened?" Sandy asked, leaning out of the window of the truck.

Richard gazed at the puddle of oil. "It's toasted," he said. "It's *gone.*"

I walked to the rear of the truck and stared at it. The tilt of its wheels, the gaily painted sponsor signs gave it the look of a derailed circus train. I stopped my thoughts just short of naming the clowns. A passing motorist pulled up in front of the truck. She opened the door of her compact pickup, leaned out, and asked if we needed help.

"Can you give us a ride to that store back there?" George asked. There was a little country market about a mile down the road and it had a phone.

"Sure. Hop in!" the woman said. As we neared her truck, she asked, "Don't you guys have food drops today?"

George wrinkled up his face. How on earth did this woman know that?

The woman smiled. "You *are* running the Quest, aren't you? The signs on your truck . . ."

"Oh, yeah," George said. "Yeah, we were just on our way to the freight depot."

"Gee, that's terrible. I saw in the paper that everything was due in today. Well, get in."

I put Kathleen in the cab of the truck and, since Sandy was making noises about having forgotten her hat, I signaled to her to climb in. George, Richard, and I huddled in the bed of the truck for the brisk, zero-degree ride.

When the woman dropped us off, she wished George luck in the race. "I guess you're getting all your bad luck over with before the start," she said.

George found the pay phone and called a Fairbanks repair shop. Since our truck was over three quarters of a ton, they referred him to a special wrecking company that could tow heavy vehicles. That done, he called the race chairman at the Yukon Quest headquarters. I could tell from the tone of George's voice that he felt small. Here he was, the underdog in the race, and now he couldn't even get his checkpoint bags to the depot. He was no longer wondering if he could finish the race. He was worried he wouldn't even get the chance to start.

"The chairman is going to send a truck out here," George told me after he hung up the phone. "They'll pick up the bags right here. I'll walk down and meet them."

"I'll walk down with you," I said.

The store clerk had been listening to our conversation. "If you can wait a minute, I'll call my wife. We live just around the corner. She can drive you down there," he said.

George and I looked over at him. "Actually," George told the clerk, "it would be more of a help if your wife could take some of us home."

"Sure thing," the clerk said. He picked up the phone and dialed. "Hi, honey," I heard him say. "Hey, I was wondering if you could help a Quest musher out."

The clerk's wife drove George, Kathleen, and me back to the truck, then took Richard and Sandy to our house. In our truck, I bundled Kathleen in the old sleeping bag we carried for emergencies. She drifted off to sleep while George and I talked, and she didn't even awake when the Quest chairman arrived. George and the chairman loaded all twenty-six bags into the chairman's truck.

"When the wrecker gets you into town, come over to the depot and we'll finish your paperwork," he told George genially. Then he drove off.

An hour passed. My feet were getting very cold. Finally, a wrecker passed us, turned around, and pulled in ahead of us. A big man with long blond hair and a beer belly hopped out of the tow truck. His wide, ruddy face was drawn up in surprise and distress. When George opened our cab door, the fellow apologized to us.

"I was told by dispatch that the truck was unoccupied, so I didn't hurry. You guys must be freezing!" His eyes fell on Kathleen. "How's that kid doing?" he asked. He didn't wait for an answer. "Get in here, ma'am," he said, opening the wrecker door. "It's nice and warm in here."

After some maneuvering, our truck was hoisted by the wrecker and George and the driver squeezed into the cab with Kathleen and me for the trip to Fairbanks. The truck was so crowded, it seemed to be made entirely of flesh.

"I think it's great you guys are gonna do the Quest," the driver said cheerily. He placed a thick-fingered hand on the gearshift and pushed the stick into second. I curled my legs closer to George.

"Yeah, you know, I've towed a lot of Quest mushers. Yes I have. Towed Jeff King's truck all the way back from Whitehorse one year. Had engine failure. That was the year before he won. He could have used the prize money that time, though. That was one expensive towing job! You know Joe Hansen?"

I nodded.

"Well, I towed his truck in from Circle one year. I think it was 1988. He finished ninth in that race. And Angel Creek—I've picked up trucks there almost every year."

No one answered him, so he continued.

"I know how it is. You mushers have gotta spend your money on your dogs. Takes a lot of time to train a good team. You don't have time to tinker with trucks. I can understand." He caught my eye and tipped his chin toward Kathleen. "How's she doin'?" he asked.

"Okay," I said. Kathleen watched him sleepily.

While the driver talked on, George stared glumly out the passenger window, his shoulder thrust against the door. Like all men, he took the breakdown of his truck personally. I was afraid that at any moment he might explode in frustration, so I kept conversing with the wrecker driver to keep a lid on things. The driver was a mushing version of an armchair quarterback. He spoke of all the top mushers as if he knew them.

"I know Rummel is good, but you know he's said so many bad things about Melissa . . ."

Melissa Woodward. Dave Rummel's archrival.

". . . he puts everybody down, so I just never could cheer the guy on, you know? I just never could. Of course, that's the Iditarod. You're running in the Quest. Did you ever consider running the Iditarod?"

"Yes," I said.

"And you *chose* the Quest?"

"Yes."

"All right!" He grinned at the windshield and slapped the dashboard. "It's just like they say . . . the Quest is the toughest race in the world. It's tougher than the Iditarod. I'd make a lot of money if I printed a T-shirt that said somethin' like 'The Iditarod—The Powder Puff Derby of Anchorage.' And who cares about Anchorage? Fairbanks was here first."

This was not my first encounter with Anchorage/Fairbanks rivalries, much less Iditarod/Quest one-upmanship, but I had nothing to say on the matter.

"You folks are from the lower forty-eight, right?" the driver asked.

"That's right," I said.

"You ever run the Beargrease?"

"Yes, we have."

This evidently made us good guys in his eyes. "Yeah, I love the Beargrease," he said. "It's my hometown race 'cause I'm from Minnesota originally."

I turned to look more closely at the man. From Minnesota? Well, he looked it. A farm boy, no doubt. Arms and shoulders like his didn't come from driving a tow truck.

"Some people in Alaska are sort of mushing snobs," he said sternly. "They don't realize what a tough race the Beargrease is. They think there's no championship racing in the lower forty-eight. Of course, I've always been a fan of Jamie's. She grew up in my town, so the whole town's behind her." He referred to Jamie Nelson, a former winner of the grueling five-hundred-mile John Beargrease Sled Dog Marathon. As he spoke of her, he blushed.

By the time we reached Fairbanks, I'd heard the driver's opinion on everything from training lead dogs to proper sportsmanship. I imagined he owned a famous mushers belt that he notched each time he encountered one of us. Still, I could not dislike the man. He was a fan, and his interest was sincere. When he dropped us off at the repair shop, he clasped our hands and said how pleased he was to meet us.

"I'll be cheering for you," he said as George paid the bill.

Our fears that the truck's engine had thrown a rod were confirmed at the repair shop. The engine was under warranty. The shop could replace it with a new engine, but we'd have to pay for labor.

"I suppose you have to send to Seattle for the engine," George said to the parts department manager. There was an edge in his voice.

"Uh, no. Not at all," the manager replied. "We have one in stock."

George looked at me in amazement. Ordinary things like sewing machine parts were never stocked in the Great Land, but heavy-duty truck engines were readily available.

It would be two days before the truck was repaired. George, Kathleen, and I walked over to the Rent-A-Wreck dealer; our funds were too limited to consider a more deluxe rental car. After securing a rental contract on car twenty-four, we went out into the lot to meet our fate. It was a red rustmobile with a large crack in the windshield. It was against the law to drive a car with a cracked windshield in New Hampshire. George walked back to the rental office. He was not fully in the door when the agent at the desk said, "If you are going to mention the crack in the windshield, it's standard. They all have it. Dirt roads, you know. We don't charge you if it gets worse."

George backed out the door and surveyed the parking lot. She was right. The windshields were in varying states of disrepair. Compared to many others, our windshield had sustained only moderate damage. We took the car.

We had transported—in one way or another—over two thousand pounds of food, equipment, and straw to the freight depot. In exchange, we were given a receipt—one pink piece of paper with some wax pencil notations on it. It didn't seem like a reasonable exchange.

Our bags were stacked on pallets with many others. Signs over groups of pallets read CIRCLE, CENTRAL, and other checkpoint names. It reminded me of our kitchen and our paper checkpoints. Here were bigger paper checkpoints, the granddaddies of them all. I glanced at a few of the piles, trying to pick out George's bags. They are in there, I told myself. They won't be forgotten.

George was over talking to the Quest chairman.

"You're not the only one," he was saying to George. "Every year a few don't make it here. We do what we can. We know it happens." He thought our crisis was neither embarrassing nor unusual. I was grateful for that.

We hobbled home in the rustmobile. Though worn out from the day's events, George decided to take the team for a short run.

"I just want to get away from everything and be with the dogs," he told me. I made no objection.

He was not on the trail more than a few minutes when he saw the glow of another musher's headlamp. The team approached, passing cleanly. When the sled drew up even with George's sled, the other musher put on his brake. George recognized the man as John Mc-Guire. He'd met him before, but did not know him well.

"Sorry to hear about your truck," McGuire said.

George was stunned. "How did you know?" he asked.

"It was in the paper tonight. Front page of the *News-Miner*."

The truck's breakdown was just the first in a ten-day string of disasters that conspired to keep us from the starting line. Under the gaze of the press, our luck went from mediocre to dreadful.

Our training runs were scheduled to end six days before the race. This would prevent what mushers called stupid injuries—last-minute accidents with a team that was already primed for competition. It would also give the team a chance to rest up, eat, and restore themselves if any limbs were sore or spirits were low.

George was still running thirteen dogs. Still looking over Abe, Essie, and Gilbert. I could tell from his comments that he was leaning toward choosing Abe and Essie over Gilbert, but he wavered.

Recently, Essie had missed a few practices. She had come into season and we saved her out from the team to keep all the males from losing *their* concentration. Often if one female comes into season in a kennel, all the other females cycle, too. We worried about this, especially because three of our leaders were females and we wanted them going forward along the trail, not standing still. Nevertheless, Minnie, Lightening, and Orah showed no onset of doggy passion. Since females will not encourage breeding until about two weeks after their cycle begins, we hoped our "girls" would hold off at least another week, so there'd be no chance of trouble during the race.

When we had to run a female in season, we always hitched her next to another female. When George was fairly certain Essie's breedable time had passed, he resumed hitching her next to Gilbert.

I happened to be driving up to the store one day. Sandy and I decided to check the mail. George's team was hooked down in the parking lot not far from Jack Patterson's team. The two men had met on the trail and, quite uncharacteristically, had stopped for coffee. Much to my horror, our team was in a huge tangle, traces intertwined. Gilbert was practically strangled, and Abe was making serious advances toward Essie. At the same time, he was growling to prevent other males from coming near her. Our usually peaceful team was at war.

I brought the truck to a halt, jumped out of the cab, and ran toward the team. Sandy came striding after me, and we threw ourselves into the team with cries of "No!" and "Stay!" There was enormous potential here for the dogfight of the century, and if that happened, we could say good-bye to the Quest. After a great deal of fumbling, we reorganized the team.

"Do you think Abe bred Essie?" I asked Sandy.

"I don't think so. I think there would've been a real fight if he had," she said.

"You little rat!" I snapped at Abe. "You'd do anything to be on this team. Even knock up Essie!" We stared each other down. He was such a bold dog. His gaze was wary and deliberate, like that of a tiger. He wasn't sorry.

I turned to Sandy. "What will we do if she's pregnant? She'll slow right down."

Sandy shook her head. I felt a burning anger swell in my chest and move up my throat to my face.

"Hold the team!" I told Sandy. I marched into the store.

George was sitting at a table in the café. He and Jack were lost in conversation. He didn't notice me until I was standing over him. He flinched when he saw my expression.

"Hi," he said.

With all the calm I could muster, I said, "You'd better go out and see what your team is up to."

This incident became a sore subject between George and me. I couldn't understand, after all the training and preparations we'd been through, how he could be so careless. He claimed he hadn't been careless and that he'd been checking on the team frequently. He said the tangle had happened "in a flash." He was probably right. It turned out that Essie was not pregnant, but even before we could establish that, George made Abe a member of the team. Though I knew he wouldn't choose a dog just to please me, I was aware that the announcement of his decision was timed to cool my anger.

It is the honest truth that Abe knew he'd made the team. Perhaps he was keying off of our actions, but he became relaxed and self-assured in those last days before the race. When I passed his house, he regarded me with an amused expression. "See, I told you I would make it," he seemed to say.

"All right," I told him one day. "So you've made it. I expect all the heroics you're famous for, all in one race. Do you understand?"

He blinked at me and, just for a moment, the thought of losing him came to me. There was danger ahead. Freak accidents sometimes happen. My throat felt tight. I gave Abe a scratch on the neck and turned my face skyward. "This is your half brother here, Dan," I said. "Look after him for me. Talk to the gods or to the ravens or whoever you know up there and get them to watch over him."

13

Our last day of training was the Sunday before the Quest. We had put 1,650 miles on the dogs in a little over five months. This was a comfortable amount of preparedness for a thousand-mile event. That evening, we treated ourselves to dinner at Digger O'Donnell's, a local roadhouse. There we found a dog-sitter for the dogs who were to remain at home during the Quest, and it was there that we heard about the virus.

Digger's was a typical Alaskan establishment. It looked fairly shoddy on the outside. Inside, its varnished log walls were illuminated by candles in cheap amber jars. The bar, the tables, and the chairs were made of oak and pine. Everything glowed the deep golden brown of a beer. Everything smelled of beer. The room seemed submerged in a beer.

The clientele varied in age and background. There were always more men than women. Children accompanied their parents, lending a family atmosphere to the place. In spite of the frontier appearance of the building and the neon signs, there was little hard drinking. The bar was a social place—a lounge in the true sense of the word. Sometimes I'd seen certain patrons become inebriated. No one shielded children from the sight. It was a fact of life, a fact of roadhouses, just as dancing, eating, and talking were facts of life.

That night, the band was a young couple. Both played multiple instruments, sometimes moving from one to another during a song. Despite how awkward this looked, they had things covered. The sound was good. In the corner of the platform they used as a stage, their tiny newborn child reclined in a baby carrier. One or the other parent rocked the carrier with a foot when the routine permitted. All the while the parent would be strumming a guitar or playing a keyboard. Once, when the baby began to cry, the parents exchanged glances and the father moved right into a soft, romantic solo, giving the mother a chance to cradle the baby. Before the song was over, the baby was quiet and back in the carrier. The mother lovingly checked the cotton she'd placed in the child's ears to protect it from the din of the amplifiers.

George, Kathleen, Richard, Sandy, Sten, and I filled a table. I glanced around the room, since we could expect to see friends there. I noticed two men by the outside door. One was taller than the other, but their faces were so similar I judged them to be brothers. They were homely in the same way and they stood alike, with their weight shifted backward, as if their bellies were hard to hold up. They ordered two beers and then turned to watch the band. They never removed their tattered green parkys, the sleeves of which were patched with duct tape. After a few more beers, which they drank at the same speed, they nodded in unison and left the bar. They were walking out when a frost-covered man walked in. The frost man looked beige all over in his canvas parky and tall Native mukluks. Slowly he shook the ice off himself and I saw that it was Robin Peters, our graduate school friend.

"Robin!" I called out. He heard me, looked around, and walked over to our table.

"Have a seat," George said, pulling up a chair. Robin began to remove layer after layer of clothing.

"Geez-um," Sten remarked, "you look like you're wearing everything you own."

"Well, I kinda am," Robin said, pulling off his hat. His shoulder-length braid fell against his neck. He flashed the quick smile of Alaskan Natives.

"Is it getting *that* cold out?" Sten fussed.

"No, but Mark is back. He brought his girlfriend, so he doesn't need me to house-sit for now. I've been living on the trail. You know, giving them some privacy."

Just then, Jack Patterson wandered over to our table and sat down.

"Campin' out?" Jack asked Robin as he came in on the conversation.

"Yeah. Just me and my team."

Jack and Sten nodded understandingly, but I was amazed.

"Robin, it's January—forty below—and you're not living indoors?" I asked.

"No, but it's all right. I'm kinda enjoying it."

I looked around at the faces of our friends.

"No one thinks this is unusual?" I asked.

"Well, hell, honey, your husband's going to be out there doin' this next week," Sten laughed.

"Yeah, I know, but he's doing it voluntarily."

"That proves he's crazier than Robin," Jack said.

"Robin, you're welcome to stay with us," I said. I had an idea. "I'll be away during the race and we'll need someone to take care of the dogs that we're leaving home. You can have the house to yourself."

"That's a good deal. Sure, I'll do that," Robin said. He looked a little embarrassed when he added, "It *has* been getting kinda chilly out there. It's hard to study."

"Ah, what do you expect? You're a grad student. You're supposed to be impoverished," Sten exclaimed. "It's good for ya. That is, if it doesn't kill ya." He looked around the room for a minute and then said, "Well, I'm gonna go talk to Hal." He wandered off to speak with a man who had just come into the roadhouse.

"So, George," Jack said, "training's over. You ready for the race? Got everything you need?"

"I think so," George told him. "I'm as ready as I'll ever be."

"Got your diapers?"

"Diapers?"

"Yeah, 'cause you always feel like you're going to piss your pants at the start, believe me." Jack finished off a beer and set the glass down thoughtfully. "Ah, don't worry. Just finish the race, that's all. You'd better finish the race. People who don't finish go crazy."

"It's true," Robin said earnestly.

I glanced from Jack to Robin to Jack again.

"Naw!" I laughed.

"Hey, just look at Sten," Jack said. "He's as nutty as a fruitcake since that race. He can't forget he didn't finish. And what about that guy . . . oh, what's his name? He was sponsored by the Canadian Postal Service."

"No wonder he never got there!" Robin quipped.

"Yeah. Anyway, that guy lives out in the bush now. He's totally nuts. He always raves about 'the virus.' His dogs picked up a virus during the race and he had to call it quits."

"If you think about it, every driver puts so much time and money into a race like that, then they go out there and they see a lot of scary things. Storms. Isolation. If they don't get through it, it can be rough on them," Robin said.

I sat back in my chair and looked at George. "Good Lord," I breathed.

"Hey, speaking of virus, anyone got it yet?" Jack asked.

"What virus?" George said.

"It's going around the dog yards. Some of my dogs have had it. Shits and vomiting. Drags 'em out for about a week," Jack told him.

"Mine had it two weeks ago," Robin said.

Robin and Jack had turned to look at the band. George leaned toward me and said in a low voice, "Kirk and Moose were off their food tonight. I didn't think it was significant . . ."

I suppressed an urge to shiver.

Kennels all around Two Rivers succumbed to the virus, but Kirk and Moose resumed eating and our other dogs remained unaffected. The *News-Miner* carried details of the epidemic as well as a story about possible last-minute changes in the Quest trail. The Yukon River ice was unusually jumbled due to a late-season thaw and refreeze. There were long stretches of open water that could thwart safe passage along the ice. An inland course was being examined. It would add another summit climb.

"Five three-thousand-foot peaks aren't enough?" George grumbled as he read the article. "They have to add another?"

There was a general lack of urgency among Fairbanks's mechanics when it came to repairing our truck's engine. We had, by that week, poured hundreds of dollars into the old engine, then the new engine, and still the truck roared and pinged and chattered. Sandy continued to borrow the truck for nightly visits with Richard. Each night, she came home later and later, claiming that the truck had stalled or refused to start.

On the Tuesday before the Quest, I awoke at four-thirty. I glanced at George, who lay beside me. He was awake.

"She's not home," he said, answering my question before I asked it.

"Did she call?"

"No."

For a while, both of us tried to fall back to sleep, but eventually George said, "I'm going to call Sten and see if I can borrow his car. She's probably broken down on the road."

He snapped on the bedside lamp and got up. I watched him pull on a pair of jeans and a sweatshirt. Then he stopped and listened. We heard our truck pull in, and Sandy opening the front door. Without looking back at me, George started downstairs. I reached for my robe and followed him.

Sandy was startled to see us both on the stairs.

"Good night," she said, and headed for her room.

"Sandy, wait," George said. She stopped and turned toward us, but her eyes were cast down and her mouth was tensed in a defiant pout. Her thick blond hair hung in her face. "I need to know if it was the truck. I can't go off on the race and leave you and Ann with a broken truck. It's dangerous, don't you see?"

She didn't answer him.

"If you want to stay over with Richard, then just do so," I offered. "We're not your parents. We're only interested in your safety."

"Sandy, we can't sleep when we don't know where you are. I keep thinking you're out there freezing to death somewhere," George told her.

"Please, just call us if you're going to be late. Then we won't worry," I added.

"Why don't you believe me about the truck?" Sandy said accusingly.

"Well, we just thought ...," my voice trailed off.

Sandy turned on her heel and made a hasty exit. I heard her door close behind her.

When George and I climbed back into bed, we lay staring at the ceiling for a while. Finally, George sighed and turned out the light.

"Hurry up and start the race," I heard him mumble, "because the world's on its side and if we wait too much longer, it will be completely upside down."

Later that morning, Sandy and George went out to do kennel chores. When they were done, we were all planning on going to Fairbanks to do our weekly shopping and take care of last-minute Quest errands. Kathleen and I were just walking out the front door when I saw Sandy stop in front of Matanuska's doghouse. She took a step back.

"Ann?" she called in a tentative voice.

I went into the dog yard and saw Matanuska lying on his side in the snow. He wasn't moving. His eyes were dull and unresponsive. I bent down and touched him. He was still warm. I felt for his pulse. It was weak and rapid.

"Get a blanket!" I cried. "Grab one off any bed."

Sandy backed away, staring, then ran toward the house. George rushed over to me.

"What's the matter?" he asked.

"It's Matanuska. I think it's a stroke or something. Take Kathleen and warm up the truck. We gotta get him to the vet."

George picked Kathleen up in his arms and started for the driveway. Sandy appeared with a blanket. We wrapped it around Matanuska and I lifted him slowly.

"I'm going to put him on my lap in the cab," I told her. "I'll carry him over. You open the door."

I was fairly sure he would die. On the way to Fairbanks, I patted and smoothed his coat and thought about all the years I'd spent with him. He was so old. I had to accept that he couldn't live forever, but did he have to go now? Sadly, I thought that maybe the answer was yes. Even if he made it through whatever this was, I knew that with the Quest, I wouldn't be home to nurse him through a lengthy recovery.

I looked over my shoulder. Sandy sat in the backseat of the cab, gazing down at the floor. She seemed stunned. She had always doted on Matanuska.

"I'm sorry you have to see this," I said to her gently.

She didn't answer me, but a minute later said, "I was going to meet Richard in town. Does this mean we can't pick him up?" George and I exchanged a surprised glance. I looked down at Matanuska and pretended I hadn't heard Sandy's question.

Within hours, we learned that Matanuska would be fine. He had suffered a slight arrhythmia and was given a medication to regulate his heart. As I popped the green pills down his throat that afternoon, I wished it were as easy to regulate what I felt in my heart.

"Handlers are a strange lot," Sten told us that evening. The atmosphere was so tense in our house that George, Kathleen, and I had gone visiting. Sten welcomed us. We slumped into his tattered recliners. "I hired a guy to help me train when I ran the Quest. He was trouble from the start. He kept threatening to quit, and as it got closer to the race, I thought I couldn't let that happen. How could I find someone else at that late date? How could I break a new person in? I didn't have the time. I had to concentrate on the race. Hell, I was working five days a week just to get enough money to pay for the race. So I asked this handler to run my team on the days I was working."

Sten paused and stared at his woodstove. Flames flickering inside its glass door turned Sten's face orange, then yellow, then orange again. "I should've let him go. In the end I was paying him fifteen dollars a run. Fifteen dollars! I was so desperate. And what was he doing? He wasn't running my dogs. No, he was hooking them up and driving them over to his girlfriend's house and then driving 'em back when enough time had passed to make me think he'd run them. I didn't know that. I didn't catch on, but I should've. The dogs always looked so fresh when they came back. I thought they were just terrific dogs."

He looked up into my eyes for a moment. The anger I saw there was startling. "Finally, he quit over some minor thing just a few days before the race. He just wanted an excuse not to have to leave the girlfriend for ten or fifteen days to follow me on the Quest. I begged everyone I knew to handle for me, but you know, people are busy. They can't just take off like that. Somebody found me a guy. I didn't know him at all. I gave him my truck and the last two hundred dollars I had and told him I'd see him in Circle. You know the rest," he said.

"No, I don't, Sten," I said. "What was the rest?"

"I got frostbitten, really badly. It was before I got to Circle. I fell in a creek. I couldn't even walk. When I got off the trail, I was in so much pain and my dogs were so tired. My handler wasn't there. There was no truck to put my dogs in. Some people in town took me in. Then the Quest officials came and told me the RCMP had called me. They told me to get my ass down to Dawson because my handler was down there. He drank up all my money in two days and they were holding him and some other handler—a woman—on drunk and disorderly charges. They said they were holding me responsible.

I borrowed a friend's truck. I couldn't even afford the gas. I couldn't feel the pedals because my feet were numb, but I got down there and bailed him out just so I could get my truck. Christ, I've been in debt ever since."

Sten put his hand over his face. I thought for a moment that he would cry and I wished that he would, because I sensed he'd been keeping a cry about this inside for a long time. When he let his hand move back to his cheek, I saw that his eyes were dry. He was not going to cry. He settled his chin in his palm.

"Aw, I don't know," he said. "I guess you can hire the best handler in the world and somehow they all turn out to be assholes. Maybe it's the job or the kind of people who are attracted to the job. That guy said he'd help me with my food drops, but he always had some excuse when it was time to do them. I ended up packing my checkpoint bags the day before they were due. I was up all night. I didn't even know what I'd put in 'em and what I hadn't put in 'em. I was just a wreck."

A cynical smile came to his lips and it grew wider. He seemed to be reliving a memory. He turned to George and said, "I hope you're not planning on eating breakfast the morning of the race."

George looked puzzled. "Why?" he asked.

"Because you just puke it all up anyway. Butterflies, you know." He pointed to his stomach. "They're awful. I know all about those butterflies."

On Thursday, George and I loaded thirteen dogs into our repaired truck and waved good-bye to Sandy and Kathleen. We were off to Fairbanks to keep our appointment with the Yukon Quest veterinarians.

At 9:00 A.M., we arrived at the freight depot. The dog trucks of our Quest competitors were lined up in front of the building's two overhead doors. When the doors opened, trucks inside would leave and Quest officials would usher in two more trucks. George drove our truck into one of the lines. As it idled, we watched our fellow entrants with fascination. It was our first close look at many of the men and women George would be seeing on the trail.

As we discussed and identified this person and that, I glanced around the parking lot. Where a week ago food-drop bags had been piled high on pallets, there was only empty space. The bags had been shipped to the checkpoints. Food from our kitchen and equipment from our dog shed were in places we'd so far only dreamed of seeing. People in distant villages awaited the mushers. They awaited George Cook, a man whose name they'd seen stenciled on our burlap bags, but whose face they couldn't recognize. I wondered if the villagers handled the bags of previous champions with more reverence, or were all the bags just dumped from a truck or plane in democratic fashion?

My musings on this subject ended when a Quest official waved our truck forward. We moved into the building and the doors banged shut behind us. George and I climbed out of the truck and set up our bumper chains. The head veterinarian walked over to me and introduced herself.

"Are you the musher?" she asked.

"No, George Cook is," I said. "I'm his handler."

She looked at her clipboard and checked George's name off a list. In an instant, two more veterinarians appeared.

George stepped out from behind the truck.

"George Cook?" the head vet asked.

He nodded.

"Drop your dogs and we'll examine each one. After the exam, you'll bring the dogs over there." She pointed to a large scale in the corner of the building. "They'll be weighed and blood samples will be taken. All clear?"

"Yes," George said.

When we hooked our dogs to their chains, they looked around, barked, and danced with joy. To them, this was a fun outing. To the Quest veterinarians, it was serious business. Each dog received a thorough physical examination. The vets paid special attention to the condition of each dog's heart, lungs, joints, limbs, and foot pads. In addition to weighing the dogs, they assessed the dogs' total body fat, making sure each animal would begin the race with sufficient fat stores.

The vets then took blood samples from the dogs. Portions of each sample were screened for banned drugs. Other portions were used to work up blood profiles. Some of the profiles would be used for canine health research. If any profile signaled impending health problems, the dog would be scratched from the race. All dogs entered in the Yukon Quest were required to pass the physical exam.

Quest rules state that teams may start the race with no fewer than eight dogs and no more than twelve. Teams may drop only three dogs during the race. Nearly all drivers opt to start with twelve dogs because, with the maximum number of dogs dropped, a team of nine has more power than a team of five. No team with fewer than five dogs is permitted to continue the race. Because dogs may fail the physical examination, and because accidents, injuries, and plain old bad luck can happen between the examination day and the start of the race, each musher may bring up to fifteen dogs to the veterinary check.

At the start of the race, the musher must declare which twelve of those fifteen he will actually run. The veterinarians keep detailed records on each dog and reexamine the dogs as necessary during the course of the race. At random times during the competition, dogs may again be screened for banned drugs.

With Shasta injured, George and I had only thirteen dogs to submit to the examination. We had twelve bumper chains, so one dog had to wait until the vets were finished with the first twelve. The exams went smoothly, with the veterinarians commenting on how well-behaved our dogs were and what good condition they were in. I knew the health records of our dogs as well as I knew my own. I could easily answer every question the vets asked of me, and I was certain all of our dogs would pass, yet I felt nervous because our dogs were Siberian Huskies. We were different, not a typical Alaskan team, and therefore not something the vets often saw.

I winced when I saw one of the veterinarians cranking on Pete's pastern, but Pete never flinched.

Another vet signaled to me and asked, "Is this dog normally thin?" He was pointing to Minnie. My heart jumped. He wouldn't fail *Minnie*, would he?

"Yes, normally thin," I said. It was the truth. She was always prim and trim.

I saw the vet write "normally thin" in the comments section of Minnie's health record. He looked up and pointed his pen toward Essie. "That's a nice-looking dog," he said. He turned to another one of the vets. "I like this little golden dog."

While Essie's coat color was not common in crossbred strains, it was a typical Siberian color usually referred to as red. She was basically a strawberry blond, but now I saw her through someone else's eyes. Her admirer had called her golden, and in the dull fluorescent light of the garage, she did indeed look like an ingot. She stood proudly as if she understood the fellow's comments. Would she be golden? I wondered silently. Worth her weight in gold?

George was loading the dogs back into the truck. He reached for Essie's collar and she hopped up, ready to return to her box.

"Last dog," George said to one of the vets. He lifted Gilbert out of his box and hooked him to a chain. Gilbert wagged happily for a moment and then stopped, realizing that the other dogs were no longer on the bumpers. He looked around as if searching for them. Then a solemn look came over his face. He was the thirteenth dog and he knew it. I don't know how he knew it. Dogs can't count, but they do feel, and he knew this didn't feel right. He stood quietly as the vet placed a stethoscope on his heart. I walked over to George and touched his arm.

"He's off the team, isn't he?" I said, motioning toward Gilbert.

"I'm afraid so. I can *trust* Essie, Ann. She'll do what I tell her."

"I understand. You know best."

George reached down to steady Gilbert while the vet checked his feet.

A man tapped me on the shoulder. He must have been speaking to us, but the sound of barking dogs was echoing off every wall and neither George nor I had heard him.

"Mike Conolly," he said. "*News-Miner*. I was wondering if I could ask you a few questions about your husband's team." He opened his hand to shake mine. I took his hand. It was cold and thin. In fact, he was all over thin: tall, raven-haired, with the pale looks and the hooded eyes of a priest. Not at all the burly Irishman his byline had conjured in my mind. This was the reporter who had been phoning us. He was the one who covered our truck breakdown. He began to fire questions at me. How did I feel in these final days before the race? Was our team ready? What did I think the greatest challenges would be?

His approach started a feeding frenzy of sorts. Reporters set down their Styrofoam cups of coffee, picked up their little pads of paper, and scurried toward me like vultures swooping in after wolves have left a carcass. They had waited for the veterinarians to be done with us. Now they could pick our minds. I looked at George. A television cameraman was filming him. A reporter held a microphone up to his face.

The reporters hoped our team was the dark horse that would upset the field. The veterinarians patted our dogs and picked out their favorites, hoping they'd been assigned to examine the eventual champions. When the race was over, they'd perhaps be able to say they'd spotted talent right there at the examination. They'd known a superior team by its vigor.

George and I stood in the warm light of their dreams. For the next two and a half days, we were loved and cheered by people with whom we'd had only the slightest contact. We were recognized by people who'd read about us in the newspapers and seen our pictures. The coverage portrayed us as approachable, everyman's mushers, so everyone in Fairbanks wanted to say hello to us and chat about the race. Strangers walked up to us in malls and on the streets. They squeezed in next to us in checkout lines. A few people pressed things into George's hands, saying, "Take this, it always brought me luck."

Our friends from home wrote or phoned us. "You can do it," they told us.

Our friends from Alaska pitched in and helped us. Sten and Robin worked with George to prepare his sled. Karen insisted on baby-sitting for Kathleen on the first night of the race.

The attention was exciting, sometimes annoying, because it distracted us from concentrating on final details. Sometimes the attention was amusing, because we'd never thought of ourselves as noteworthy. It was strange to have fans.

We assumed many of the other Quest entrants knew the odds were against us. We even overheard one driver boasting that he could "dust" our team, but all the other competitors treated us with respect. At the Friday afternoon drivers' meeting, where all the drivers were briefed on rules, regulations, and trail conditions, several of the elite veterans of the race offered George words of encouragement. Few of them forgot their first time on the trail. They understood that a rookie seldom races to win.

Our darkest thought was that we might fail altogether. We might have to withdraw from the race. Like a bird shot out of the sky, we would tumble down and flutter in the agony of public humiliation. We had lived through disappointing races before. No team is ever perfect, but in the past, our disappointments had been our own— measured on our private scale. This time the world would be watching. Try as we might, there was no way to throw off the pressure this uninvited stir created.

The Start Banquet was held at a Fairbanks dance hall on Friday night. It was an enormous affair attended by mushers, fans, race sponsors, local politicians, celebrities, and, of course, the media. People gave lighthearted speeches and mushers drew for their starting positions. One by one, the twenty-seven drivers walked onstage to choose a number out of a hat. George drew number fourteen. We had hoped for a lower number, but fourteen was an acceptable position. That would give him some teams to travel with early in the race.

After the draw, there was an auction. Framed Yukon Quest posters signed by the entrants were offered up for bid. George and I were afraid that no one would bid on his poster. We were relieved when there was competition for it and shocked when it brought the second-highest bid in the auction. The highest bid was for the defending champion's poster.

As I scanned the crowd, trying to identify the bidders, I fought a choking sensation. I was going to cry, I thought. Or perhaps I was going to laugh. In either case, I wished the moment wouldn't end. I wished we wouldn't have to start the race. Then people could believe in us forever and there would be no hour of reckoning.

A band began playing at the conclusion of the auction, but we, like other Quest entrants and their families, did not join the revelers on the dance floor. We returned home to our beds, knowing sleep would be hard to come by in the next two weeks.

The next thirty-six hours of waiting were neither joyous nor sad. George and I were numb. We wandered around the house in a mild state of shock, while Sandy kept to herself. I went through the motions of motherhood with Kathleen, but my thoughts kept drifting back to George.

Our Alaskan experience had brought him closer to me. We'd shared the crises and the laughter, the depressive self-doubt, and the bright revelations. We were, as George said, worried out.

We weren't aware of the curtain falling between us. It would not block our mutual support, as a curtain cannot stifle sound, but it would remove us from each other's sight. Until that day, I had shared all of George's thoughts and actions. What tasks I did not perform myself, I could easily imagine. I had driven a team, raced, cared for dogs, strategized, but I had never run the Yukon Quest. George would soon be on the other side of the curtain. He was passing into another world. I could only await his return.

On his last night at home, while he slept in our bed, I crept downstairs and found his logbook. I folded a small portrait Kathleen had drawn of George and the team and taped it inside the log. On the inside front cover, I copied a verse from Isaiah:

> But those who trust in the Lord
> will renew their strength.
> They will soar on wings like eagles.
> They will run and not grow weary.
> They will walk and not be faint.

Quietly, I returned to bed.

Loading the team into the truck for the trip to the starting line was a liberating experience. Action replaced suspended motion. At nine o'clock in the morning on Sunday, February 9, we fetched Minnie, Lightening, Orah, Kirk, Essie, Abe, Moose, Pete, Boomer, Bandit, Scamp, Taro, and, just in case, Gilbert. I dressed Kathleen in her heavy Native parky with the bright braid trim and buckled her into the carseat. Sandy and George reviewed a final checklist, decided it was complete, and hopped into the truck.

The overcast sky was clearing as we started into Fairbanks. Temperatures were climbing into the low thirties. By midday, when the race began, it would be too warm for the dogs to perform at their best. We ignored this glitch, knowing that every team would have to contend with it. Bad luck shared by all was no issue after the personal ups and downs we'd faced.

The staging area for the race was a municipal parking lot in downtown Fairbanks. There, parking spaces were reserved for entrants. Each musher's starting number was spraypainted on the snowbank in front of his or her space. Teams would hitch their dogs at their trucks, cross the lot, and head down the short, steep bank of the Chena River. Once on the surface of the frozen river, they would follow the trail along the ice to an arch of gaudy banners that marked the starting line. One at a time, at two-minute intervals, the teams would be given the signal to depart the line.

When we arrived at the lot, Quest officials ushered us to our space. We parked, got out of the truck, and looked around. About half of the teams were already in the lot, busily preparing for the trip. Kathleen and I wandered to the edge of the riverbank and watched the spectators gather. At first, there were a few distant forms moving down from Golden Heart Park at the city's center. Fairbanks looked gray and white, its modest skyline rising only a few stories from the solid white cover on the Chena. The parkys of the spectators were bright patches on this dull scene and, in a short time, the river became stippled with color. People were everywhere.

I turned back to view the staging area. More trucks had arrived. More dogs were out on chains. Spectators and reporters were visiting the teams. I saw George filling his bag with gear. "Kathleen," I said, taking her tiny mittened hand into mine, "come help Mommy count out harnesses for Dad."

While Kathleen counted aloud and plucked twelve harnesses off a carabiner, Sandy and I let the dogs out to stretch. We offered them water baited with meat and watched carefully to see that they drank.

Sten and Robin showed up and offered to help, but there was little to do once the sled was loaded. Richard arrived with a few friends. Sandy introduced them to our dogs and then handed them our video camera, so someone could film the start. Karen and Alan appeared and took charge of Kathleen. I was touched when Mary Ann from FrigiDesign appeared and handed George a little paper bag. He opened it and smiled. It contained a headband she'd made and a huge chocolate bar. "For the trail," she said. "Best of luck."

When George walked off to view the place where the teams would descend the riverbank, I followed him. It was our last moment to speak in confidence.

"Are you real nervous?" I asked him.

"Not nearly as nervous as I thought I'd be," he said.

"Me neither. Strange, isn't it?"

"Yeah, maybe it's because we have everything on our side."

"What do you mean?"

"Well, you sewed a Saint Christopher's medal into my coat pocket."

"He's the patron saint of travelers," I said defensively. "My sister sent it from home."

"And I have every lucky charm in Fairbanks."

"You didn't take that hat that guy gave you, did you?"

George shrugged. "Sure I did. He said his cousin wore it all the way to the finish in the eighty-eight Quest."

"Your sled is going to weigh ten extra pounds just from all that stuff," I said. "Your fans are killing you with kindness."

"What I'm worried about is how all this stuff is going to get along. Do you think Athabascan talismans will mix okay with Catholic medals?"

"If they don't, just dump them all in the Yukon," I suggested. "After all, you've always got Dan. I know you still talk to him."

"I've always got Dan," he agreed.

Aurora

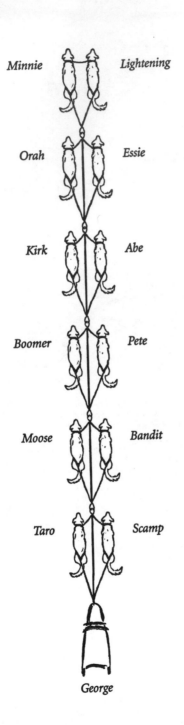

Minnie   Lightening

Orah   Essie

Kirk   Abe

Boomer   Pete

Moose   Bandit

Taro   Scamp

George

14

1,000 MILES

Sandy took the leaders' neckline. I jumped on the runners with George. The team was lunging in their traces. We fell in line with the other teams moving up to the starting chute. People rushed along beside us, calling out last-minute encouragement. Up to the banners we rode. Over our heads it said START OF THE YUKON QUEST. The sled holders caught the sled and held it for the count-down. Dogs were barking, people were shouting and cheering. The PA system was saying something about George. I stepped off the sled and ran up to Minnie and Lightening to say good-bye. They pawed the snow, ready to burst forward.

"Do well girls. Do your very best. I know you can," I told them.

I was going to run back and give George a farewell kiss, but there was no time. The count reached "Go" and the team bolted ahead. They were off.

Sten, Robin, and the others moved into the crowd, anxious to see the next team. Sandy caught up with Richard. I slipped behind the chute lines and watched the other teams, but little of what I saw sunk in. My thoughts turned inward. I saw again and again the flash of maroon parky that was my last glimpse of George.

When the start was over, there was nothing to do but go home. Sandy and Richard rode back to the house with me, and they went out around five that evening to watch the teams pass by our house. I cautioned Sandy not to let our dogs see her. If they did, they might think this was a practice run and turn off the trail into our yard. For this reason, I did not go with her.

Alan phoned, then Sten, and surprisingly Jeffry, all to tell me they had seen our team pass beyond our kennel with no incident.

"You know, that doesn't always happen," Sten said sternly. "There was a fellow who ran it the year I did. His yard was about twenty miles out on the trail. He couldn't get his dogs to go by it, so finally he stopped, thinking he'd give 'em a rest and then get started again. He tied 'em off and went into his cabin. Well, he never left. He just stayed there. That was as far as he got."

"Only twenty miles?" I gasped.

"Yep. It happens sometimes. But don't worry. George is on his way to Angel Creek now. What time do you expect him up there?"

"Between ten and twelve tonight."

"I'll be there. You want a ride up?"

"No, thanks. I've got Sandy and Richard. We'll drive there together."

Sten began to chuckle.

"What's so funny?" I asked.

"Richard," he said. "She coulda had anyone in Fairbanks, not just me. I know I'm an old man. I liked the grad student, though. What's his name? Robin? He would have been a good choice, but instead she chose Richard. He's not even an Alaskan, you know. He's from New York, of all things. He's just pretending to be an Alaskan."

"I know, Sten, but what can I do? I'm not her mother."

"Laugh. That's what we all can do. See you up at the Creek."

"Yeah, see you." I hung up the phone and looked around the kitchen. Richard, the cad of the century, and everyone but Sandy knew it! I hated the way he affected Sandy. He'd put a wedge between the two of us and I was helpless to dislodge it.

A disturbing thought came to me. It was more of an unpleasant sensation at first. Then it took form: My relationship with Sandy had changed. I didn't know when the change had begun. I didn't remember any day or any particular incident that signaled it, but we had changed and we weren't close anymore. I admitted to myself that my feelings for her were on a downhill slide.

As I thought about the last couple of months, I realized there had been an ongoing battle between us. Her long-faced silence had been pitted against my loquacious attempts to cheer her. I could not get to the heart of her moodiness. For some reason, she'd shut me out. Richard was merely the key with which she'd locked the door. She seemed to enjoy rejecting me and I was tiring of that. Had I done something to hurt her? Had I not done something to help? Had I just been so busy with George that she felt overlooked?

I thought that we had agreed that getting away to Alaska was best for her. For years, she had complained to me about her mother's control, and so I'd created a means for her escape. The bargain we struck seemed simple to me: Sandy would work hard for our cause and enjoy some independence in return. Now I wasn't sure she wanted that independence. It seemed to overwhelm her. She had turned away from all the newness of our journey, choosing to spend her time writing to old friends instead of making new ones, cataloging her old photographs, rereading books she'd brought from home. Perhaps I'd forced too much change on her in too short a time.

If I read Sandy's actions correctly, what she wanted was attention, the all-encompassing attention her mother gave her. However suffocating this relationship was, it apparently provided some sense of grounding and security for Sandy. In a way, her life at home had given her a freedom that she couldn't have in Alaska; her mother orchestrated her life, freeing her of any responsibility for herself and her decisions. Now that Sandy's mother was absent, Sandy constantly pushed me into the mother role, acting out in ways that demanded a response. When I insisted on negotiation instead of domination, I lost her. She found Richard. Now he was in charge of her life. My attempts to make her choose her own path had only made her resent me.

I comforted myself with the knowledge that after tonight there would be no Richard for two weeks. Sandy, Kathleen, and I would be spending long hours on the road. I decided this would be an opportunity to reestablish our relationship. Surely I could get our friendship back in balance. Surely things would work out.

Angel Creek was bustling when we arrived at nine that night. The single building in town, a tiny lodge, was nearly hidden among dozens of cars and trucks. Every vehicle that could force its way within a quarter mile of this establishment had done so. Four-wheel-drives were perched on snowbanks at the edges of the parking lot. There was absolutely no place for our truck to squeeze in, so I parked it out on the road and Sandy, Richard, and I walked to the lodge.

We entered the low wooden lodge through a thick door. A rusty spring hinge snapped the door back, but a layer of frost on the threshold kept it from actually banging shut. Despite this ample air gap, it was warm inside. The place was packed with racers, handlers, and fans. Smells of wet wool, fryolator grease, and chili filled the air. Many people were talking, but I doubted anyone could hear in such a din.

I spotted a big blackboard that read YUKON QUEST 1992—ANGEL CREEK. I indicated to Sandy that I was going to push my way past the crowd at the bar to see what else the board said. I was offered several beers by happy, drunken men before I made it across the room. Finally, I got close enough to see that the board was marked off in columns. The header on one column read DRIVER'S NAME, the next read TIME IN, then TIME OUT. There were only three drivers' names posted, all fast veterans of the race. I glanced at my watch. It was nine forty-five. Most of the drivers should have arrived.

"You lookin' for a driver?" someone yelled from the bar.

I turned to see a middle-aged woman. She looked unfriendly.

"I'm looking for George Cook," I said.

"Who?" she yelled.

"George Cook," I said a little louder.

"Haven't heard of him." She turned to face the bar. "Hey, where's George Cook?" she shouted over the room.

Another equally intimidating woman yelled back. "Who wants to know?"

The first woman pointed to me as if she were singling me out to be executed. The other one shouted, "George Cook? A rookie! You'd better sit tight. It's gonna be a long night." She began cackling and I retreated from the bar.

As I worked my way back to Richard and Sandy, one swarthy fellow asked me to dance. When I shook my head no, he seemed disappointed. Perhaps he hadn't noticed that no one else was dancing, and there was no dance floor.

Amid the commotion, Quest mushers sprawled on the seats of diner-style booths, trying to catch a bit of sleep before traveling out into the night. Judging from the number of them, there were many more mushers in the checkpoint than the board indicated. Short booth seats made rather inadequate sleeping quarters for them, and one drunken bar patron after another stumbled over the dangling knees and feet of the sleepers. Not only had these fans all but forgotten the race, they'd become something of a menace to the competitors.

I surveyed the faces of the sleepers hoping to see George, but I knew it was too early for him to be in. Mushers' wet clothes steamed on the chairs that encircled the potbellied stove. None of George's things were there.

Someone tapped me on the shoulder I turned to see that it was Sten. "Checkpoint's out back," he said.

"Have you seen George?" I tried to sound casual.

"Not yet. Three teams have already gone through."

Three teams had already gone through and George hadn't arrived! I knew it would be like this. Eventually, there might be days between them all, but I felt uncomfortable just the same. I looked around for Sandy and caught her eye. I motioned that I was going outside. She nodded firmly and nudged Richard. He had apparently run into some friends, so he stayed inside, but Sandy followed me outdoors.

We walked out behind the building to the checkpoint holding area. We could hear the loud chugging of a generator working to power the strings of floodlights overhead. A huge yellow banner hung from the strings. Bold red letters proclaimed WELCOME TO ANGEL

CREEK—CHECKPOINT #1 OF THE YQI. Checkpoint officials stood under the banner with clipboards in hand. They paced around and talked with one another, passing the time until another team came in. Handlers and spectators milled about. Mushers hovered over cookstoves and dogs.

In a plowed area alongside the incoming trail, the checkpoint bags were laid out in rows. I could read the names on a few of the bags and I could see the reflective tape on George's. Beyond this lot, small parallel paths had been snowshoed—angle parking spaces for each team. Unfortunately, the spaces were rather close together, and many teams were not yet tired. Though the mushers broke bales of straw open and lined the paths to make beds for the dogs, the dogs were too excited to sleep. They rustled about in their traces eyeing the other teams. There were smells of new and different dog foods, barks from unknown challengers, and fragrant females to fight over.

While mushers attempted to sleep, handlers watched over these dogs. Race rules did not permit handlers to touch or in any way aid the teams, so if a team took it upon themselves to move, investigate another team, or fight, the handler had to rush off and inform the musher of the trouble. Race officials were allowed to separate teams and step in where necessary, but they seemed reluctant to do so.

The barking and canine pandemonium outside the lodge were more than equal to the human chaos inside. Shouts of "Whoa! No!" caused Sandy and me to turn our heads. A team had pulled up their snow hook and broken free. They were driverless, heading full tilt for the outgoing trail. A cloud of snow powder went up as race officials and veterinarians dove on the sled and dragged until the team stopped. Another noisy incident began when an incoming musher pleaded with the officials to separate his team from another one that kept hopping the snowbank to visit one of his females.

"She's gonna get bred, damn it! I can't have that!" the musher complained. The trail officials seemed unsympathetic until some snarling erupted between the two teams. Two veterinarians came to the rescue.

"Is this what the whole race is going to be like?" Sandy asked me.

"I don't know, but this is terrible," I said. "I've never seen dogs so fired up. They're just crazy."

A tall fellow in sealskin mukluks and a Native parky stood near us. He leaned over to Sandy and said, "Don't worry. The first checkpoint is always wild. They settle down after the first night."

Sandy and I both looked at him without saying a word. He grinned at us through a blond handlebar mustache.

"I'm Dave," he said. "And you are?"

We told him our names and he told us he was handling for one of the teams. "But my driver's not in yet," he said calmly. There was a faithful sound in his voice as if he would wait forever if necessary. I glanced over at the checkpoint bags. All but four of them had been claimed.

"We're handling too," Sandy said.

"Our team's not in yet, either," I added.

"Who are you handling for?" Dave asked.

"George Cook," I said. "He's my husband."

"Oh, yeah. A rookie. I read about you guys."

Sandy and I rolled our eyes at each other. "Who hasn't?" Sandy said.

"Yeah, but you can't let that get to you," Dave said knowingly. "You gotta run your own race. Do what you can. Like my team: My driver's not fast, but he has a good time out there and he's finished it twice before. He knows what he's doing."

One of the race officials shouted, "Team coming!" Everyone strained their eyes to identify the driver making his way through the darkness. I held my breath and crossed my fingers inside my mittens, but the headlamp in the distance looked low to the ground and bobbed up and down rapidly—a short driver peddling the sled. It was not George, with his tall body and long, sweeping kick. Two lead dogs appeared under the floodlights, then the point dogs came out of the shadows. *Not Minnie or Lightening.* The team pulled up under the banner and Dave strode proudly toward it. He towered over the jockey-sized driver. A race official handed the driver a sign-in sheet and pointed out the checkpoint bags. The driver nodded and started up the team while Dave ran along next to the lead dogs to guide them into a parking space. Jealously, I watched them go.

A long time passed. I dared not look at my watch to see just how long. Sten, Robin, Richard, and Richard's friends all came to check on George's progress, but we had no word for them. I forced back thoughts of "last place, already" and reminded myself that the day had been very warm for heavy-coated breeds like our Siberians. First days of long races were not often accurate predictors of the days to come, and in an endurance race, where you finished was not as important as the fact that you *did* finish. In any case, it was important for the handler to inspire the musher by being enthusiastic and welcoming, regardless of where the team was in the standings.

Finally, a headlamp appeared. "Team coming!" someone announced. Sandy and I waited side by side, eyes trained on the far-off glow. I knew it was George, but I didn't say it was him because I felt it might jinx the possibility. "Almost home, Minnie," I heard him call.

"It's him!" Sandy said. We scrambled to the edge of the trail. Minnie and Lightening trotted up under the banner.

"You're here!" I heard Sten call from behind me. George gave him a tired smile and then noticed Sandy and me standing beside him. Sweat, no longer contained by his headband, rolled down his forehead.

"How are you?" I asked as a race official handed him the sign-in sheet.

"Okay," he said vaguely. "It's hot out there. Where am I supposed to park?"

The race official pointed out a space.

"Do you need the vets?" she asked.

"No. Everybody looks fine," George told her. Then he called out, "Okay, Minnie. Okay, Lightening." He talked the dogs over to the space and hooked them down. I overheard one race official say,

"There's a team that isn't going to finish." I didn't know if he was talking about our team, but I suspected he was.

"Like hell," I said aloud, but not to the race official.

George had walked over to get his checkpoint bag. He dragged it back to his campsite and cut it open with his knife. Sandy and I stood watching him, our hands thrust into our coat pockets to keep us from any action that might get our team disqualified. Watching, when ordinarily I'd be helping, made me feel anxious for George, but he seemed confident as he fed the dogs, bedded them down, re-filled his fuel bottles, and worked down a checklist he held in his mind.

"So, how was it?" Sten asked. I turned to notice that he, Robin, and Richard had walked up behind us.

"Well, the trail was really soft, so it was slow going. I got passed a lot, but then I kind of caught up. I think a few of these guys were surprised to see me still with them." George paused and smiled. "When Sonny Lindner passed me, he said, 'Nice-looking bunch of dogs.' Do you think that's a compliment or an insult?"

Lindner was known as a man of very few words. A former Quest champion.

"I guess you should be flattered he said anything at all," Sten said.

"When I passed through Fort Wainwright, it was incredible," George continued. "There were all kinds of army people out there with lawn chairs and barbecue grills set up. Some guy was handing out sloppy joes to all the teams, so that was my lunch. There were people who'd been stationed in Massachusetts and soldiers from New Hampshire who yelled out the names of towns they were from and cheered me on. It was even more amazing when I got to Nordale Road. The place was packed with people. Our whole neighborhood was there. It was a good place to watch, I guess. There is a tough, almost vertical climb off the river right there."

"A harbinger of many climbs to come," Sten said.

"Yeah," George agreed. Then he recalled his checklist. "Well, I'd better get some food."

"There's food at the lodge," I told him. He looked around, glancing to see that the team was settled down.

"Point me in the right direction," he said.

I walked him to the lodge while Sandy watched the team. The party had wound down a little since I'd last been inside. Some of the mushers had departed, and there was chair space where George could hang his wet clothes, and a booth where we could sit down. Chili was available to the mushers, so George ordered a bowl.

"Have you eaten?" he asked me.

I thought for a moment. I couldn't remember eating anything since breakfast, so I ordered a bowl of chili, too.

George ate hungrily and then had seconds. I could hardly choke down half a bowl. I couldn't stop checking the Alaskan Ale clock over the bar. George was supposed to be ready to run again in five hours. If he was going to get any sleep at all, he'd have to bed down soon.

Halfway through his second bowl of chili, his eyelids grew heavy, his conversation ceased to make sense, and his face hung a precarious few inches from his food. He was shutting down. Just then, Sandy charged up to our table and reported that the team parked next to ours was challenging Minnie and Lightening to a fight.

"George, you've gotta go out there and stop them!" Sandy cried. George looked at her blankly. He got up slowly and wandered toward his coat.

"Sandy, I can probably shout them down," I said. "Get George out there as quick as you can." I pushed through the crowd and sprinted out to the team. There I saw that Minnie was behaving herself, but Lightening was returning the snarls of the other team.

"Lightening!" I shouted. "Cut it out!" She turned to me and a sweet expression came over her face. She wagged her tail innocently.

"C'mon, Lightening. We can't risk any fight wounds now," I scolded.

George walked up to the team, urged on by Sandy. The excitement had awakened all of our dogs, and some of them were on their feet. George bedded them down again and trudged back to the lodge.

"I'll take this watch," I said to Sandy. "Go get yourself something to eat."

An hour passed. All the remaining teams arrived at the checkpoint. Some teams had gone on down the trail. Our dogs were fast asleep, as was the neighboring team, so I returned to the lodge.

George was asleep in a booth, and Sandy sat across from him staring into space. A few other mushers slept nearby. Most of the revelers had gone, and the ones who remained were lulled by gentle country music coming from the speakers over the bar. I checked the Alaskan Ale clock. It was one-thirty in the morning. George would have to wake up in an hour so he could prepare for a four-thirty departure. I crawled into the booth next to Sandy.

"Should I go out?" she asked.

"Not for a while. Everything is quiet and it's getting a lot colder."

She nodded, sat back, and resumed staring. I put my head down on the table and brought my arms up over my face, but I was afraid to let myself go to sleep. I'd close my eyes, but they'd pop open again. Eventually, motion drew my glance to the next booth. There was the fellow that Dave was handling for, passionately kissing a young woman. The two were entwined from head to foot, pursuing the moment without the slightest bit of self-consciousness. Dave sat a few booths away, resting his chin on his hand. He caught my eye and shrugged. I couldn't help but smile.

As the lovers continued their embrace, I searched for something else to look at. I noticed that George's parky had slipped off the chair and was down on the damp floor. I also noticed that two race officials were at a nearby table. I wanted to return the parky to the chair, but knew that the race officials could construe my actions as special help for George, so I sat there, looking at the parky and feeling miserable about it. After a few minutes, one of the officials stood up and walked past the woodstove. He noticed the parky and replaced it on the chair.

Perhaps I'd reached him by telepathy. I rose from the table and set off to check the team. Dave followed me and we walked together past the chugging generator and toward the floodlights.

"I don't think your musher's getting much sleep," I told Dave.

"Naw. Well, this is a new girlfriend and she doesn't like the idea of him mushing. She doesn't want him gone for two weeks and all that."

"He's never going to get the chance to leave if she keeps him in that headlock!"

"Oh, I'll get him out of here somehow. I always do. I've handled for him in all three of his Quests, and the first year he had a great girlfriend. She loved the dogs and helped in the kennel. I can't see why he'd dump a great girl like that. It was worse in the middle year. That's the year he'd just broken up with the one he dumped the first one for. Man, he was depressed. I didn't think he'd get through the whole race. Yeah, he's bad when he's got a girlfriend, but he's worse without one, believe me."

Dave's driver never did close an eye that night, but he departed on schedule, as did George. When it was time to leave the checkpoint, both teams' dogs came to their feet quickly and headed toward the dark opening in the spruce forest that was the trail. In seconds they vanished, leaving Sandy, Dave, and me gazing at nothing at all.

"You going on to Central?" Dave asked after a while. We told him we were.

"See you up there," he said. He walked off.

Sandy and I raked up the straw where our dogs had slept and set it in the checkpoint's burn pile. Then we were free to leave.

"Where's Richard?" I asked. I realized I hadn't seen him in some time.

"He got a ride home with Sten."

"Hours ago?"

"Hours ago."

We walked back to the truck. So many vehicles had left before us that ours stood alone on the edge of the road. We drove home, checked on the dogs that remained in our yard, and went to bed. It was 6:00 A.M. when I crawled under my blankets. I fell asleep immediately.

My alarm clock was set for nine-thirty, the time when Karen would arrive with Kathleen and Robin would move in to become our kennel sitter. Before the alarm sounded, I was awake. I showered, dressed, and packed a bag for Kathleen and myself to take to Central. Sandy was up early, too. We made coffee to share with Robin and Karen.

The morning drifted by on schedule. By one o'clock, we'd filled our truck with supplies. We included food, fuel, extra clothing, blankets, sleeping bags, shovels, chains, a well-stocked medical bag, a rifle, and a small cookstove. We were traveling the Steese Highway, and it was often closed by storms. We wanted to be prepared.

Just before we left, I checked and fed all the dogs in the kennel yard again. Perhaps I only imagined that Shasta and Gilbert looked especially wistful.

"Your feet are looking better, girl," I told Shasta. She thumped her tail on the snow. "Just keep healing. That's your job now."

I turned to Gilbert, squatted down beside him, and patted his chest. "I'm sorry, buddy," I said, "but it's not the last race. Next season, who knows? The important thing is, you tried your best and I love you for that." I ran my hand down his ribs and he leaned against me. "Well, good-bye," I said to the whole kennel yard.

I had asked Sandy to call the Quest hotline for an update on George's whereabouts. She came out on the porch and said, "He's in twentieth place."

Robin leaned out the door. "He's moved up since last night," he said.

"Well, we'd better get going then," I told him. Kathleen wiggled past Robin's legs. Her boots were untied and she was dragging her parky behind her. "Let's go see Daddy," she said.

"Let's go see Daddy," I repeated, working her arms into the parky. "Let's all get in the truck."

Sandy and I took turns driving. The road was miles of packed snow. It was about fifteen degrees outside. Skies became increasingly gray and, as we progressed northward, it became obvious that snow had been falling in that area for hours. Fine flakes came down at an angle. I took out the chart George had given me, listing his predicted arrivals and departures from checkpoints. He thought he'd be in Central sometime between midnight that night and 5:00 P.M. the following day, depending on weather conditions. Well, there goes midnight, I thought.

When I wasn't worrying about driving conditions, I was worrying about how our team was coming along. Sandy passed the time playing music on the tape deck. Most of the songs were New Wave pieces that made "The Eve of Destruction" seem optimistic, but she shared no interest in the lighthearted oldies and country music I preferred, so I steeled myself to the notion that everyone has a right to his or her own taste. Kathleen, sleepy from the previous night's excitement, napped peacefully through jangled chords and repetitive phrases.

The trail from Angel Creek to Central is only eighty miles long, but it is perhaps the most treacherous portion of the Quest. Seventeen miles out, teams encounter Rosebud Summit, a three-thousand-foot mountain with a rough, rosebud-shaped peak with petals made of stone. The ascent up Rosebud is so steep that teams can and do slide backward down the slope if the dogs let up on their harnesses for any length of time. The reward for making it over Rosebud is the chance to try Eagle Summit, some thirty miles farther down the trail. I thought of that peak, desolate even in the fall when we'd passed it. Winds commonly roared up to seventy miles per hour there. It did not look like a good evening to attempt the ascent.

Four hours into our trip, I began to see orange and white stakes—Quest trail markers—along a trail that emerged from the scrubby high-elevation woodlands. For a while, the trail paralleled the road. We came upon three teams stopped near a marker and peered through the dim light of the stormy afternoon, trying to identify them. We decided that none of them looked like our team, so we drove on.

Finally, we encountered another team close enough to see clearly. Dogs and driver moved along silently through unpacked powder. I slowed the truck and rolled down my window.

"Quest team, who are you?" I called out.

"Buck Williams," the driver called back.

"How are you doing?"

He shook his head. "It's slow going out here. How far to Highway One-oh-one?"

He referred to an area at the base of Eagle Summit, mile 101 of the Steese, where a Quest radio operator was located. Though it was not an official checkpoint, teams could rest there and, if necessary, drop dogs off with a race veterinarian.

"By our guess, it's about five miles," I said.

"Okay." He seemed relieved. "That's good. Do you know my handler?"

"No."

"Well, he should be up at One-oh-one by now. If you run into him, tell him to wait for me, would you? I'm gonna be dropping a dog there."

"Will do," I said. "By the way, have you seen George Cook?"

"Yeah, he passed me quite a while ago. He's lookin' good."

"Okay, thanks. We'll catch your handler if we can."

We speeded up and soon reached 101. There we saw a few other handlers' trucks parked in the northbound lane of the road. I pulled up to each vehicle until I located Buck's handler. The handler seemed grateful for word of his driver.

I moved our truck on to investigate 101. It turned out to be a set of old gas pumps and a tiny, long-closed service station that sat well off the road. In the last light of day, I could make out the shapes of dog teams parked near the pumps. The driveway to the station was not plowed, though a few officials' trucks had braved the route. I parked beyond the driveway. Sandy and Kathleen waited in our truck while I walked in toward the pumps. I could feel the full force of the wind. Icy flakes pelted me, and I waddled along in the tracks of the trucks, the only place where the snow wasn't up over my knees.

Just as I neared the pumps, I saw our team. The dogs lay bundled in the green coats I had sewed for them. Two by two they slept, still in their traces. I wanted to touch them, but it was against the rules, so I tiptoed past them and approached the decrepit station, opening the door with authority. I did not expect to find six mushers, a Quest official, and two radio operators jammed into this eight- by ten-foot space. Sleepy, angry eyes snapped open and focused on me. I stepped in and closed the door gingerly to avoid bumping anyone. In the glow of a single oil lamp, I saw mushers huddled against the walls, trying to sleep, but also trying to avoid collapsing onto the floor, where thawing boots had created a puddle from baseboard to baseboard. I could hardly believe anything could have thawed in that room. The walls were so thin, the wind blew right through them. In one corner, the two radio operators sat on the only available chairs, their arms drawn in as if they were in fear of being attacked. One of them, a grandmother for sure, sat with her headset around her neck while the radio's speaker whispered unintelligible messages. She looked as tired as the mushers.

My eyes fell on George. He sat squeezed into a corner, hunched over his knees. He smiled faintly, stood up, and ushered me outside.

"Hi," I said when we were back out into the wind. "How are you doing?"

"I'm okay. Rosebud was a bitch."

"How are the dogs?"

"Good, Ann. Really good. They're doing well. Some didn't eat much tonight, but I think they're just tired." His speech was somewhat slow. I could tell it had been a long day. "I'm leaving here as soon as the storm lets up. The radio operators have told us it's a whiteout on top of Eagle Summit. Some teams went through a few hours earlier and they're caught in it."

"Oh, that's terrible."

"I hear the road is closed up to Central, too."

"We got this far, but the weather has gotten a lot worse . . ." My voice trailed off. I decided not to trouble him about *our* passage. "Well, I'm glad to see you, but you'd better go back to your nap."

In our heavy parkys, we embraced, bouncing off each other like cloth dolls. Through the fur ruff on my parky, I gave him a kiss.

"See you in Central," I said. "Good luck."

"I'll be there," he said. He turned back toward the building and I forged on to the truck.

When I got to the road, a Quest official's truck was parked in front of mine. Sandy had been talking with the driver.

"This official just told all the handlers that they've sent a road crew up to plow past Eagle Summit," she said. "They plan to open the road for an hour or so, so if we want to go through, we should all make a run for it now. Do you want to go?"

"Yeah," I said, dismissing all caution. I started the truck and briefed her on our team's condition as I drove along.

Eagle Summit by night was even more terrifying than Eagle Summit by day. The road follows a ridge line. A car could fall a thousand feet if it were to go over the edge. By the time we reached the highest elevation of the roadway, the snow had abated, but the wind was still wild. It was so profoundly dark up there that we could only navigate by following the reflective markers set high on poles here and there along the route.

On the ridge, our windshield wipers froze to the windshield. Gusts of wind blew snow over the truck, then carried it away, intermittently blinding us. At the height of land, the fan belt, or something under the hood, began to squeal. Sandy and I never even looked at each other.

"What's that sound?" she asked through clenched teeth.

"I don't know," I said. My jaw never moved. My hands held the steering wheel in a death grip. The squealing stopped as we started downhill but returned every now and then as we made our way into Central and down a spur road to our hotel. Wearily we gathered our packs and checked in for the night.

The hotel, one of two within a 150-mile radius of the checkpoint, was a famous old hot springs resort. Tourists had been lounging in the big wooden frame building since Victorian times, and the decor had changed only a little in a hundred years. Heat for the place was supplied by steam pipes filled with the springs' 140-degree water. It was cozy there. The rooms were warm, the showers were hot, and even though it was past kitchen hours, the owners of the place put together a little dinner for us.

"The road must've closed right after you got through," one owner told us. "We weren't expecting anyone else tonight, but thank goodness you got here, because they've put up the gate." Indeed, during storms or threat of avalanche, the road was barred by two large metal gates installed at either end of the section that traversed Eagle Summit. Since the road was not frequently patrolled, the gates were there to keep fools from taking chances.

15

875 MILES

Shortly after I'd left George at 101, there'd been a break in the weather. The clouds had lifted and George saw stars in the sky. He packed his cooker, roused the dogs, and prepared himself for a night run on the summit. Despite a fierce headwind, the team moved steadily along with Minnie and Orah in the lead. The first hill they climbed was concave, like a bowl. The trail swooped up and around the bowl in a fashion that made George wonder if some trail-breaker wasn't deliberately making the trek more difficult. He followed the markers up to a reflecting tripod, then used his headlamp to scan the hillside for more markers. He saw several that did not line up. Confused, he moved the team to the closest marker, then to the next closest. Eventually, he was back at the tripod. The team had gone in a circle.

There was no discernible trail. The wind had swept the markers off course. George brought the dogs to a halt on the bare, rocky hill. While he scanned again for markers, Minnie grew impatient. She turned the team away from the wind and led them down the fall line! George scolded her and jammed on his brake, but the metal claw was useless on the frozen shale. He tried standing on his snow track, but gravity was against him. His heavy sled began its rapid descent, nearly overrunning the dogs. In desperation, he capsized the sled and threw himself on top of it. Team, sled, and all fell two hundred feet before coming to a stop.

"Minnie, stay!" George commanded. There was still a long way to slide if he lost control of the team again. Carefully, he rose and worked his way up the gangline to the leaders. Minnie looked at him indignantly. Orah averted her eyes nervously. "It wasn't my fault. I was just following my mother," she seemed to say. Taking a deep breath, George remembered Ron MacArthur's words. Lightening would be good at getting him out of trouble.

"Okay, Lightening," George said as he unhitched Orah and swapped her with Lightening. "It's your turn at lead." If Orah couldn't stand up to Minnie, he'd put someone up there who could. Minnie would obey commands if Lightening were next to her, simply because she wanted to prove she was the boss.

This combination got George and the team up out of the bowl, but then he faced an ever-steeper climb up an old streambed and along a ridge. He discovered that he had to lift his chin higher and higher to locate successive markers. When his chin was practically as high as it could go, the beam of his headlamp struck on a huge tripod. It was completely covered with reflectors. *So that was it. The summit.* To his amazement, a long bolt of green, shimmering northern lights seemed to shoot directly out of the tripod. He looked around at the eerie scene. The team ahead of him probably had made the summit an hour earlier. The team behind him was trailing by three hours. He was truly alone in this hall of the Mountain King.

Up he climbed along a steep ridge. The drifted snow was soft. It was a constant fight to keep the sled tracking in the bottomless powder. His sled bag was so heavy that George dared not push too hard on the sled's handlebar for fear of breaking it off. The dogs could gain only two markers—about two hundred feet—before having to rest. Then the only way to get the sled moving again was to have all twelve dogs and George pull in unison. During each rest, George would visit each pair of dogs, patting them and encouraging them so they'd be ready to pull again.

He slogged through the snow, not daring to think of what would happen if the weight of the sled overcame the team. He focused only on reaching the green beacon of light, and all at once, he was there.

There was no time to reward himself or the team, for as soon as he crested the peak, the trail began a hair-raising descent. He had just enough time to glance at the tripod before Minnie and Lightening disappeared over the edge of the summit. Two by two, the dogs passed out of sight, then the sled nosed down. As the team careered down the hill, George hung on. He managed to look for markers. He saw one to his right at the bottom of the drop-off, and one below to his left. Then he lost control of the sled. It tumbled sideways and down the hill, plowing up a huge furrow of snow and dragging the dogs and George with it.

Just before the sled buried itself so far into the snow that it came to a stop, George heard the zipping sound of Velcro. Something flew past his face. His mittens! His big overmitts had popped out of his sled bag, coming to rest on the slope above him. He couldn't go on without them. He'd freeze if the temperatures dropped much more. Lying in the snow, still holding the handlebar of his sled, he looked at the fleece gloves he was wearing. No, they weren't enough for the whole trip. He lifted his head up off the snow. There was still a lot of steep slope to come.

The dogs were momentarily quiet, unharmed by the fall but confused. They shook the snow off themselves and turned to look at George. He fumbled for his snow hook and tried to plant it, but the snow was so deep and loose that the hook was completely useless. He would have to make a run for the mitts even though it could be a fatal mistake to separate himself from the team. If they moved when he moved, they might be swept down the slope and he would be left behind. In a sudden burst of adrenaline, he leaped up from the snow, half dashed, half crawled back to the mittens, snatched them up, dived for the sled, and grabbed the handlebar. His heart was racing, but he'd made it! All the dogs were up on their feet. They were starting to whine impatiently.

"Okay, Minnie. Okay, Lightening. Easy!" George told them. They continued down the slope faster than George liked, but a little more in control, at least.

When he was finally on safe trail, George glanced back at the slope. In the glow of his headlamp, he saw that the trail down from the summit was designed to be a series of switchbacks. The markers he'd seen to both his left and his right suddenly made sense. He also noticed crater marks from at least a dozen teams who had come down from the summit in the same fashion he had.

There was a hierarchy to the rooms at the Circle Hot Springs Hotel. First-floor rooms were beautifully furnished and very spacious; second-floor rooms were quaint, if a little cramped; third-floor rooms were "dormitories"—literally walled-in dormers with doors that opened out onto a central hall and common room. These rooms were unfurnished. Guests were advised to bring their own sleeping bags.

When I'd reserved one dormitory room for Sandy, Kathleen, and myself, I'd had no idea how small it would be. Only at the very center of the room, under the ridge line of the dormer, could Sandy or I stand erect. Nevertheless, we rolled out our sleeping bags and stuffed all our heavy gear into the eaves. Kathleen was enchanted with the bizarre accommodations, but Sandy and I hadn't planned on sleeping in a dollhouse.

"I hope you're not claustrophobic," Sandy laughed.

"Gosh, this *has* to be against fire regulations. How would you even know if the place was burning?" I said. "It's like sleeping in a tomb! You can't hear or see the rest of the building, and the frost is so bad on the window, you can't look outside!"

We giggled and another funny thought grabbed me.

"Sandy *this* is what we get for being mushers."

"What do you mean?"

"Well, this must be what it feels like to sleep in a dog box. Just a little hole to the outside world, all shut in for the night."

"Yeah, all we need is to sprinkle a little sawdust on the floor and it would be *just* like a dog box!"

One laugh led to another and released some of the tension the race had built in us. The room had given us a serious case of the sillies. We fell asleep smiling.

Sometime in the night I awoke again. George is on the summit now, I thought. I wondered if the storm was over. To comfort myself, I turned to look at Kathleen. I could just barely make out her features in the darkness. She was breathing softly, unconcerned about her rough-and-tumble life. She had her father's happy, daring personality. That was what I loved in both of them, but loving them took a lot out of me. I dared not think of what Kathleen might grow up to be.

Gauging George's times for the trip from Angel Creek to 101, I assumed he would not be into Central until ten the next morning, so Sandy and I set our sights on leaving the hotel at about nine forty-five. When we drove up to Crabb's Corner, where the checkpoint was located, I was very surprised to see our string of dogs all napping in their green coats again. My heart leaped.

"Sandy—he's here! He's here already," I cried. We parked the truck and scrambled out into the minus-twenty-degree day.

"We've been trying to call you since six this morning! Something's wrong with the phone up at the Springs!" I heard a familiar voice say. It was Sten. He came marching across the parking area. "George has been in since seven or so."

"Is he inside?"

"You bet."

Sten led the way into the little corner store. To the left of the register was a doorway that opened onto a small restaurant and bar. Though the place was crowded with locals, mushers, and race officials, I saw George immediately. He was sitting at a table, devouring a plate of steak and eggs. He looked up, caught my eyes, and beamed. The dreaded Eagle Summit was ours!

"If you race it more 'n once," Sten said, leaning against the table where George sat, "I guess you know what's coming. Merle Hoskins says he just sits down at the top and rides it out like he'd ride a toboggan."

George finished up his steak and put his fork on his plate.

"They give you a steak dinner for free if you're a Quest musher," he said brightly, "only I didn't get here for dinner, so I had to have it for breakfast." He looked terrible. The race had been on for forty-eight hours and he'd had about three hours of sleep. His hair stuck up in greasy spikes. A beard sprouted from his normally clean-shaven face. His eyebrows were raised in a vain attempt to keep his eyelids open, and his lips were drawn up in a permanent simper.

"There's a shower here and a Laundromat," he said. "I'm gonna take a shower and dry my clothes." He got up from the table and headed toward the door to the store. I thought perhaps he was hallucinating, but I followed him to a back room where race veterinarians were gathered around a pool table. A plastic tablecloth was stretched over the table. One canine patient sat upon it having his shoulder examined, while other injured dogs, tethered to the legs of the table, awaited their turns.

Behind the pool table, in a room no bigger than a bathroom, was the laundromat: three ancient Maytags and a dryer. In one corner of the room, there was a shower stall. Mushers, male and female, were lined up to use it. I saw one musher pulling a huge green parka from the dryer. Then he fished around inside the drum and pulled out a pair of beaver-fur mittens. I hadn't known fur was wash and wear!

While George tended his own soggy clothes and stood in line for the shower, I talked to some of the other mushers and handlers. Their moods varied. A couple of front-runners were just packing up to leave. They seemed optimistic, almost cocky. The middle-placers of the group were friendly; most had an even attitude. The rookies wavered between laughing about the troubles of being new to the race and panicking when things weren't going as planned.

After his shower, George joined some napping mushers in a big box trailer set up at the checkpoint. He got a couple hours of sleep while I walked a very impatient Kathleen around and around the parking area. The temperatures were so low that I was afraid she'd freeze, but she was full of activity. She needed to get out and run around.

Meanwhile, Sandy found a phone and made a few phone calls. I presumed she was calling Richard.

Before George awoke, our dogs had finished their own nap and were up looking around at the other teams. As I walked over to them, race officials kept a careful eye on me.

"Hi, guys," I said to them. They looked at me expectantly. My arrival always meant pats or food, but not that day. Instead, I just spoke to them and apologized to them because I couldn't do more.

"Bandit, you old beast! We're going to have to call Ted and tell him you're still young enough to climb mountains," I told the oldster. He looked a little more subdued than the rest of the gang, but overall, I was amazed at how chipper all the dogs seemed.

I checked on Essie. "How's my rookie girl?" I asked her. She blinked sweetly.

Minnie and Lightening lounged at the head of the line. Unlike the other dogs, who snuggled together with their running partners when they were bedded down, these two preferred to have the neckline that joined them detached while they slept. That way, they could extend their tug lines out like a Y and get as far from each other as possible. Even at that distance, they slept with their backs to each other.

"They look pretty good. How does George feel?" someone asked. I turned to find Mike Conolly standing next to me. He was wrapped in a big parky. Under it, he wore a hooded sweatshirt that he'd pulled up over his head. He looked like a monk.

"George is sleeping now. He seems pretty good," I said.

Mike engaged me in a conversation about our team, our goals, and our feelings to date. He referred to our breed of dogs as slow but steady animals. I was tired of this theme.

"We're not here to set the land speed record," I said a little testily.

Mike noted my tone and changed to more inspirational chatter about how various underdogs had come out near the top in other Quests. He spoke to me as if we were friends. His nice-guy act was designed to make me let down my guard, but I had no interest in reading my unguarded comments in the next day's *News-Miner*. I watched him talk. I saw his mouth move, but I hardly heard his words.

Mentally, I toyed with wild things I could say to him. Wild, *truthful* things. If the fans wanted to know, if Mike demanded a story, I could give him a dose of reality. I could tell him my truck was falling apart and give the name of the garage that had repeatedly failed to repair it. I could tell him how Sandy and I were not the happy team we appeared to be. I grinned, imagining an exposé. If people really knew the bizarre entourage that comes with professional sports: the handlers, the helpers, the trainers, the families. No one does something like this alone. For each racer entered, there are dozens of lives involved, and sometimes those lives aren't going very well. Still, we cope. I'd never be the one to spill the beans.

Mike returned my grin, never knowing why it was there.

"Well, I'll see you down the trail, won't I?" he asked.

"Yeah, I'll be in Circle tomorrow," I said.

Rookie fatigue was starting to envelop George. He departed Central at two-twenty that afternoon, almost two hours behind schedule. His late exit, coupled with the time he'd lost waiting out the summit storm, dropped him to twenty-third place.

Though George seemed dazed when he left, our dogs were lively, barking, and ready to go. George pulled the snow hook and they lurched ahead, eager to follow teams that had started out before them.

Dave passed by, heading for the restaurant. "So, he's off," he called out.

"Yeah. It's good-bye until Circle, I guess," I said to him. "How's your driver doing?"

"Oh, Bobby's okay. He's got one leader that's pretty sore on one shoulder, though. He may have to drop him. The vets are looking at the dog right now."

"Well, I hope it works out for him."

"Did you hear Buck Williams dropped out?"

"No. Why did he do that?"

"I don't know. I heard the hills got to his team. He's from the flat-lands, you know. Maybe he didn't have enough hill training."

"That's a shame." I shook my head. It was always sad to hear someone else's race was over before it was done. Back in New England, I'd felt sorry for teams that dropped out of races, but their disappointments had little reflection on our team's performance. George had always finished and finished well. In the Quest, the notion that another driver had been overwhelmed was more unsettling. What was too much for an Alaskan, I reasoned, could easily become too much for a New Englander.

After another stuffy night in the dormitory, Sandy, Kathleen, and I set off for the checkpoint at Circle City. On the road, we encountered a dog truck loaded with dogs. I recognized the driver as one of the Quest competitors and realized that this meant another team had scratched. It was a strong team that had completed quite a few Quests. I couldn't imagine what troubles they might have had. Seeing them caused me to utter a silent prayer for George.

With the snowbanks built up, the road into Circle was only slightly wider than a single lane. It was not difficult to find the community center where the checkpoint was located. There was only one road in Circle and it looped around the village. What buildings were not directly adjacent to the road were connected to it by footpaths and driveways.

Three small log buildings stood in a row at the south end of the loop. The adornments on one indicated that it was a church. The middle building bore a yellow Quest banner. It was evidently the community center. The building to the right was painted a bright blue color—a color one would find on final sale at a hardware store closeout. A sign tacked on the front door read CIRCLE HEALTH CENTER—CHIEF ISAAC CLINIC. Dog teams were bedded down all around these buildings. Some mushers were out tending to their teams. Quest veterinarians, resplendent in the red and royal blue parkys that came with their job, hovered about, checking on dogs.

I parked the truck and surveyed the teams. The front-runners were gone, but many of the drivers in the middle of the pack were still in the checkpoint. George's projected arrival time was late that morning, but now the schedule he'd made for me was off and I wasn't sure when to expect him.

For a while, I waited in the brilliant winter light. Kathleen and I walked past the checkpoint. We stood on the edge of the Yukon River and looked out at its mile-wide expanse. The distant banks were tinged with silver sun. There was no sound or movement between the banks. The ice was still, solid, giving no hint of the treacherous conditions that lay below its frozen cover.

Returning to the checkpoint, Kathleen and I climbed an icy set of steps and entered the community center. Inside, a small common room was filled with an assortment of people. I saw that Sandy had seated herself at one of the long sawbuck tables. Dave sat opposite her, and they were talking. I led Kathleen to their table and we sat down beside them.

As I helped Kathleen remove her parky, I noted that the press had holed up in one corner by a huge woodstove. Complicated-looking cameras lay among the mittens, hats, and paper coffee cups piled on their table. Mike Conolly was typing away on a laptop computer.

On the other side of the woodstove, a ham-radio base station was set up on a folding table. A fierce-looking operator sat at the controls, his leathery face surrounded, forehead to chin, with curly white hair. Now and then he spoke gruffly into the radio, then he'd shout a message to the room. "Anybody here named Joe Brayton? Message for Joe Brayton!" No one responded. In fact, no one responded to any of his messages. "Naw, nobody knows any Joe Brayton. He's not here," he yelled into the microphone. A few requests came in for information on drivers. If the team was out of the race the operator would say "Scratch" with a note of evil satisfaction. Someone must have asked about George. "George Cook?" the operator boomed. "Number fourteen? He ain't here yet. Naw, he's way back! I dunno when he'll come in." I felt personally chastised by this fellow, even though

I'm sure he was unaware and uninterested that I was waiting for George.

One end of the center housed a small kitchen and a little ante-room. Off-duty veterinarians were sleeping in the little room, stuffed into bunks with their sleeping bags and gear. Well-picked-over trays of sandwich fixings rested on a kitchen counter along with a partially consumed roast turkey. Pots of moose-burger chili and spaghetti drowned in tomato sauce simmered on the stove. The food was free for mushers and members of the community. Everyone who entered the building wandered over to peruse the offerings. "Watch out for the turkey," I heard one Native man whisper to another as they eyed the carcass.

"Why?" the other asked.

"It's been there since the start of the race." He paused momentarily and scowled at the bird. "And it wasn't too good then."

His companion nodded, grateful for the information.

Three young Native men strode in. They had long black hair and wore leather jackets.

"Where's Bobby?" one of them said, almost to the crowd. He turned to the chart on the wall that listed all the mushers and their standings and glanced down the list.

"He's not here yet," Dave called out. All three men turned to Dave. When he stood up, they walked over to him.

"Hey, hey, Dave!" one of the men said, his lips opening into a smile. He patted Dave on the shoulder. "When's he getting here?"

"Well, not for a while. I dunno, really. It was tough out there last night."

Dave chatted amicably with the men. I started listening to the conversation, but my attention was drawn to a large plastic barrel next to the door. On the wall over the barrel was a sign that read WATER. A hand-drawn arrow pointed toward the barrel. I had no-ticed a couple of thirsty trail crew workers dip mugs into the bar-rel and drink from the mugs. Then I saw a musher walk in with a dog watering bucket. He plunged it into the barrel. A race official finished up a sandwich, looked around the room questioningly, then dipped his hands in the barrel to rinse them. A few minutes later, a woman minding the kitchen filled up a coffeepot with the help of a huge metal ladle that was fastened with a greasy rope to the side of the barrel. I decided that an additional message should be added to the WATER sign; AT YOUR OWN RISK might have been appropriate.

Dave's voice penetrated my thoughts again. He was saying good-bye to the Native men.

"Be back later," one of them said as he headed out the door.

"Bobby hunts with them," Dave explained to me, though I hadn't asked. "He sees them every year. He met them out in the woods some-place up north of here. They were freaked out to see a white man so far out in the bush, hunting where the Natives hunt. I guess they were impressed, so they get together with him and go out each fall now."

Someone standing at the window said, "Team coming in!" Two race officials who'd been hovering around the radio put down their coffee mugs and pulled on their coats. A veterinarian who'd been chatting with Mike Conolly jumped up from the press table. Mike signed off on his computer and snatched his parky off the back of his chair.

"It isn't George or Bobby," Dave said.

"No, it's too early," I agreed, but I walked to the window just in case.

We saw Larry Grout's team come loping in, then we returned to our seats.

Kathleen told me she was feeling sleepy, so I settled her down on a bench and covered her with my parky. She was worn out. The skin under her eyes looked thin and dark. I touched her face. It felt very warm and clammy. Maybe she's just overtired, I thought. Despite the commotion around her, she closed her eyes and drifted off to sleep.

"Tired?" I heard Mike Conolly say. He had returned to the community center and was standing in front of me looking down at Kathleen. "I think we all are," he added.

"Siddown," Dave suggested. Mike quickly took the seat opposite me. An hour passed, during which we traded the latest gossip on which drivers had scratched and why, which teams looked good, and which were failing.

At one point, a spectator butted into our conversation. "Hey," he asked, "where are all those drunk and crazy snowmobilers that are always roaring around this place during the race?"

"They were here last night," Mike said, with a hint of disdain.

The spectator grinned. "Did they have a wild party like usual?"

"Just one knife fight. Two women claimed the same pair of gloves."

"Really? Women? Did they go at it?"

"Like tigers," Mike told him. He shook his head and smiled at me. The spectator scurried off with his news.

All at once, Kathleen awoke, sat upright, and vomited on the floor. She began to shriek. Dave grabbed some napkins off the kitchen counter. Sandy made noises about cleaning up while Dave and I set to work. Mike moved my parky out of harm's way just as Kathleen brought up another round. One of the veterinarians came over and pitched right in, wiping the floor with a handful of cotton dressing.

"It always happens at times like this with kids," he said cheerfully.

I wiped Kathleen's face and tried to calm her. "I don't feel good," she kept saying through her tears. What an understatement!

I rocked her in my arms and tried to avoid meeting curious glances. Still, I could not avoid the motherly guilt that crept in on me and built on itself. Perhaps I was responsible for her illness. I'd pushed her too far. Too much on-the-road, not enough sleep. Who could I have left her with? Her grandparents, aunts, and uncles were four thousand miles away.

My father had warned me that Alaska might be too much for children. He'd wondered what would happen if we lived too far from a hospital. No, I told myself, I was being silly. Kathleen probably had a little flu bug, some twenty-four-hour thing. Nothing serious. It would pass.

As the day wore on and Kathleen's vomiting attacks continued on to dry heaves, I was less inclined to dismiss the malady. She became listless with fever and I began to wonder what, if any, medical attention I could get for her. Perhaps I'd have to ask the veterinarians to examine her.

The veterinarian who had helped me clean up seemed approachable. He had pulled up a chair and was reminiscing about the times his children had been sick. He told his stories in graphic detail, yet his tone was that of someone recounting something pleasant.

"I haven't seen my kids in three weeks," he said after a while. "I came up here from Ohio for this race. I miss them."

If only George would arrive, I thought. I had really hoped to see him by noon, but what would his arrival do except give me less time to deal with Kathleen? It didn't matter. I wanted to see him so I could get at least one worry off my mind.

"They are probably together," Dave said as he watched me watch the clock. "Does George have any sense of humor?"

"Yes, why?"

Dave pretended to be smoking a joint. "Maybe they stopped for a little break."

I smiled, but I didn't think that was what George had in mind.

Several mushers entered the room and began gathering up the mountain of clothes they'd left drying by the woodstove. They each donned parkys, mitts, and windpants and waddled outside. They were leaving the checkpoint, off to Eagle, some 180 miles away. Their leaving made me more desperate to find George.

"Are you the person with the sick kid?" a Native woman asked me. I looked up at her face. She was little more than a teenager. Her expression was soft and friendly. "There's a health clinic in the next building," she said, tossing her chin in the direction of the door.

I brightened, recalling the place, but then I stopped. "It's for ... Is it okay if I go there?"

"Sure. Where else would you go?" she said.

"Well, then I guess . . . I guess I'll go. Thanks." I gathered Kathleen into my arms and headed for the Chief Isaac Clinic before I had a chance to change my mind.

The clinic was warm and quiet, an oasis of cleanliness and order in the frontier town. A heavyset Native woman heard me walk into the waiting area. She peeked out from one of the exam rooms.

"I'll be with you in a minute," she said pleasantly.

While Kathleen slept on my lap, I read perhaps a dozen posters that had been artfully arranged on the walls. Most of them pictured Alaskan Native people. Most of them had anti-alcohol messages. Two cautioned about the dangers of mixing alcohol with pregnancy. One recommended simple aseptic techniques to prevent infection of wounds. Another suggested ways to prevent teenage suicide. In the context of that room, my problems seemed minor. "You'll be all right," I whispered to Kathleen. "It's just a bug, really. It could be much worse."

Just then, the woman from the exam room came down the hall and handed me a clipboard with a form on it.

"Fill this out," she said. "Treatment is free, but we need some information."

I glanced at the form. It had some questions I could answer, such as patient's name, address, parent or guardian. It had other questions about what tribe and band Kathleen came from. I left those sections blank.

The woman took the partially completed form and led Kathleen and me to an exam room.

"Sorry to keep you waiting," she said cheerfully. "I was cleaning up in here. I had to stitch up two women last night. Knife fight. I was here until morning."

"That's terrible," I said.

She smiled. "No worse than usual." She put down the clipboard and addressed a drowsy Kathleen. "So your daddy is running the Quest and you got sick? Where do you hurt?"

I never asked the woman if she was a doctor. I knew it was likely that she was a nurse practitioner or diagnostician trained to handle routine and emergency medical care in the absence of a doctor. After examining Kathleen, she gave me some Tylenol and amoxicillin.

"I've heard a lot of people around Fairbanks have been getting this," she said. "It's a virus. It should pass in a few days." She brushed Kathleen's sweaty blond hair back up off her forehead and I saw the contrast of her darker red skin against Kathleen's pale cheek.

"You try to feel better so you can cheer for Daddy," she said to Kathleen. Kathleen nodded solemnly. I thanked the woman and she smiled at me like a loving mother.

"*You* try to feel better, too," she told me, and we laughed. I was grateful to be understood. Renewed, I returned to the community center.

I met Sandy in the doorway.

"He's here!" she said. Dave was right behind her. Race officials and reporters pushed by me. With Kathleen in my arms, I jogged down to the parking lot to see our team come trotting in. The wait had been so long that I was certain there'd be something wrong, but I couldn't see any dogs hobbling or loafing, so I knew we'd just had a slow night. George looked very tired and not very happy. He barely greeted Sandy or me before he signed the checker's clipboard. Race officials were anxious to ask him about trail conditions. Dave wanted to know if George had seen Bobby.

George looked blankly at Dave when the question was asked. Slowly he replied, "Bobby? No. Not since Central." Dave's face darkened, and he faded out of the conversation. I could feel his pain and anxiety. He'd been certain Bobby had been traveling with George. Now Bobby was out there alone, unaccounted for in eighty miles. Even figuring in starting time differentials, he was last in the race.

"I saw Larry Grout and Jim Kublin," George offered.

"How was the trail?" one of the race judges cut in.

George smiled faintly. "Rough," he said. "Birch Creek is so windy. You just think you're getting somewhere and then you turn and you're almost back on yourself. One minute the moon was behind me, then on my left, then in front of me, then behind again. It really screws up your sense of direction."

"Was there any overflow?" Mike Conolly asked. I saw his pen poised against his flip pad.

George looked in the direction of Mike's voice. I could tell he was trying to answer the question, but fatigue wouldn't let words come to his lips. "I gotta get these guys fed and bedded down," he said, gesturing toward the dogs. The phrase sounded memorized. He pulled his snow hook and called to Minnie, directing her to an empty corner of the parking lot. The team went willingly, knowing it was rest time.

Sandy and I took turns watching Kathleen as she napped, and watching George attend to our team. The veterinarian from Ohio carefully examined each of our dogs. He thought Moose's back feet looked swollen, so he helped George slather Moose's pads with foot ointment, then he wrapped both feet in plastic wrap to hold the ointment.

"Keep the wrap on until you're ready to leave," he instructed George. "I think he'll be okay to run by then. Everyone else looks good. You're doing good work."

When all the dog chores were done, I walked George to the community center.

"There's food here," I briefed him. "But I heard the turkey is old, so don't eat it. Also, Kathleen is sick. She's got a virus, so don't get near her. She won't understand, but I'll explain it to her. And George, there are a bunch of teams still here, so if you hurry up, you can leave with them. Maybe you can move up."

George regarded me with annoyance.

"You're still in there. You just had a slow night. Don't give up."

"Did I say I was going to give up? Did I say anything about it? I'm not giving up," he said testily.

I was surprised at his response. This was not my patient husband talking. "I didn't mean it as a criticism," I said softly. "I meant it as encouragement."

We stepped into the center. He stopped in front of the standings board and paused. He was reading the mushers' times, but I doubt any of the information was sinking in.

"I'm having trouble with my hand," he said, never turning to look at me. "I did something stupid at Central. It was before you got there. I was filling my fuel bottles for my cooker. They had a big drum of methanol there with a pump on it and I couldn't get the pump to work. But then the fuel came out all at once and I spilled some on my glove. I frostbit two of my fingers and my thumb. Now I can't keep my hand warm."

"What will you do?"

"Keep it covered and hope for the best, I guess." His mind wandered onto another subject. "I'm gonna get some food and some sleep," he told me.

Mushers slept in the church in Circle. George curled up on a hard wooden pew and never moved for two hours. In the meantime, I sat in the community center watching other mushers come and go. I was starting to recognize all of them, and I recognized their handlers as well.

There was a fellow with long curly hair who seemed to be having a devil of a time getting organized to leave the checkpoint. His gear was strewn all over the snow. I learned that his name was Jim Kublin. He was a rookie, driving a second-string team for a powerful Alaskan kennel. His handler was a pretty young woman named Jenny who chain-smoked to pass the time.

A redheaded musher with a big beard came into the center looking distraught. I realized he was Roger Hocking. He spoke with race officials for a while. Then one of the officials wrote SCRATCH next to his name on the standings board. I turned away, trying not to look at the ugly word, but I couldn't avoid seeing Mike Conolly scribble the news on his pad.

The young men who were Bobby's friends returned and joined what had become a serious vigil for the missing musher. Outside, the light was fading, temperatures were falling. Race officials talked of sending snowmobilers out to look for Bobby. Then someone said the magic words "Team coming in."

Everyone in the community center rushed out to welcome Bobby. I wanted to sweep Kathleen up into my arms and hurry along with the others. I didn't know Bobby, but by now I cared about him and his team and his handler. I contented myself by leaning out the door of the center.

Bobby seemed in good spirits despite his long journey. He talked with his friends, the race officials, and the reporters while he patted his dogs. Then he asked to see the veterinarians and a look of concern came over his face. Both of his leaders had suffered shoulder injuries. He wanted the veterinarians to determine how serious the injuries were. He had dropped dogs in Central and was now dangerously close to dropping the total allowable number of dogs, yet he was only one third of the way to the finish line.

George awoke from his nap and walked to the parking lot where veterinarians were poring over Bobby's team. He watched the scene wordlessly, then checked on our team. Minnie poked her head up when she heard him coming. Then Pete looked up, and Taro stood up, bringing all the rest of the team to attention—all except Essie, who lay curled in a ball, tail over her nose in characteristic Husky fashion.

Gazing at her through the window of the community center I thought, She's just a baby. She's never been on a trail this long. What must she think? That George has gone mad? That this trek will never end?

She opened her eyes, blinked for a minute, and then looked up at George with an expression of complete devotion. If he'd gone mad, she evidently planned to go with him.

George set to work, hovering over the team. He took no notice of an Athabascan man who'd been standing next to our dogs for quite a while. While George unwrapped Moose's feet and massaged Pete's weak pastern, the man stood still, watching, never flinching in the twenty-below weather.

George took a leash from his sled bag, unhooked Pete from his traces, and started off to walk the dog. When he passed the man, he recognized him. It was Johnny—the fish seller.

"Johnny!" George said, extending his hand.

Johnny shook George's hand and said with concern, "You're *not* dropping out?"

"No, just limbering up this dog. He injured a pastern in the fall and I want to make sure he doesn't reinjure it."

A look of great relief passed over Johnny's face. "You will finish this race?" he asked.

"Of course. Of course," George told him.

Johnny smiled broadly. "Good!" he said. Then he stepped back and resumed his watch, this time with an air of satisfaction. He waited for George to pack his sled and bootie the dogs. Then all at once, he was gone. George and I never saw him leave.

George pulled out of the checkpoint about eight-thirty that night. Two other teams were not far ahead of him, while Jim Kublin's team tailed him by less than half an hour. The veterinarians had advised Bobby to rest his dogs and himself before making any decisions, so Bobby and Dave had gone to the church to nap.

After a musher leaves a checkpoint, handlers may collect any gear or clothing their musher has left behind, so Sandy and I loaded bags of used booties, George's sweaty clothes, and extra dog food into our truck. We planned to return to the Hot Springs that night and then strike out for Fairbanks in the morning. In preparation for our departure, I'd jockeyed the truck up to a spot near a parking lot plug-in, so the block heater had been running for a couple of hours. The truck started up easily enough, but the engine sounded terrible. The squeal we'd heard driving up Eagle Summit had become louder, and something sounded like it was misfiring. For the second time in a week, the oil gauge read low.

I switched on a headlamp and popped the hood of the truck. I knew very little about engines, but I figured I could recognize any obvious problems. I found no broken hoses or leaking chambers. Sandy climbed up on the bumper.

"Shut it off," she said. "I'll check the oil."

I reached into the cab and turned the key. The truck sputtered, backfired and stopped. Sandy leaned around the hood, dipstick in hand.

"It's down three quarts," she said. Her words were almost a question. I dug around in the back of the truck and found the two cans of oil in our road emergency kit. Deftly, Sandy tapped the spout into the first can and tipped it into the filler neck. The oil was nearly frozen. Refilling was a tedious process. When I tried to start the engine again, it wouldn't turn over.

"Could the engine have cooled that quickly?" I asked Sandy. She didn't know.

"Well, let's plug it in again," I said. "Maybe we can get someone inside to help us."

Sandy gave me a sour look. "This damn truck!" she grumbled.

"I know, but what are we going to do?" I released Kathleen from her carseat and we all walked back into the community center. Stepping through the door seemed like a defeat. We had said our good-byes to the veterinarians and the few reporters left, and now we were back.

"You're having truck trouble?" Mike Conolly asked. There was a note of real sympathy in his voice.

"Yes," I sighed, "and I'm not exactly a mechanic. It started fine a few minutes ago, but it didn't sound good. Then we had to stop it and put more oil in because it's been burning oil all the way from Fairbanks. Now it won't start and I can't see what any one of those things have to do with each other." I slumped down on a bench. Mike looked at the photographer from the *News-Miner*.

"Know anything about trucks, Bruce?" he asked.

"Not much, but I guess I can take a look." Bruce stood up and picked up his coat. Sandy knew more about engines than I did, so I handed her the keys and stayed behind to watch Kathleen.

"You're not having it easy," Mike said.

I shrugged.

"I'm writing about the back of the pack," he told me. "That's what I'm focusing on in some of these articles."

"Really?" I wasn't interested.

"Yeah. I know it's hard. I've been there."

"Have you?"

"Yeah, I finished last in this race two years ago."

"No kidding?"

"It's hard to be in the back, and it's hard to handle for people in the back, but what you're doing is important. You're showing your support for George and that will get him to the finish line."

I shook my head. I felt my guard coming down and I let it go. I was too exhausted to keep it up.

"You sound like a cheerleader, Mike. I dunno. George seemed so surly the whole time he was here. What could I have done for him? The kid's sick. Maybe now he'll get the flu. I wonder if I should have stayed home."

"No, you shouldn't have stayed home, believe me. George is just tired. He wants you out here, I'm sure." He got up from the press table and sat down in a closer chair. He folded his hands and looked thoughtfully at them.

"When I ran the race, I was going out with this girl. She came to the start and some of the checkpoints. She left messages for me with the radio operators if she couldn't follow me for a few days. I really looked forward to each checkpoint. She made each part of the trip seem worth it. Then, all of a sudden, about two thirds of the way to the finish, the messages stopped coming. When I got to Whitehorse, I found out why. She'd met the winner and, well, dumped me."

"Oh, Mike, that's terrible. How could she?"

"Well, I didn't *own* her," Mike said wistfully. "She liked him and at least I got through the race. I mean, I *thought* I had someone waiting for me, and that was what counted at the time." He looked away from me for a little while. At last he said, "I wonder what's happening with your truck? I guess we'd better go see."

We rose and pulled on our parkys. Mike waited patiently while I cajoled a limp, semiconscious Kathleen into donning her coat, gloves, and hat.

Sandy and Bruce were attempting to jump-start the truck off of one of the officials' trucks. The race official was revving his truck's engine. Nothing much was happening on the other end of the jumper cables. Bruce reached under the hood and adjusted something.

"Try it now," he yelled to Sandy. She turned the key, pumped the accelerator, and the engine started. It sounded worse than ever, but it was running. Everyone looked at Bruce for an explanation.

"I don't know what I did, but anyway, it worked."

"Thanks, Bruce," I told him. "Really, thanks a lot." I lifted Kathleen into her carseat.

"Are you sure you're going to be all right?" Mike asked.

"Sure, no sweat."

"See you in Eagle."

"No, in Dawson." There were no roads to Eagle and it was prohibitively expensive to fly there.

"Well, I'll say hi to George for you when I get there," Mike said.

"Yeah, do that."

It was 10:00 P.M. Sandy backed the truck around and we started the thirty-mile drive to the Hot Springs.

16

760 Miles

George felt a strange sense of elation when the team pulled out of Circle. He traveled through the darkness, guided by his leaders and his headlamp beam. Turns were tight along the heavily forested trail and steering the sled took quite an effort, but the dogs enjoyed the constant weaving back and forth. They accelerated on each corner and took advantage of the momentum gained on the banks of the sloughs they passed over. Veteran Quest mushers used to scrawny spruce forests and open tundra had cursed this portion of the trail, but George found that he didn't share their opinion. New Hampshire trails were all like this. He was reminded of home. Perhaps the dogs were reminded, too.

His hour of confidence ended when a sweeper hit him squarely in the chest, almost knocking him off his sled. The near miss seemed to use up whatever adrenaline he had left. He started to doze on the runners and was brushed awake by another branch, then another. Late at night, the team arrived at the banks of the Yukon River, and George realized that if he did not stop to rest he would run the risk of losing his team on the ice.

The wind had picked up, so he bedded the team down against a slough bank that offered good protection. He gave the dogs snack burgers. They gnawed on the frozen cakes before napping. George slept for an hour. He opened an eye when Jim Kublin's team tiptoed past him. Then he sat up, ready to continue the race. He switched on his headlamp and walked to the mouth of the slough. As he was examining the approach to the river, his headlamp caught the glint of many eyes; dogs out on the Yukon. Someone else's team was camped far off the trail. He wondered whose team it could be and why a team would camp way out there.

Returning to his own dogs, he woke them and bootied their feet. He put Orah in lead and moved Lightening back into the team. As he pulled out of the slough, his headlamp again caught the distant eyes. The other team seemed to be moving closer to him. Perhaps he'd gained a traveling partner, but he saw no musher's headlamp. Sometimes mushers turned off their headlamps so they could sneak up and pass another team before the leading team realized it was being pursued. But who, so far at the back of the pack, would bother with such games?

On the flat, open trail, Orah came to life. The team glided along behind her through the clear night. The other team followed, but gradually fell back. George peered at them. Though the moon was bright, he could not see them distinctly because they were shadowed in the trough of the trail. Then, suddenly, they seemed to bunch up. A couple of the dogs turned broadside. George's heart raced as he realized that they were not dogs at all, but a pack of wolves! Fortunately, they had chosen to turn back. Nevertheless, he passed the next hour looking over his shoulder.

When at last he convinced himself that he was alone with his team, he settled back and watched Orah's long, speedy strides. He became mesmerized by her movement, so mesmerized that he forgot exactly where he was on the trail.

He found himself at a cabin at daybreak. Veteran mushers knew the location of this and of other cabins along the trail. They were not official checkpoints. Some were unoccupied remnants of the days when mail and freight were carried into the area by dog teams. Others were occupied by miners or homesteaders who welcomed the mushers into their homes as a service to the race and as a diversion from a long winter of isolation. Merle Hoskins had mentioned these cabins to George. He had described their locations as twenty-eight, forty, and ninety miles up the Yukon, respectively. Vague reference to these cabins was made at the Quest drivers' meeting, too, but rookies were left to guess their whereabouts. Evidently, Quest officials did not want the mushers becoming dependent on these cabins. Like the veterans, George had hoped to use the cabins to his advantage, but the cabin at daybreak confused him.

He could see that many teams had stopped there. The surrounding snow was tromped down, and a dozen or more sets of sled tracks had beaten a path to it. He knew, given Orah's speed for the last few hours, that he had to have traveled more than twenty-eight miles. However, even if she had been moving the team along at top speed, he didn't think that he had covered forty miles. That would be too good to be true. So this had to be the cabin at twenty-eight miles, unless he'd missed that cabin in the darkness. Deciding that it was the twenty-eight mile cabin, he continued past it without stopping. All at once, he felt discouraged. Only twenty-eight miles in all that time— and he'd thought he was doing so well! Eagle seemed very far away. He dared not think of Whitehorse.

The team trotted on for three more hours and encountered no other cabins. George could then deduce that the cabin he'd passed had, indeed, been the one at forty miles. He would need to take a major rest break before Biederman's cabin at ninety miles, but this had not been in his plan. He had figured to travel from the twenty-eight-mile cabin to the ninety-mile cabin in one repetition of his run/rest cycle. He carried on, hoping that Merle's estimates had been inaccurate. If the ninety-mile cabin was closer than Merle had predicted, perhaps he could push the dogs a little farther and make it there by nightfall.

Extending the dogs' run time proved to be a mistake. They slowed up and plodded along in a fatigue gait. After a while, they were making no time at all, so in the late afternoon George stopped them and camped on the river.

There was no shelter available out on the ice, but the wind was light. Temperatures weren't bad, perhaps ten to fifteen below, George guessed. The snow around him looked pearly under pink, cloudy skies. As he hauled out his cooker to start boiling water for the dogs, he heard a familiar *zip-zip* sound. Minnie was removing her booties by opening the Velcro closures with her teeth. This was a habit she had developed during the race. As soon as she saw the cooker come out, she knew she could settle back and stretch her toes. She always placed the booties in a neat pile just in front of her nose, and then sat in sphinx position, looking superior.

George filled the cooker with snow, poured fuel into the fuel chamber, and lit off the stove. Then he collected Minnie's booties and worked his way down the team, taking off old booties, examining feet, and wrapping dogs in their coats. Essie had a small fissure in a front pad, but it didn't seem to be bothering her. Some of the dogs bedded down while George worked and were asleep before he could get a meal into them. They were more tired than hungry. He knew this was a bad sign.

I've mismanaged them, he thought glumly as he dropped his own meal into the cooker. Now he would have to do something to bring them back. He didn't know that Bobby had dropped out of the race. He figured there was still one team behind him, and he doubted Kublin had built up much of a lead. The rest of the pack was forgotten. They were off in some world on which he could no longer focus.

When his meal was hot, he placed it in a small metal dish and started eating. After the first bite, the meal was cold, the noodles were sticky, the steak tepid and tough. Soon the green beans became frosty bullets. As he ate one mouthful, the fork froze to his lip. He pulled it away carefully, but it tore tine marks into his skin, and all he could taste after that was blood.

It was time to sleep, but he couldn't sleep. He tossed about on top of his sled bag and thought about what he could do to get the team moving again. Not eating— that worried him. Had they picked up a virus? Were they just not able to go on? He closed his eyes again. Someone was snoring, and loudly, too. He looked and saw that it was Bandit. George had to laugh. Whatever the camping trip, there was always a snorer in the tent! At least someone was getting some sleep, he thought. He glanced at the faces of each of his dogs. Their eyes were shut tight and their tails were drawn up over their noses. Gradually, he felt his own lids droop. He drifted off.

He woke with a start an hour later and was instantly aware of the hand he'd frostbitten back in Central. It felt strange, more numb than painful. He removed his mitt and placed the hand inside his parky. In a few minutes, it started to warm up, and the pain became much worse. He moved his fingers and the sensation made him dance around his sled in agony. Finally, his hand warmed up, his fingers felt less wooden, and the pain subsided. He put his mitt back on and loaded his sled.

After four hours on the trail, George came to a cabin and spotted Jim Kublin's team sleeping in the dooryard. Jim was just walking out of the cabin.

"You stopping here?" he called to George.

George touched the brake of the sled and slowed his team to a stop.

"Which cabin is this?" George asked. He was still mentally juggling cabins.

"Slaven," Jim told him.

"Biederman's must be farther on?"

"Yeah, I think ten or fifteen miles."

George hesitated. It was too soon to stop again, but if the trail to Biederman's was rough, he might have to camp short of that cabin to feed and rest the dogs. Another night on the trail would take more out of them and more out of him. This cabin looked warm and inviting.

"No, I'm going on," he said. His words were sudden, a declaration. "I'll probably see you at Biederman's."

"See you there," Jim said. He watched George leave and then returned to his dogs.

Searching for something to soothe his disappointment over the cabin mix-up, George concentrated on the sunset. He followed the trail beyond the cabin and started down through a beautiful stand of spruce. The sky was gold and he thought how fitting the hue was for this land where miners toiled. Eventually, he came to an old gold dredge. It was still and snow-covered, just an artifact along the historic trail. He hadn't heard anyone mention that dredge. No one had referred to it as a landmark or reference point. That seemed unusual. Come to think of it, he hadn't seen a Quest trail marker for . . . half an hour?

He stopped the team. Kirk and Minnie looked back at him.

"We're off the trail," he told them. He was sure of it. Setting his hook, he called to the leaders to bring the team around. Back to Slaven cabin they went.

On his way through Slaven, George encountered Jim and his team stopped in the trail. Two of Jim's dogs were mating. Dogs cannot be physically separated when they breed. They are literally tied together. This unhappy accident was costing Jim a half hour's time.

Jim flashed George a chagrined smile and George continued down the correct trail. As he passed Jim, he felt compelled to offer him an explanation of where he'd been. "Guess I took a wrong turn. Took a tour of a gold dredge."

Again Jim said, "See you at Biederman's."

"If I ever get there!" George mumbled to himself when he was out of earshot.

The trail up the Yukon ran along the bank, and the trail bed was tilted, causing the sled to slide toward the downhill runner. This "side-hilling" is hard on the musher because he must constantly push and pedal with one leg while leaning full weight on the uphill runner. It is also hard on the dogs, whose forward motion is constantly countered by the sideward force of the sled. When the trail left the riverbank and traversed the frozen surface of the Yukon, the team and driver gained some respite, but once they crossed the ice, the trail would parallel the other bank, where an equally bad side hill existed. This pattern continued all night, traversing, side-hilling, traversing, with the traverses becoming bumpy where the ice had formed, broken up, and refrozen.

To save the wheel dogs, on whom the strain was greatest, George rotated Scamp, Bandit, Taro, Pete, Boomer, and Moose, changing the back pair each time he stopped to rest the team. While the dogs seemed willing to continue after each break, they failed to make good time, so George shortened the intervals between stops, hoping this would pick them up a little. He dug around in his sled bag and brought out salmon snacks and lamb strips with which to reward each dog. Some of the dogs were delighted to hear the sound of the plastic snack bag, but Orah, Moose, Pete, and Kirk were still too tired to eat much. Taro and Bandit continued to be powerhouses, immune to fatigue. They gobbled up whatever the other dogs left behind. Finally, even Bandit turned up his nose at a snack. So Bandit became a gauge for the team: If he was too tired to eat, George knew he was pushing the team too hard and would back off a little.

Scamp was also a gauge of sorts. He took break time seriously, eating his dinner or snack and then bedding down immediately. After a good sleep, he'd start to stir. If there was no sign that the team was departing, he'd begin to bark. This would wake any dogs that might still be sleeping and get all of them up on their feet, lunging to go. He was the drill sergeant. His excited yaps even inspired George to hurry back to the trail. When Scamp said the team was leaving, it was leaving. Rest break was over!

A few hours past Slaven cabin, Jim Kublin's team trotted by George's team and disappeared into the darkness. There was nothing but Quest markers to see until shortly after 3:00 A.M., when George's headlamp beam picked up a cardboard sign.

BIEDERMAN'S CABIN, it read. THIS IS IT! MUSHERS WELCOME!

George looked for cabin lights but saw none. The lead dogs began to turn the team slightly. He cast the beam in their direction and saw that the spur trail to Biederman's made a long, steep climb up the riverbank. Kirk and Minnie were starting up, but Kirk was having a hard time of it. His small, light frame was exhausted from holding the front of the team up on the side hills. George hooked down and removed him from the line. He brought the dog back to the sled and loaded him into the sled bag. He'd done an excellent job that night. George saw no sense in asking him to go beyond his capability. With ears down and a look of embarrassment, Kirk accepted the lift.

"I sure hope this climb is worth it," George told the team.

He called to Minnie to go forward and, with a last burst of enthusiasm, the team marched up the hill. They had smelled the rich wood smoke before George had and knew the checkpoint was near. Somewhere up ahead, a dog barked. The team put their ears up and then dropped them again, pulling straight toward the sound.

Biederman's cabin lies at the confluence of the Yukon and Kandik rivers. It is approximately halfway between Circle and Eagle on the Quest trail and has served as a rest stop for mushers since gold rush times. Though no longer a roadhouse or mail stop, the cabin is open during the race and is operated by a Kandik River couple, Mark and Lauri Richards, who mush fifty miles south from their own cabin to provide food and radio communications for the racers and officials.

The long, low log building looked lower still in its blanket of winter snow. Yellow light came from a single window. George brought his team into the dooryard and tied them down.

Not far from where he stopped, Jim Kublin bent over his own team. George greeted him and began routine dog chores. Jim held up a section of gangline. It was dreadfully frayed.

"Active use," he said. His amorous dogs had chewed the lines to get to the female in season.

"Is there water here?" George asked.

"Inside."

The cabin had an arctic entrance, a small vestibule so low that George had to duck to step into it. The inner door opened on to a sparsely furnished kitchen. The Richardses welcomed George and directed him to two big stockpots of water. He filled his cooker and returned to his team.

When the dogs were settled in, George joined Jim in the kitchen. He wolfed down the cheese, homemade bread, and hot chocolate the Richardses offered him, but passed on the inevitable bowl of moose chili. Despite his exhaustion, he found himself drawn into conversation with Mark and Lauri. He discovered that they had come to Alaska from Los Angeles. They had given up the rat race for a self-sufficient life in the wilderness.

Something stirred in the room beyond the kitchen. George was startled. He didn't think anyone else was in the cabin. A little girl appeared at the door of the room, apparently the Richardses' daughter. The sight of her made George think of Kathleen. She hadn't crossed his mind in days. Now, for a long moment, he missed her and wondered what she was doing. Then it came to him that it was four-thirty in the morning. She would be sleeping, of course, but where? Somewhere on the road to Dawson. He pushed the subject from his mind. It brought on worries about things he couldn't control and took his thoughts away from the race.

Mark Richards agreed to wake George in three hours. George wandered into the back room, hung his gear to dry by the barrel stove, and crawled into a bunk. He was vaguely aware that children were sleeping in two of the other bunks. In the dim light he saw that the walls were lined with books. He read some of the titles. Everything from classics to crossword puzzles, several winters' worth of entertainment, but he was too sleepy to think about reading; he wanted to think about sleeping. Indeed, it was heavenly to sleep in a bed, the first bed he'd seen since Fairbanks, five days ago.

Before dawn, the Richardses cooked up a huge breakfast of eggs, bacon, home fries, and toast for George and Jim. Mark explained to the two delighted mushers that his sympathies lay with the "rear guard" of the race, so it pleased him to cook a special meal for them.

While they ate, Mark briefed them on the condition of the upcoming trail and then started packing up the kitchen. By the time Jim and George had loaded their sleds, the Richardses had readied their own teams. They were bundling their children in thick coats for their journey back up the Kandik.

Surveying the scene, George turned to Jim. "Bobby dropped out?" he asked.

"That's what I heard. I don't think he ever left Circle. We're the back door now."

George nodded and looked over at his team. The back door was not much of a spot, but if the weather stayed clear and the trail flattened out, he might make better time that day. Though Kirk was up and wagging his tail, George put Orah in lead with Minnie, hoping to use her speed to catch up to the teams ahead.

Jim's team pulled out while George was still harnessing. This excited the dogs, who were anxious to go. This rest had finally been productive. George wondered if, like humans, the dogs needed to feel they'd gotten somewhere to really be at ease. Camping out on the trail left a human pondering how much farther it was to a cabin or a checkpoint. Once at a cabin, these concerns disappeared. It seemed the dogs understood this and their goals were consistent with the musher's.

When George called to Minnie and Orah to hike up, the team charged forward. Their renewed energy left George clutching the driving bow to avoid falling off the sled. The trail curved around the cabin, and George took a last look at the place. He knew it would generate special memories for him, memories of bush hospitality. Turning back to his driving, he realized that the dogs were towing him toward the riverbank. An image of the hill he had climbed to get to the cabin flashed in his mind and he remembered he was up over the Yukon. The trail ahead made a steep, dangerous descent to the ice. It took him just a few seconds to drop the 150 feet to the on-trail marker that indicated he was headed for Eagle. The team, enthused by the wild ride, continued along the riverbank at a gallop. George laughed to himself. He was awake after that eye-opener!

His hopes of a trail with less side-hilling were soon dashed. The trail upriver was worse, and the traverses were full of sharp, broken hunks of packed ice. The weather remained clear and the sun came up bright and beautiful, but temperatures hovered around twenty below zero. Orah soon tired on the side hills, so George moved Lightening up to the lead; eventually both Minnie and Lightening were being dragged down the fall line. Scrutinizing the team, George decided to take a chance and put Abe next to Minnie. Abe arched his neck proudly as he took the lead. He glanced back at the team, looking for acknowledgment of his new status. As the team went forward, Abe used every muscle in his compact body to hold the front of the line tight and on course. He was not a fast leader, but he was a dedicated one. For the moment, Minnie was willing to coast along next to him. The going was too difficult for her to fuss about hierarchy just then. Getting to the next rest stop was plenty to think about.

While Sandy, Kathleen, and I stayed north of Eagle Summit, storms raged just south of the mountain range. We had planned to leave Circle the morning after George departed for Eagle, but the road to Fairbanks was closed. We were delayed a full day, long enough for Kathleen to recover from her illness. When the sun finally came out, we drove down the summit pass in light so bright we could not distinguish the roadbed from the sky. The blinding glare proved more dangerous and disorienting than the gale we'd braved three days earlier.

After several hours on the slippery road, we arrived in Two Rivers. It seemed strange to be there, back home again, our handler's duties temporarily suspended. We knew the eighteen-hour interlude was merely time spent waiting for a new rush of activity to begin. We watched television coverage of the race on our tiny black and white TV and tried to organize our thoughts.

"Geez, I'm glad you made it back," Sten said as I poured him a cup of coffee. He watched Sandy walk from her bedroom to the front door with a heavy duffel bag. "Have some coffee, Sandy."

"No," she mumbled. She turned the doorknob and tossed her weight against the door. It slammed behind her.

Sten glanced at me. "What's eating her?"

I shrugged. "I wish I knew."

"Nerves."

"Do you think so? Because I'm beginning to wonder if it's home-sickness. She's a grown woman and lately she's been calling her mother every day. At first, I thought it was just to update her on the race, but now I don't know. She's telling her the truck isn't working and I think she's terrifying her. What can my aunt do about it but alarm my parents, too? They're a whole country away. Funny, she didn't think of the dangers when she was chauffeuring Richard around. Anyway, we'll make it to Dawson and to Whitehorse, too. I've put every piece of survival gear known to man in that truck. If I have to push the damn thing half the way, I'm going to get to Whitehorse."

Sten smiled at me. "That's the spirit," he said.

The door swung open and Sandy marched through the living room again. Her bangs were hanging in her eyes. She blew them off her forehead with a strange gesture—a combination of an exhale and a chin thrust. It was a gesture I was getting to know well.

"What else?" she said to me. She was asking what else needed to be packed in the truck before we left for Dawson that evening.

"Relax," I told her. "We've got until six. I'll help you when I'm done with my coffee."

"I just want to get it *done*," she said tensely and disappeared into her room.

"Nerves," Sten whispered with a nod.

Just before six o'clock, Robin arrived at our house. He called the Quest hotline for me. I always preferred that someone else ask for information about George. That way, if there was bad news, I could react to it privately. I'd not be left gasping on the line.

"George was into Biederman's cabin last night," Robin told me. "Officially, he's still ahead of Jim."

I looked down at the floor.

"The race is young, Ann," Robin told me. "He's still in there. That's what's important."

"I know," I said. "I know." I considered his words and felt a little brighter. "Well, we're leaving, I guess. On to Dawson and all that."

"Have a safe trip," Robin said.

"I'll try."

With me at the wheel, our truck roared down the Alaska Highway bound for Tok. The truck guzzled oil, but I'd taken a case of it from our shed and stacked the cans behind the backseat. Like a spouse unable to control an alcoholic mate, I'd given up on trying to cure the truck. I was just letting it have its fix. That evening when Sandy, Kathleen, and I stopped in Delta Junction to fill the gas tanks, I had trouble getting the engine restarted. The strange squealing noise returned when at last the engine fired.

It was 10 P.M. and terribly cold when we pulled up to a hotel in Tok. We kept the engine running while we registered for a room. Then we drove across a large parking lot to a small market that sold gas. I wanted to top off the tanks so we'd be ready to move early the next morning. I shut the engine off and, this time, was unable to get the truck started. Sandy trudged into the gas station and asked if someone would help us. A young man volunteered. We waited while he fetched a car with which to attempt a jump start.

The cab of the truck cooled off quickly. Kathleen's teeth were chattering and she was starting to blubber about the cold. My own hands were freezing inside my heavy mitts.

"You should take that little girl inside," the young man said to me while he unraveled a set of battery cables. His statement made me feel like a neglectful mother.

"Do you want to take her over to the hotel?" I asked Sandy.

"No," she said. Her tone indicated martyrdom.

"Then I'll go. Come get me if you need me." I pulled my overnight bag out of the cab and started off at a jog, encouraging Kathleen to follow me. I thought the exercise would warm us, but the slight wind chill caused by running made our extremities even colder.

When we got to the motel room, I put Kathleen's pajamas on the electric heater and turned the fan up to high, then stripped off her clothes and dressed her in the warmed pajamas. We sang a bedtime song and soon she was asleep. Still, there was no sign of Sandy and our truck.

A half hour passed. Finally, I heard the distinct roar and squeal of our truck's engine. I went to the window and saw Sandy maneuver the truck up to a nearby plug-in. She stepped out of the cab and walked quickly to the door. I opened it before she knocked.

"My God, you must be frozen!" I said.

"I am." She threw off her scarf.

She seemed to expect an apology, so I gave her one. "I'm sorry I left you out there. I mean, I'm sorry it was necessary, but I couldn't let Kathleen stay out there and I wouldn't leave her in here alone."

"The guy who got the truck going says there's a good mechanic in town. He's on Route One, about a mile from here."

"We've got time to take the truck there tomorrow. George won't be to Dawson for a couple of days. I just hope I can afford to pay whatever this guy will charge us. I mean, we're sitting ducks—two handlers who have to make it to Dawson. Everyone in Alaska knows that."

"Well, these people at this market are born-agains. They say the guy is honest."

"I'll have to take their word for it. We'll call first thing in the morning."

Miraculously, the truck started in the morning. We were soon on our way to Burley's Garage. The place was a greasy concrete building with a two-bay setup. Racks of tools lined every wall. Burley was indeed a bear of a man in the physical sense, but he seemed pleasant and, best of all, sympathetic. We rolled the truck into one bay and then Sandy, Kathleen, and I all waited in a small, overheated reception room where there was nothing to read but a single frayed issue of Road & Track. I saw a tiny bathroom in one corner of the room. It did not appear to have a door. After two hours, I really needed to use the toilet and passed the time considering how I might drape my parky over the door frame, but I never quite dared to do so. It was just too immodest, even for a woman well used to Alaska. Among friends, it might not have been the worst thing, but with strangers I drew the line.

Burley emerged from the garage holding up his oil-blackened hands like a surgeon after a scrub.

"The dealer in Fairbanks put in that engine?" he asked.

"Yes," I said.

He shook his head sadly. "Well, the alternator wasn't even bolted down. There's a lot of things wrong. The engine wasn't tuned right, so there's been a lot of damage to it. Is it under warranty?"

"Yes."

"Well, I'd take it back there and tell them to get me a new engine."

"But I can't do that until after my husband finishes the race," I explained.

"I know. I think you'll be okay for that length of time. But, just in case, I've made a list of mechanics between here and Dawson. Guys I know, who I know will help you out if you get in trouble. I wrote the phone numbers and addresses on the back of your invoice. If you have a problem within fifty miles of here, call me. If it's past there, call the next guy on the list. Okay?"

As I took the list from him, I felt a sense of redemption. Burley was no mere mechanic, but an angel sent by God. I gladly paid his very reasonable bill and put the precious address list in my safest shirt pocket. Soon I was back on the road in a truck that, although not purring, did sound reasonably roadworthy.

The address list worked like a lucky charm, warding off evil engine spirits. We bumped along the icy highway, made it to Whitehorse on schedule, stayed one night, and then drove on to Dawson City.

The single light in the darkness between Biederman's and Eagle was Trout Creek cabin. Late at night, Abe and Minnie led up to the log building. George felt a sense of déjà vu as he glimpsed Jim's team asleep in their bedding. This tortoise and hare game in which they were caught was actually somewhat comforting. When it seemed they would never see any of the other racers for the rest of the competition, at least they knew they would see each other. There would be some guarantee that one other human and one other dog team was somewhere within reach; a daily reality check. The front-runners had a couple of days on them by now, leaving Jim and George to slug it out in a separate world. George was even starting to learn the names of Jim's dogs—an accident of togetherness.

There was no food at Trout Creek. It had been consumed by all the other racers who'd passed, so George sat down to a meal he'd taken from his sled bag. While he ate, Jim and a race volunteer from Eagle discussed the history of the cabin. It had been the residence of a trapper and his family. A few years ago, the federal government had taken over the property and several thousand contiguous acres to create the Yukon-Charley Rivers National Preserve. The family had been allowed to remain on the land, but were ordered to file permits to use the cabin and to continue trapping. Local feeling was that the "feds" deliberately created a morass of red tape to confound the family and cheat them of their rights. Ultimately, due to "permit violations," they had been forced to leave their home.

Ironically, some Alaskans who are pushed off their land by eminent domain are later hired by the U.S. Department of the Interior to work for the National Park Service (NPS). At Trout Creek, the trail volunteer expressed open hostility toward the federal government, nevertheless admitting that he worked for the NPS each summer. He said that many other residents of Eagle shared his dilemma. Some visited Trout Creek cabin regularly and found its declining state a reflection of their own situation.

With this sad subject in mind, George crawled off to the loft of the cabin and fell asleep. He awoke again before dawn and prepared for his run to Eagle. The trail volunteer was asleep, but he had stoked a boiler outside the cabin after the mushers had turned in. The boiler was a common northern design. The top was cut off a steel drum and welded inside the drum to create a false bottom some ten inches above the actual bottom. Holes were then punched in the sides of the barrel below the false bottom, and an opening was created to accommodate some fuel source, liquid or solid. Thus a burner existed under the barrel and could be used to heat whatever might be in the barrel. In this case it was dog water, but as George scooped the water into his cooler he noticed the usual remnants of dog food and meat circulating in the liquid. The rinse water from other racers' dippers and buckets had again created a checkpoint broth. Our dogs had begun to enjoy this smorgasbord.

"Here you go," George told the dogs as he carried the water to them. "A canine version of the Baskin-Robbins thirty-one flavors."

Scamp was on his feet at once. In a few minutes he started barking. Then the whole team began to fidget. They drank their broth voraciously and leaned into their harnesses with enthusiasm. George shared their interest in leaving: Jim's team had departed a short time ago. His trail was still fresh. Perhaps Jim could be caught.

Sunrise brought another clear, cold day. The scene on the Yukon was otherworldly. In places, upended plates of ice towered over George's head. Angular and sharp, they jutted into the trail, ready to catch and tear clothing and sled bags, ready to bruise or cut dogs and drivers. For hours, George carefully maneuvered the sled over the bumpy maze of a trail. He felt like an insect working his way through a vast expanse of glass shards.

"Here comes a dragonfly," he said aloud. Then he realized what he was saying. He'd heard the sound of a plane engine! He looked up in the sky and saw a red and white Piper Cub. It flew over the team, then circled at a lower altitude. It was surely one of the trail volunteers trying to identify him. News that he was on his way into Eagle would soon be radioed back to the checkpoint. He waved to the plane, a confident, one-stroke action to indicate that he was doing fine. The plane dipped its wings, then climbed and flew off toward Eagle.

Up ahead, strange clouds hung over the surface of the river, forming a bizarre ground fog under an otherwise blue sky. As the team drew closer to them, George could hear a rumbling noise. It became louder and louder until it sounded like a train rushing by. Some of the dogs looked about uneasily, but they kept moving. George took a deep breath. He was coming to open water. Beneath the clouds lay a huge hole in the Yukon ice.

The trail passed within twenty feet of the hole, and George could see the deep black water roiling. He tried not to think about his margin of safety. He just guided the sled along, reassuring the dogs. Still, he knew that on a river as large as the Yukon, no margin was enough. There was nothing to keep the hole from growing once it had started, and such holes tended to grow suddenly, catastrophically.

Hearing tension in his voice, the dogs picked up the pace. He was surprised and pleased by their burst of energy. Then he felt, more than heard, a cracking noise. The dogs felt it, too, and began to lope away from the vibration.

When at last the clouds were behind the team, George stopped for a brief rest. He took some lamb cubes from his sled bag and rewarded the dogs. He went up and down the team, checking their pads and adjusting booties, patting every dog. They had recovered from his mistakes during the cabin mix-up. They had energy again and were eating well. They'd escaped the water and were making good time. Eagle was just minutes away.

The last river crossing before the checkpoint proved to be the worst. George found himself wondering how a snowmobile had managed to break the trail. His sled skidded about on the bumps and he was slammed back and forth between walls of ice. At last, the trail left the river and continued on a packed, unplowed road. The team trotted past a speed limit sign and George laughed. It was very, very good to be on solid earth and headed for a town. He'd been feeling like a tiny speck in the wilderness, a small, insignificant snowflake blowing along the river, but now he could again see humans and fool himself into thinking he had control of this wintry world.

He passed residences and a general store. People waved to him as if he were a passing motorist. There was a bright yellow checkpoint banner in the center of town, and a checkpoint official hobbled down the slippery steps of a white clapboard building to sign George in.

The official was a middle-aged woman with a cheery, cherub face. She welcomed George with every bit as much enthusiasm as if he'd been the first team in the race, directing him to park his team in a large yard beyond the banner. "There's food in the schoolhouse and you can sleep in there, in the back room," she told him, gesturing toward the clapboard building. "Make yourself at home."

George thanked her and drove the team over to the yard. To his delight, he saw five teams resting in the checkpoint. He glanced around and located Jim's dogs. It had become habit to look for them.

Steve Ketzler, a rookie who had at one point been leading the race, wandered over to look at George's team.

"Your dogs look great," Steve marveled. "They don't even look tired. My guys are really beat. They don't want to go on."

George had no chance to answer him. A race official, a veterinarian, and three reporters had joined them. The race official wanted George to hurry up and pack any used gear he might want to send back to Fairbanks. Apparently, the mail plane was due any minute and the race officials wouldn't be responsible for any later shipments. The veterinarian wanted to look over the dogs, and the reporters wanted a story.

One reporter, flip book in hand, stepped forward and said, "Mr. Cook, to what do you attribute your tardy arrival?"

George eyed the man. He was a little, chubby person with beady black eyes. He wore a fluffy wool scarf around his neck and a seafarer's cap that was pushed back in an affected way to reveal his neatly styled dark hair. He shivered in the cold as he awaited George's reply. It was obvious, at least to George, that the man hadn't an athletic bone in his body. He'd likely perish in a race such as this.

"Tardy?" George asked. "I haven't seen but one team since Circle City. I pull in here and there are five teams. Hell, I'm right on schedule!"

He breezed past the man and headed over to the cache of checkpoint bags to find his supplies.

The push to Eagle had taken its toll on George. He sat in the school building, barely conscious, and stared at the standings board. None of it made any sense to him. He'd start to calculate the difference in times and forget the numbers. Next to Steve Ketzler's name, he saw the word SCRATCH. He vaguely remembered a moment somewhere early in the race when a reporter had asked veteran racer John Schandelmeier what he thought of Ketzler leaving the Angel Creek checkpoint ahead of the front-runners.

"I think he left the checkpoint too soon," Schandelmeier had said with confidence. He'd been right. Ketzler had run the team without giving them adequate rest. There was also a rumor he'd not had a proper cooker. So there in Eagle—415 miles from the start—his team was through, on strike, out of gas.

Through the haze in his brain, George contemplated the thrill of speeding toward Eagle in the front of the pack. He gazed out through a small clear patch in a frosty window and saw Ketzler loading his gear up for the flight to Fairbanks. Dave Dalton was also dragging a sled bag along without a sled. George's eyes shot back to the standings board. Dalton was out, too.

Looking down, away from the board and away from the scene outside, George thought, I'm not Ketzler or Dalton, but I'm still in this race. He wandered over to the pot of chili that was simmering on a cookstove. A trail volunteer who was buttoned into three layers of plaid jackets graciously served him. He perused the offerings on a bake-sale table but was too tired to make a decision between brownies and oatmeal cookies.

When he could no longer find his mouth with his spoon, he returned the chili bowl to the volunteer and staggered into the sleeping room, an old infirmary attached to the back of the single classroom. Larry Grout and Jim were just bedding down. He could see their breath when they spoke to each other. George found a bunk and passed out.

Village children roaring around on snowmobiles woke all three mushers in less than an hour. Angered, they stumbled out of their bunks, all figuring that if they couldn't sleep, they might as well return to the trail. As George passed the bake-sale table, he saw that new items had arrived, and he purchased a good-looking fruit square from a little boy who was minding the table.

"Do you go to school here?" he asked the boy.

"Yes," the boy answered dutifully.

"How many students go here?"

"Eight."

"Are they all in one grade?"

"No. This is kindergarten through eighth."

George nodded and took a last look around the place. With its oak trim and formal carpentry, it looked like a building straight out of New England history. He wondered what transplanted teacher had commissioned its construction. His ponderings were interrupted by the chatter of race volunteers who were packing to leave. A janitor was sweeping the floor, sweeping him back out onto the trail.

17

585 MILES

Out in the sunshine, Abe lay with his teammates. He had rolled onto his back and was sleeping with all four feet in the air. A small crowd of spectators had formed around him, but he was oblivious to their amusement. His soft snores were flutelike, contrasting with Scamp and Bandit's tuba-toned din. George tiptoed past the dogs, packed his gear, and waited until the last minute to wake them.

At 6:00 P.M., George made a final note in his trail log. "Feet to watch: Essie front L (rosie). Pete rear L (biozide). Abe front R ankle. Taro front L crack." This way, no matter how exhausted he became, he could remember which dogs needed special care, and he could recall which one of the three ointments he carried should be used to remedy their conditions. One ointment was an astringent, one a disinfectant, and another was a multipurpose pink concoction of Fairbanks origin known as Rosie. Earlier in the day, he'd held all three ointments up in front of the veterinarians who examined the team. Worried that he might not be medicating Essie correctly, he asked, "Which one?"

The vet pointed to the Rosie, so Rosie it was, and now it was noted in his trail log and he could be off, back out of town and onto a bush trail. No more Yukon River for a while.

Grout and Kublin left the checkpoint just as George departed, and the three teams traveled together up the unplowed Taylor Highway. Temperatures fell as the climb got steeper, and though George's hands were cold, he was sweating under his parky. He opened the vents on his parky, knowing that if he soaked his clothes he could later freeze.

His team made steady progress. Minnie and Orah seemed to enjoy the challenge, and George felt pleased that he'd done his hill training. All his effort was paying off as he approached the 3,420-foot peak known as American Summit. After three and a half hours of constant uphill grind, George stopped the team for a rest. Grout and Kublin went on.

George was just hiking the team up after their break when he met Grout's team coming back down the mountain.

"What's the matter?" George called to him. "Are you okay?"

"I'm going back. My dogs need more rest. They seem to be sick, so stay clear of them. Pull your dogs to your side of the trail and I'll pass as far away as I can." He hauled his leaders over toward the tall berm.

"You're not thinking of scratching, are you?" George asked.

"Naw. I'm just gonna see the vets. Maybe get more fluids into these guys."

"I think you could catch Jim and me if you don't stay too long back there. You're still moving along okay."

"Yeah, no doubt. I'll see you," Larry called. He was on his sled, moving out of earshot.

George knew this was Larry's third try at the Quest. His last two attempts had been unsuccessful. While George plodded along contemplating Larry's situation, darkness fell. After a while, he noticed that the wind was picking up.

"It's already thirty-seven below zero," he grumbled to no one at all. "I don't need any damn windchill."

As if the wind were responding to his comment, George suddenly found himself engulfed in a howling blizzard. He'd come out of the shelter of the wooded trail and hit tree line. There had been no warning that the weather would be so different at that altitude. He hurried to tuck his face mask into his collar and pull his hood tight over his hat. His headlamp, his only beam of light, was being blown off his forehead.

The team advanced slowly. George could no longer see Minnie, Orah, or any of the front-end dogs—they were lost in the whirling snow. What dogs he could see struggled along, their tails blowing straight out to the left as the wind hit them broadside. He knew he was supposed to be traveling along a road. In the troughs of huge drifts, he could see grass and occasional glimpses of pavement. Then the team would plow through another mound of soft, deep snow and he'd lose the trail. He expected to find a level bench in the hillside that indicated roadbed, but there seemed to be no such thing. There was only side-hilling, pressing along at a forty-five-degree angle on the edge of a ragged slope. Now and then, he found a trail marker, and that gave him comfort, but the markers were caked with snow, their reflective surface rendered useless. He easily missed as many as he found.

For a while, George sensed the team was climbing still further. Then things seemed to level off. Perhaps he was at the height of land, but he didn't want to get his hopes up in case this was another version of Rosebud Summit and he had further peaks to navigate.

The gangline started to slacken, and George waded through a drift to check the leaders. Orah seemed nervous. She was turning her head from the wind and tucking it into her sheltered shoulder. The chances of tumbling down the side hill were great, and George did not dare risk a roller-coaster ride to the bottom, especially since he could not see what lay below. He unhitched Orah, put her back in the team, and brought Lightening up front.

"Get me out of trouble, girl," he told her as he fumbled with the frozen lines.

He started back to his sled and got blown over. He lay on his chest in the snow, his heart pounding. He grabbed for the gangline. Slowly he worked his way back to the sled, never letting go of the line until his hands were firmly on the side rail. Finally he reached for the driving bow and stood behind the sled. He had to kick around to find the runners. They were already buried in the drifts.

He called to the team to start up again. His words were carried off by the wind. Then his face mask was peeled from his face. He heard its Velcro fasteners go *zip* and saw it fly off into the darkness, spinning as it went. He tried to think of it as no loss. It had been frozen stiff anyway, but where it had frozen to his nose, it had now left with the upper layer of skin. His nose stung so badly his eyes teared up. The tears froze instantly, forming an icy crust on his eyelashes. He had to get off this summit!

The team maneuvered along the ridge. George saw a little line of grass tufts and reasoned that they marked the edge of the road. He tried to direct Minnie and Lightening to move along the right side of the tufts. Still, he felt a crippling fear that up ahead, where he could not see, there might be a drop-off. He peered into the blowing flakes, straining his eyes. The team went on. No cliff appeared. He was now convinced that this grass was his line to safety. All at once, he saw Minnie bumping Lightening's left shoulder, forcing Lightening to turn uphill. George realized in an instant that if the team turned, the sled would slide toward the fall line, dragging him and the dogs down the mountainside. "Minnie, no!" he shouted, but she disobeyed him and leaped over both Lightening and the grass. Abruptly, the team swung around to follow.

"You'll kill us all!" George screamed at her, but in a few seconds he realized that he was not falling. His runners were tracking on level snow. His headlamp caught something off to his left . . . a road sign! It was almost buried, but he could see the edges of it some ten feet away. He gasped out loud, finally understanding that he'd been following the downhill shoulder of the road. Somehow, Minnie had known and had dragged them up to the surface of the roadbed. George's plan would have sealed their doom. Immediately, George began the first of three recitations of the Lord's Prayer that American Summit squeezed out of him that night.

Two hours passed. The storm continued, and the team crept along, barely moving. The occasional sight of markers told George he was moving along a knife edge—a narrow spine of land with drop-offs on either side. The snow was deep there, loose and soft, so he was surprised and shaken when his sled struck something hard in one of the drifts. The snow fell away and the object revealed itself: Jim Kublin's sled.

"Jim, where are you?" George yelled, but as he spoke he heard Jim's muffled voice coming from inside the buried sled bag.

"George? Is that my buddy out there?"

"Yeah. Are you all right?"

Jim unzipped the sled bag just enough to poke his face out.

"Do you want some help?" George asked.

"Yeah. I've got a thermos out here in the snow somewhere . . ."

George dug around in the snow next to Jim's sled. The entire contents of Jim's bag had been unloaded so that he could take shelter.

"You've got to get outta here," George urged Jim. "You can't spend the night up here."

"My dogs won't go. I can't get any farther."

"Tree line can't be far. I think I see something dark on the horizon. It's probably trees. There'll be shelter there."

"I can't go. I'm stuck here."

George found the thermos and handed it to Jim.

"Thanks, buddy," Jim said. "See you in Dawson." He zipped up the bag.

George was astounded. He didn't want to abandon Jim, but he knew that if he hesitated at all, he would find himself in the same danger. Despite the ferocity of the storm, George's dogs had been making headway. He couldn't afford to interrupt them.

He looked in the direction of Jim's dogs. They had settled themselves into the drift, letting the snow fall on them for insulation. They hadn't moved once during the commotion. He knew he wouldn't be able to entice them to follow when he passed.

Reluctantly, he started up his team. He *would* pass. The plain fact was that Jim did not want any assistance.

"Wait!" Jim yelled.

"What?" George felt his stomach wrench. He jammed on his brake.

"There's one more thermos!" George stopped, searched again,

and found a second thermos next to Jim's sled. The two men said another good-bye, and George continued on through the storm.

An hour passed before George made it to the dark line on the horizon, and eventually he could make out that it was, indeed, a column of trees. The team had been trudging along at barely one mile an hour. Looking back toward the summit, George hoped to see Jim's headlamp or some sign that Jim was up and moving again, but there was nothing but blowing snow.

"Trees!" he yelled at the top of his lungs. "Jim, it's the tree line!"

There was no answer but the wind, so George didn't try to sort out his feelings just then. He was safe, his dogs were okay, he was ahead of Jim, but how would Jim survive the night? A few minutes later, George and the team moved down into the shelter of the woods. George wanted to rest the dogs at the first windbreak but reasoned that he should continue on long enough to be sure they were past any break in the forest. At last, in a thick grove of spruces, he halted.

Starting with the leaders, he patted and hugged each dog. "Thank you, thank you," he told them. When he had cuddled every one, he looked up at the sky. "Thank you, too."

One of the race officials in Eagle had mentioned a cabin to George. It was supposedly on the trail on the far side of American Summit, somewhere among the trees, switchbacks, and stream valleys that the team negotiated that night. The going was rough. By 4:00 A.M. they'd been on the move for ten hours with just two breaks and no cabin had appeared. They'd outrun the summit storm as it headed down the valley. At last, the dogs were too tired to go on, so George made camp. Another night on the trail.

Preoccupied with his search for the cabin, he had not realized how cold it had become until he stopped the team. After he fed the dogs, he floated his own metal dish in the hot water in his trail cooker and ate over the steam, a method he'd devised to prevent his dinner and utensils from freezing. Still, his feet and fingers ached. He considered lighting a fire but worried that he might expend too much energy searching for wood. He couldn't risk any further chilling.

Pushing the most fragile contents of his sled bag down toward the brush bow, he carefully lay down on his sled and drew the sides of the bag up around him. He pulled a pair of dry mittens out of a pocket in the sled bag and put them on, then he took his wet overmitts and pushed them under his body. He would need the mitts in the morning and wanted to prevent them from freezing. After that, he pulled the drawstring on his hood tight, covering as much of his face as he could. Placing his mittened hands in his pockets, he tried to sleep.

For a while he dozed, but in the very first light of day, he opened his eyes to a sight he didn't want to see: The storm was catching up to him. Quickly he roused the dogs and put their booties on. There was no time for breakfast or a snack. Up in lead, Minnie and Kirk sensed the urgency. They turned their ears, listening to the sounds around them, and pointed their noses into the wind to sniff the air. Some of the team dogs whined softly and pawed the snow. At George's signal, the team took off at a lope.

Within an hour, they reached the cabin George had hoped to find. There was evidence that many teams had stopped there. A ski plane had left tracks in the yard, and two big fire circles contained the charred remnants of bonfires. Now the cabin was closed up tight. George hurried by the scene, reminding himself that a closer look might alter his determination to finish the race.

Late in the morning, the team reached the Fortymile River and followed the trail down a bank, out onto the ice. Once again, they'd managed to put distance between themselves and the storm. Skies over the river were cloudless and indigo blue. The high banks of the river were white with dark blue details etched into them. George viewed the scenery, savoring the beauty. It was the only way to forget how cold it was.

At midafternoon, after hours of solitude, he noticed something moving in the distance. It was a man working at the river's edge. The man was starting up a chain saw and appeared to be cutting the ice. A closer look revealed that he was working driftwood out of the ice and loading it onto a sled, which he pulled around on his own without the aid of a dog. The man had made numerous treks of this sort, evidenced by a network of trails that went to and from trapped chunks of wood.

The man noticed George, stopped his saw, and began walking toward the team. All at once, George felt apprehensive. He recalled a story Quest champions Jeff King and Bruce Lee had told at the rookies' meeting. Jeff and Bruce had encountered a lonely cabin dweller one night during a previous Quest. The fellow had rushed from his cabin to welcome the mushers. He waved a warm pot of coffee and begged them to come share it, which Jeff and Bruce had pretty much decided to do, but as the man came within range of their headlamps they saw he was dressed in nothing at all but insulated bunny boots. Hastily, they drove on.

The man on the river greeting George was well bundled up in a green parky, beaver hat, wool pants, and air force surplus mukluks. He looked young and friendly. Best of all, he looked sane. He introduced himself as Mark and asked George if he wanted to come in for coffee. Uncertain as to when he'd see another human, George accepted.

"In" turned out to be a teepee-type structure draped entirely in ten-mil plastic Visqueen sheeting. The structure stood on the river's edge and housed Mark, a woodstove, stacks of books, furniture fashioned mostly of crates, and a suction dredge that operated through a large hole in the surface of the river.

"I've lived out here for six years," Mark told George. "I have a claim that runs along these two miles of riverbank. One winter I broke my ankle and I couldn't get around, so I experimented and found I could bring the dredge in and keep it going all winter. That winter was long. I only get into town twice a year, fall and spring, to get supplies, but usually I can hunt if things run short. Well, I couldn't hunt that year. I couldn't even walk. If it hadn't been for the Quest, I might have starved. I was down to rationing my food. Down to just cans of beans. When the trail packers came through, I knew I was going to be okay. The mushers gave me food. They were lifesavers."

George was glancing around the teepee. Mark smiled at a memory and said, "I like the Quest. I don't have any way to put in a trail. No snowmobile or team, so it's hard to get around until the trailbreakers come through. Then the options kinda open up, you know?"

When George had finished his coffee, he went out to his sled and rummaged around in his food bag. There wasn't much he could give away, but he settled on some instant oatmeal and farina, and offered them to Mark, who gratefully accepted them. Then Mark gave George a message.

"Nineteen miles down, there's another cabin. Klaxtons'. Tell the folks there that Mark in the Visqueen Palace says hi."

"Will do," George told him. "Thanks for the coffee." He called the team up and started downriver. Another cabin! Nineteen miles. He could make it by nightfall and get a chance to dry out his clothes. He estimated the temperature was about thirty-five below. This was one cabin he wasn't going to miss.

Kirk and Minnie set a blistering pace. The wind picked up, but it only served to excite them. For a while, George wondered if they smelled game or another cabin, but time passed and they continued without a letup. Suddenly, they rounded a bend in the river and plowed into deep snow. The whole team came to a complete stop. Feeling certain this was just a brief drifted stretch, George encouraged the dogs to wade through it, and they did, finally dragging themselves back onto a packed section of trail. In just a few seconds, they encountered another drift, a deeper one. George set his hook and walked to the front of the team. What he saw made his heart sink. The trail ahead was completely blown in. There was only a slight V impression in the snow where the trail had been.

The cabin by nightfall. With this complication it might not be possible, but he had to try. He returned to the runners, pulled the hook, and encouraged the dogs to start into the drifts. For a half an hour, they made a good effort, speeding up in the shallow spots where they could sense the hard-packed bottom of the trail, and forcing their way through the deeper drifts. At times, Kirk looked back at George, threatening to balk, but Minnie was unfailing. She moved on like an icebreaker sailing frozen seas. Nevertheless, the team made little headway, so George stopped them, pulled his snowshoes from his sled bag, strapped his boots into the bindings, and walked up in front of the team. For the next several hours, he was the lead dog. Where the drifting exceeded chest height on the dogs, they marched behind him as he broke the trail. When they would come to a fairly easy stretch, George would take off his snowshoes and ride or pedal the sled. It was tedious work, and each time George removed his outer mitts to fasten or unfasten the snowshoes, he would feel his hands start to freeze.

The sun set and the moon began to rise. It had been a long time since George had seen a trail marker. He scanned the surface of the river with his headlamp and saw no trace of the orange and white stakes. However, he did see, here and there, an indication of the trail, a line broken by drifts, stretching off into the night. He *couldn't* be lost. The steep-sided gorge of the Fortymile surrounded him. There was no way off the river but to follow it. This *had* to be the trail, he told himself. It wasn't marked because there was nowhere else a team could go. He snowshoed on, feeling a vague sense of doubt.

By his reckoning, even at this painfully slow pace, Klaxtons' cabin would be near, but when his watch read ten that night, there was still no cabin. He'd run through every leader on the team, rotating them when they tired. Now even Minnie balked at the sight of another powdery mound. In disgust, she stopped and lay down. Lightening looked at her for a minute. She wanted to disagree with Minnie, just to disagree, but after a few seconds she lay down, too, grudgingly admitting that it was time to quit.

George walked quickly to the front of the team, stumbling through the snow.

"No, no, no, Minnie," he said softly. "Please go on. C'mon. Please. Up on your feet."

Minnie flattened her ears back and gave him a withering look.

He flashed his headlamp over the team to look for a more willing prospect. Orah and Kirk avoided his eyes. Bandit had already curled up and drawn his tail over his face. George walked back to Abe, but Abe was digging a little bed in the snow, indicating his vote to stay put.

George returned to Minnie and Lightening. He tugged on their harnesses and got them standing again. He felt around in his pocket and brought out some lamb snacks. The two dogs devoured the snacks and then lay down again.

For forty-five minutes, George continued to coax the dogs. He tried pushing the sled a foot at a time to put slack in the line. This can excite a team into taking up the slack, but not a team that has spent all the energy it has to give. He tried commanding, happy talking, and even pleading, though the latter was hardly a posture recommended by dog trainers. Anything that worked was all that mattered.

"Minnie, there's a cabin up ahead. It must be right around the corner. We could get warm there. We could be dry. Minnie, please. I'm going to freeze to death out here." He ran his big mitten along her neck, but she was unmoved. She merely snuggled deeper into the snow.

"All right. All right," George sighed. "I can see your point. You're tired and you want to go to bed, but Minnie, you have a fur coat. Here might be as good as anyplace for you, but I'm human and I need shelter. I'm only asking for twenty more minutes of your time!"

He realized he was raising his voice. Anger would get him nowhere. No dog team responds to temper tantrums. Resigned, he dragged the dogs' coats out of his sled bag and distributed them, strapping each dog in for a cozy sleep. Then he started his trail cooker, hoping the heat from it would warm him. He fed the dogs and himself, and tried entertaining himself with the beauty of the moon and the brightness of the stars, but he wasn't able to escape the fact that he was cold, dangerously cold. He set off toward the riverbank to look for firewood, fantasizing about a huge bonfire as he made his way through the snow. He scoured the alders that grew there, but found only a few dead branches, hardly more than twigs. At last, he thought he'd found a good-sized dead trunk. He hacked it from the bank with his ax and hauled it, along with his other precious sticks, back to his campsite. There he chopped the trunk into several pieces. The loud cracking noise of the wood breaking convinced him that this was, indeed, dead, dry wood.

Stomping down an area for a fire, he fetched a few worn booties and soaked them with fuel from his cooker, then laid them among the pieces of wood. When he set a match to the booties, the alcohol flared, but the wood did not catch. Quickly, he hunted for anything that might stoke the fire. He grabbed more booties and stripped plastic bags off his dog snacks. He searched for food wrappers left in his sled bag and parky pockets. He tossed all this on the fire. A noxious cloud went up and a few smaller pieces of wood caught, but as George stretched his hands over the flames, he could see that the larger logs were sizzling with molten sap. They were frozen, not dry. It was ice that had caused the loud report of his ax. Glumly he watched the fire die out. He poured the last of the water in his cooker into a cup of instant soup mix and curled his hands around the cup, hoping the warmth would work into his mittens. In a few minutes, the soup froze.

Handwarmers! George thought. I have handwarmers! He jumped up off his sled and fumbled through his bag. Somewhere in there he had several packs of chemically activated handwarmers. He found them, read the directions by headlamp, crumpled them, and placed them in his gloves. Then he stood there, arms tucked against his chest, anticipating warmth. Nothing happened. He crumpled them again. Nothing.

The bastard who invented these has never been to anything colder than a Minnesota Vikings game, he thought angrily. And probably in November, at that. He doesn't know what winter is. He doesn't know he's just cheated me out of my hands!

He climbed into his sled bag, raving about what he was going to do to that inventor. Removing his outer mitts, he forced his hands down into his pants. The sensation of his icy fingers touching his warm thighs made him feel faint. "My brain is jamming," he whispered to himself. "Too many signals! I must analyze. My hands are glad to be warm, but they hurt because they're thawing and my thighs are screaming to stop the cold."

He was not aware that he'd fallen asleep. When he opened his eyes, he didn't recognize his surroundings. Suddenly, he thought of his hands. The one he'd frostbitten in Central rested on the edge of his sled bag. He had moved it there in his sleep, exposing it to the weather. He sat up violently and wiggled the fingers on both hands. He could move them, but they did not feel like part of his body. When some circulation finally came to them, he felt the now-familiar ache and tingle. George hopped out of his sleeping bag, waved his arms around, clapped his hands, and tried to get his body moving. He searched for his big red overmitts and found them, not in his sled bag where he'd always put them, but on the snow next to his sled. He snatched them up, but it was far too late. They were frozen solid, the palms still cupped. They reminded him of two giant lobster claws. He shrugged and, realizing he had no choice, forced the mitts on over his inner gloves.

He began to notice tracks all around his campsite. They went every which way. They were his snowshoe tracks, made while gathering wood and tending the dogs, but he hadn't thought he'd roamed around so much. Beyond the tracks, there was no more trail to follow, no V in the snow. For a moment he wondered if the team was headed in the right direction. He couldn't recall which end of the Fortymile River he'd come from. His chest felt tight. He started to panic. Then he took a deep breath.

"No," he told himself. "Stop that. The team hasn't moved. They *are* headed in the right direction. Get ahold of yourself."

He strapped on his snowshoes and started down the river, leaving the team to sleep a while longer. He marched through the snow, swinging his arms to fight off the cold. After a few minutes, he came to a place where a short section of trail remained. This tiny bit of encouragement had to do, he decided, and he hustled back to the team.

Less than a mile downriver, the trail opened up. George passed Klaxtons' only seventeen minutes after he started his run. Cheerful signs were stuck in the snow around the cabin. MUSHERS WELCOME, they read. HOT SOUP, SANDWICHES, COFFEE. COME DRY YOUR GEAR.

It was quarter to six. An oil lamp burned in the window, but it was unfair to stop the dogs so soon, and unfair to wake those kind people so early, so George passed by. Later he was struck by a terrible thought. He hadn't seen Jim Kublin since American Summit. The cabins after the summit had all been closed. Perhaps Quest officials needed to know Jim's whereabouts. Perhaps they needed to know his own whereabouts. He should have stopped. The cabin had a radio pole.

It was too late to turn back. He would go on and look for another cabin.

18

REST

A red pushpin held a folded sheet of paper to the message board at the Dawson checkpoint. "Handler for George Cook" was written in black marker on the outside of the fold. I took the message from the board and opened it. "Call Kathy Webster, Sunday afternoon," it read. A local number was scrawled beneath the name. I refolded the paper, then folded it again and put it in my pocket.

It was no longer Sunday. It was Monday. The race was in its eighth day. Kathy Webster was no doubt one of many helpful people who provided lodging in their homes for Quest drivers and handlers during the mandatory thirty-six-hour layover. *Kathy Webster was waiting for us.*

I glanced around the room. It was a small office in the back of the town's community center. Checkpoint officials appeared to be barricaded behind two metal desks. Some balanced sleepily on folding chairs. Others had sacked out on a pile of parkys. Used Styrofoam coffee cups littered every surface. Beyond the barricades, two more people lay sandwiched in parkys, sleeping away. Though I couldn't see the faces of these two, I recognized one of them by his mukluks: Dave.

"I'm George Cook's handler. May I use this phone to call the person we're staying with?" I asked one semiconscious person behind the desk.

"Sure," she said with a wave of her hand that meant "What do I care?"

I dialed Kathy Webster's number. As it rang, I wondered what she looked like and if her house was clean. I wondered if she had running water. I let the phone ring fifteen times. There was no answer. Of course not. It wasn't Sunday. It was Monday.

Before returning to the truck, I tried to compose myself. "Call Sunday." There was no wound intended by those words. This was a friendly note—an offer to stay in someone's home, the home of a caring stranger. But the stranger had expected us earlier. She hadn't counted on us being at the back of the pack. Now we were here, rudely late. Her neighbors had no doubt housed the front-runners. They'd regaled her with stories of thirty-six hours with the fascinating champions of the sport. Now, after the excitement had worn off in Dawson, she would have to feed and change linens for a straggler and his lackluster crew. I folded the paper again and stuffed it back into my parky.

Out the door I went into the cold afternoon. Our truck was idling in the community center parking lot. The engine chugged and squealed and exhaust poured out of the tailpipes, engulfing the whole vehicle in ground fog.

"We've got someone here we're supposed to stay with," I told Sandy as I climbed into the truck. "I tried to call her but there's no answer."

Sandy said nothing. She sat slumped against the passenger door with no expression on her face. Kathleen snoozed in her carseat.

"It's pretty here," I said. "Lotta mining history. Maybe we should drive around town for a bit and try to call that woman again later."

"Okay," Sandy said. Just then, Dave came walking out of the community center. "Look, there's Dave," she added with more enthusiasm. She opened her car window and called to him. He walked over to the truck.

"Hi there," he said, leaning in the window. "How's the truck running?"

"Better," I told him. "At least for now. By the way, we're sorry about Bobby."

"Yeah. Well, he went home to his girlfriend and I . . . I just decided to follow the race. You guys heard about the storm, didn't you?"

Sandy nodded. "Someone on the Quest hotline said it was pretty bad on American Summit when George was crossing it."

"Yeah, he was in it all right. He's okay, though. I heard one of the cabins radio in this morning. They spotted him at about quarter to six."

This *was* news.

"How far was he from Dawson?" I asked.

"Oh, I think about fifty miles. He probably got slowed up yesterday. I heard the trail was blown in on the Fortymile River. But don't worry, he's back on the Yukon by now." He paused for a moment then said, "You heard about Jim Kublin?"

"No," Sandy and I said at once.

"They can't find him. They've sent the planes out. He spent the night on American Summit in the storm."

"And they haven't seen him since?" Sandy asked.

"No."

We were all quiet for a moment, then Sandy said to Dave, "Want to get in? We're just going for a ride around town."

"Sure. Don't mind if I do."

We drove through the snow-covered streets, viewing the lovely old Victorian buildings. Once an obscure Indian fishing camp, Dawson City jumped into the world spotlight when, on August 17, 1896, George Washington Carmack, Skookum Jim, and Tagish Charlie discovered gold in a nearby creek. News of their find reached Seattle in 1897 and created a stampede up the Klondike and Yukon rivers as close to forty thousand fortune seekers risked illness, injury, and death to stake claims in the territory. Dawson was not prepared for its sudden popularity. A frontier town, it depended on steamboat traffic for most of its food and building materials. Goods gathered in the summers were stored for wintering-over while the rivers were frozen, but no one had planned for the arrival of the stampeders.

In the winter of 1897, Dawson's citizens, new and old, faced terrible hardships as supplies were quickly exhausted. Graves, dug in the fall in anticipation of the usual number of winter deaths, filled up early. Extra corpses remained uninterred, grisly reminders of the shortages. Nevertheless, spring breakup brought new hope in the city, new supplies, new gold strikes (although most residents had staked large claims prior to the arrival of the stampeders), and new businesses. Soon Dawson became known as the "Paris of the North." Downtown streets were lined with busy mercantiles, hotels, and fine restaurants. Theaters, dance halls, opera houses, and saloons provided entertainment for the miners and entrepreneurs who had plenty to spend on such delights.

In 1903, news of a gold strike in Nome caused many Dawson dwellers to head farther north, and by 1910, Dawson's rush was over. Its population began to dwindle. Buildings were abandoned and became dilapidated. The place took on the appearance of a ghost town. Once the capital of the Yukon Territory, Dawson lost even that honor in 1953. Whitehorse, serviced by railway, roadway, and an airport, became the new capital. Freight companies canceled their Yukon River steamer lines in favor of Whitehorse-bound boxcars and trucks, and Dawson ended up at the end of a long road that few chose to take.

In the 1960s, the Canadian government declared Dawson a national historic site. Since then, many buildings in the town have been restored. Momentarily tourists ourselves, Sandy and I dug out our cameras and photographed the restored buildings and their graying cousins. Some of the most elegant buildings were the ones in the worst state of decay. Their turrets and porches sagged under four or five feet of snow, leaning into the streets as if begging for salvation.

I piloted the truck up a steep, windy road that climbed the riverbank where most of Dawson's residences stood. Some were older structures made of wood or logs, others were newer prefab houses, the sort that are prevalent all over the Northwest. I wondered which house belonged to Kathy Webster.

The road looped back to Dawson's downtown area. There, old buildings lined the waterfront, clinging to the wharf that was once their only port of supply. A huge stern-wheeler was trapped in the ice, and barges and small riverboats had been pulled up on the shore. The entire scape was frozen into the snow and frozen in time as well. We passed a blue, frontier-style building. LOWE'S MORTUARY was painted across its flat, square-topped facade. Behind the facade, it was merely a long, low log building. Like several others in this section, it had been dressed up on the street side to impress customers or, in this particular case, the customers' kin.

Over the main street of town, a banner displayed the words WELCOME MUSHERS TO DAWSON CITY—HALFWAY POINT OF THE YUKON QUEST. I put the brakes on, not so much to look at the banner, but to prevent the truck from rolling over three dogs who had positioned themselves under the banner. One was a Malamutish pup, one some sort of yellow hound, another a ragged-looking collie. They were not concerned that my vehicle had been moving down the road toward them. In fact, they never flinched. They waited for me to drive around them. I got the impression that these three knew the significance of the banner and had appointed themselves the canine welcoming committee. Still, loose dogs are not a welcome sight to a musher. They often chase teams much the way they chase cars, barking and challenging. The team may perceive that the dog is attacking their pack and choose to defend themselves. At the least, such confrontations may cause the team to become tangled in their traces. At worst, a dogfight could ensue.

"They shouldn't let these dogs roam loose," I said angrily.

"Well, they can't do much about it," Dave said.

"Of course they can! Someone should insist that the owners tie them up or put them in kennels or bring them in the houses."

"Not so easy in Dawson."

"Why not?"

"No one will enforce the leash laws. No one dares," Dave said. "Getting elected dog warden here is like a death sentence. Seems people want to let their own dogs run loose, but they don't want their neighbors to do the same, so everyone is always complaining about the dogs, but everybody adds to the problem. For years, the laws said that loose dogs should be shot, you know—on account of the threat of rabies and all that—but every time any warden shoots a dog, somebody shoots him. So after a while, the town officers decided that the identity of the dog warden would be a secret. It's a small town, though. Word always gets out, and the death threats begin. So right now, nobody will take the job. The dogs rule."

My thoughts drifted back to Kathy Webster. Did Kathy Webster have a dog? "I'm going to stop at the checkpoint and call this lady we're supposed to stay with," I said.

There was still no answer at Webster's place, so Dave guided us to the campground where the teams were laying over.

We drove down to the wharf and headed across the river on a plowed ice bridge. I felt a little fearful as I steered the truck onto the river, but at a solid, windless fifty below zero, I realized the ice wasn't going to give way. Still, it seemed odd to be driving onto such an enormous body of water. On the far bank, a narrow road led to the campground. Dog trucks were corralled in the campground parking lot, where they remained under the watchful eyes of race officials. This prevented mushers from illegally acquiring fresh dogs or new equipment. Handlers hauled permissible supplies to their musher's campsite, dragging the supplies in on children's sleds or carrying them in on their backs. We had come prepared with Kathleen's coaster and her toboggan. We loaded two plastic tarpaulins, rope, a tent, two shovels, a stake-out line, and a campstove onto the sleds and started down toward George's preassigned campsite.

We passed the cache of mushers' drop bags and picked up George's straw bales. Once at our site, we dug a trench for the dogs, lined it with straw, and stretched a rope over the trench from tree to tree. When the dogs arrived, we would bed them down in the trench and use the tarpaulins to form an open-ended shelter for them. This way, the dogs could rest undisturbed. We set up our tent and our cookstove, creating a little sentry post for Sandy and me, and then we were done. We just needed our musher to arrive.

• • •

At the highest point of land in Dawson, Kathy Webster had built her home. It was spacious, made of logs and salvaged pieces of Victoriana. As Dawson's grand buildings declined, Kathy rescued their stained glass and door sets, their fixtures and floorboards, and incorporated them into her own dwelling, making it a living history lesson. This was fitting. She was a teacher at the Dawson City Elementary School; within a few minutes of meeting her, I knew she must be popular with the students. She exuded positive energy. Her unadorned good looks gave her the aura of a cheerleader. She focused on understanding and encouraging others.

She swept Sandy, Dave, Kathleen, and me into her home and insisted we all stay for dinner. As soon as our coats were in the hall closet, she pulled an enormous plate of lasagna out of her freezer and popped it into an oven. We sat in the warmth of her kitchen getting to know one another. Kathleen was delighted to meet Kathy's eight-year-old son, Matthew. A perfect young gentleman, he shared his toys with her. They played on the floor by the woodstove while Kathy's two old Malamutes dozed nearby. The day's last light passed through the leaded glass windows, casting long rays of red, violet, and green light across the room. Kathy Webster couldn't have been nicer. The fact that it was Monday didn't matter to her at all.

I was dismayed when Dave did not leave at a polite time that evening. He stayed on, finally getting an invitation to sleep on the living room couch. Kathy graciously showed Sandy, Kathleen, and me to our rooms upstairs. Sandy had called the checkpoint at 10:00 P.M. and learned that George was on his way into Dawson, but we calculated that he'd arrive no earlier than 6:00 A.M. I set my alarm clock for quarter to six and we all went to bed.

At four-thirty, Kathy knocked on my door.

"Someone from the checkpoint is on the phone. George is in."

I jumped out of bed and woke Sandy.

"Get the truck running," I told her. "When the cab is warm, just scoop Kathleen up in all her blankets. She can sleep in the backseat.

Meet me at the checkpoint, and put on your warmest clothes so you can take the first shift at the campground."

I raced downstairs and grabbed my parky, throwing it on over my long underwear. My boots were knee height and the parky lapped over them. No one would see what I wore underneath. Bracing myself for the shock of cold air, I dashed out Kathy's front door and took the porch steps three at a time. Through the darkened streets of Dawson I ran, all the way to the checkpoint.

In the yellow spotlight outside the community center, a race official checked George's sled bag for its mandatory gear. George leaned on his driving bow and chatted with a few race volunteers who had come out to greet him. I could see the dogs in the shadows. They were lying down relaxing on the snow. When I walked up to George, we just grinned at each other for a few moments. His face was gray from windburn and frostbite. His eyes were watery and bloodshot.

"Well, I'm here," he said with all the joy of a man who has been saved from death.

"You're here," I laughed. "And you look like shit!"

George was pleased. This was actually a compliment among mushers. The race volunteers chuckled.

"How's everyone?" I asked, looking at the team.

"Everyone's fine," George said. Some of the volunteers nodded accord.

I turned to the race official. "Can I touch them now?"

"Yup. They're all yours for the next thirty-six hours."

"Oh boy!" I scurried up to the leaders and hugged Orah and Minnie. They looked a little tired, but still bright in the eyes. They wagged their tails and licked my gloves when I patted them. Lightening and Essie were at point. "You're halfway there. Yes, you are!" I said to them. They wiggled happily, hearing my cheery tone. I congratulated each dog. It felt especially good to hold the big wheel dogs in my arms. "We're going to get you all some rest and lots of good food real soon," I cooed to them.

Lights flashed across the parking lot. Our truck rolled up to the team and Sandy and Dave stepped out.

"Hi." Sandy called out to George. She glanced at the dogs. "Wow, they look good!"

"Orah was *hot* tonight," George said proudly. "I know she could tell we were coming to a checkpoint. She pulled me straight to the lights of town. I haven't needed to give her a command in twenty miles."

"Oh, they know. They know where they're going," a volunteer said. She patted Boomer and he sniffed her hand as if to say, "Do I know you?"

"We'd better get you to the campground," I reminded George.

"Bed the dogs down before they get stiff," he added. I took the leaders by their neckline and guided them across the street, releasing them at the wharf. George rode along behind them.

"Follow the trail across the river," I called to him as he passed. "We'll meet you there with the truck."

He waved to signify that he understood and, as the team moved away, I saw the frost on the dogs' backs glistening. I looked up and became aware of the huge pale moon that hung above the Yukon. All at once, the land and sky dwarfed the team, their tiny forms sparkling now and then in the distance. The scale seemed right to me. We were no more than a flash in the night, and we could not control the power of the river or the temperature of the air. We couldn't make night into day, but I wasn't afraid of that anymore. I felt strong.

A muffled cry came from Kathy's bathroom.

I put my face up to the door. "George, you okay in there?" I asked.

"Come in," he said. He sounded frightened.

I opened the door. He was standing in front of a mirror peeling off his hat. Black strings of something connected his ears to the mink lining.

"Oh my God! Does that hurt?" I asked.

"No," he said tentatively. "I . . . can't . . . remember . . . frostbiting my ears. They're black! I'm going to lose them!"

Leaning toward him, I took a careful look at the damage.

"I don't think that dark stuff is skin. What is that *smell*? It smells like something burned. Geez, George, your hat looks like a road kill!"

George's shoulders started to shake. He broke into a fit of giggles.

"What?" I said. I was starting to laugh, too, but I wasn't sure I got the joke.

"Oh, there was a cabin last night—a place called Cassiar Creek. I was freezing," he said. "My clothes were wet and the dogs needed feeding, so I stopped there. I caught Jeff Bouton's team. He was just leaving. Anyway, no one else was there after he left, so I stoked up the fire and hung most of my clothes on a drying rack over the stove. My hat was frozen solid like a helmet, and it fell off the rack when I was outside getting more wood. I saw all this smoke pouring out of the chimney and went running in to see my hat had landed on the stove. It was sizzling and hopping around like bacon in a pan! Well, you know, when it dried out, I didn't have any choice. Even though the fur was all burned, I had to put it back on."

"You have another hat in your sled bag," I offered.

"Yeah, but it's not as warm. I figured it was better to smell than to freeze. It was sort of turning my stomach at first, but I kinda got used to it."

He sat down on the edge of the elegant claw-footed tub and picked burned fuzz off his ears.

"I feel kinda guilty about taking a bath here," he said. "It's all so nice and clean." He looked around at the brass fixtures. In his trail-filthy long underwear and with nine days' beard on his face, he looked like the frontiersmen who'd frequented Dawson's bathhouses at the turn of the century.

"Something tells me this tub has seen your kind before," I said.

He reached down to remove his socks and winced when he bent his knees.

"I'll take them off," I volunteered, hardly believing I was going to touch something that odoriferous.

"Thanks. They're soaked. I went down a steep bank about twenty miles out of town. The brush bow of my sled wedged in the ice and I heard a big crack. I thought it was my sled breaking, but it was the ice. This whole big plate of ice moved, and the water came up over it. I got wet up to my knees. I was afraid I'd freeze my feet, so I just kept moving."

"Mother of God! You could have drowned."

"Yeah, but I didn't." He smiled at me. He looked a little crazy. "I didn't," he repeated.

Somewhere along the Fortymile, in a place that is unpatrolled in winter, Quest mushers cross the Alaskan/Canadian border. Mushers arriving in Dawson during regular business hours are required to check in with a customs official when they sign in for their layover. Mushers arriving after business hours must report to the customs office within twenty-four hours. However, when nothing much was happening in town, officials made house calls. George was no sooner clean and asleep in bed when a uniformed Native woman appeared at Kathy's door. I woke George and he wandered downstairs. Searching through his parky pockets, he produced his passport and twelve rabies certificates and handed them to the officer. She examined them, poker-faced, and then asked George if he had any goods to declare.

"No," he replied.

Her face brightened and she dropped all pretense. "Welcome to Canada," she beamed. She shook George's hand. "Sorry I had to wake you up. I'll let you get back to sleep. Good luck with the rest of your trip."

"Yeah, thanks," George said.

After the official had gone, George shared a laugh with Kathy and me.

"Now *what* would I have to declare?" he asked as he wandered back up the stairs.

George slept deeply. The dogs did, too. Sandy and I took turns watching over the team. It was bitterly cold, too cold to let a child play outdoors, so whenever one of us was tending the dogs, the other one stayed with Kathleen. Dave followed Sandy about and, though I guessed he was older than me, I wondered if he had some romantic interest in her. They seemed to be in rapt conversation each time they drove up in the truck and, since he'd surfaced at the checkpoint, Sandy had curbed her incessant need to phone her mother.

Our shifts at the campground were timed to keep the dogs on the same eating schedule they'd become accustomed to during the race. We made soups out of meat and warm water and urged the dogs to drink them to rehydrate. We crawled into their tent to serve them. We doctored their feet, massaged their muscles, and took those who seemed stiff or sore in the joints for individual, limbering walks. In short, we treated them like royalty. They stayed cozy in their straw and their tent.

In the constant forty- to fifty-below chill, we were forced to make the truck our base of operations. We never stopped the engine. Jugs of water and broth filled the backseat. Foot ointment was kept thawing on the dashboard defroster. We would work with the dogs for a while and then run, groaning, back to the truck to warm ourselves.

Late in the morning, I stopped in at the checkpoint and saw the woman who was Jim Kublin's handler. She looked more than downcast, and though I wanted to ask her if she'd had any news, I hesitated, deciding she might prefer to keep to herself. I checked the standings board. There was no indication that Jim had scratched. I noticed Larry Grout was out of the race. Apparently he had spent the night of the storm in Eagle and had started out again on Monday, only to return that same afternoon. So now there was only Jim to account for. I glanced back at his handler. A wave of sympathy washed over me.

By one o'clock, I was performing triage on George's clothing, worst cases first. I couldn't risk washing his parky. It had a synthetic lining that might not dry in time, so I hung it on a beam over Kathy's woodstove. It was damp with sweat and, as it steamed, the kitchen began to smell like a gymnasium.

I had retrieved four frozen stuff sacks from George's sled bag. They thawed near the woodstove. When I could get the drawstrings open, I poured the contents of each of them on the kitchen floor. One was full of dirty socks and underwear, two contained used booties that could be reused after they were washed, one held mittens and a spare face mask. I was grateful that Kathy was at work so she could not see the mess I was making in her house. Of course, she knew about mushers. We were not her first Quest guests. She had showed me how to operate her washer and dryer less than thirty minutes after we met, and she had encouraged me to help myself to the big box of laundry soap stashed in the utility room. Still, I was glad she didn't have to see—or smell—what I was seeing and smelling. All the gloves were covered with grease from lamb and salmon snacks. Some booties were caked with dog excrement. I rushed to get these items into the washer before they warmed up.

I pulled George's boot liners from the shells and, holding them at arm's length, marched into the bathroom. I plopped them into the tub and filled it up with hot water. It was all I could do to keep from retching.

Finally, there was the hat. What could I do with a burnt hat? I examined it carefully. In one area, the mink skin had merged with a synthetic seam binding, causing a hard, sharp substance to form. I'd noticed that George had a corresponding scrape on his face, although in that weather it was unlikely he'd felt the injury occurring. I took a pair of scissors from a kitchen drawer and chopped the seam out of the hat. It was shedding black, singed hairs as I worked with it, so I fluffed the fur and broke off all the loose ends. With a sewing kit I'd stashed in my handling gear, I sewed the ragged seam, but the hat still looked pathetic. I had to think of some way to get the loft back in the fur or it would be useless.

"Well," I said to the hat, "we'll have to try something radical. You have nothing left to lose so—" I tossed it into the washing machine.

A half hour later, the spin cycle was complete, and I observed that the hat had sustained no further damage. I became even more daring and put it in the dryer. It needed some additional sewing after that experience, but by dinnertime it had joined the growing pile of clean clothes that would return to George's sled bag.

Shortly after Kathy and Matthew came home, George awakened from his daylong nap and Dave returned from the campground full of news about Jim Kublin. He'd made it into Dawson no more than a half hour after I'd seen his handler.

"We saw him," Dave said. "Was he ever frostbit!"

"How bad?" George asked. "He's going to go on, isn't he?"

"Oh, yeah," Dave nodded. "His face looks rough, but I think it's just superficial bite. You know, no blisters. He seems in pretty good spirits."

George sat back in a kitchen chair. "That's good," he said with a note of relief in his voice.

"He said he was going up on a ridge on American Summit and his dogs didn't like the wind, so they went over the edge of the ridge thinking they'd get shelter," Sandy reported. "Instead, they got going downhill and he fell off the sled and was holding on to the team by the end of his snow hook."

"Jeez-us!" George cried. "*That* ridge? He's lucky he wasn't killed. I thought I was going over that edge myself. It's a hell of a drop-off."

"Well, he got back up somehow and then the dogs wouldn't go at all. He said he talked to you up there," Dave said.

"Yeah. I ran over him . . . literally. I couldn't see where I was going."

"I guess the storm never let up, but he finally got out of there in the morning," Dave added. "He spent the whole night trying not to go hypothermic. Do you know what the temperature was?"

"It was very cold," George said, "but I was so nervous I was sweating."

Dave tipped his head and looked sideways at George. "Trail checkers say it was ninety below counting the windchill."

"Holy smokes!" I said.

"Yeah," Dave continued, "and it wasn't over yet for Jim. He told us he came to a steep bank on the Yukon, went screaming down it, and plunged into a hole in the ice. He thought he was gonna freeze on the way in. Said he was wet up to the elbows."

"I know the place," George said wryly. "I feel bad. The hole wasn't that big when I hit it. I just got wet up to my knees. I probably made it bigger. Poor Jim."

Dave pulled a kitchen chair out from the table and sat down. He loosened the laces on his mukluks then said, "Well, Jim's gonna sleep well tonight."

I took the midnight shift, watching over the dogs at the campground. Sandy relieved me at 3:00 A.M. By 6:30, I was driving across the ice bridge again. When I returned to Kathy's house around eight, Sandy, Dave, and Kathleen were just finishing breakfast.

"Dogs are okay," I told them as I hung up my parky. "I looked over George's sled. Some of the bolts are sheared off and the runners need changing. There's a gas station in town that's letting mushers use their garage. We can bring the sled in there and work on it. Also, George asked if we could pick up some handwarmers. He says some of his were duds, so we'd better make sure we buy one and try it before we buy any more."

George walked into the kitchen.

"Hi," I said. "How're you feeling?"

He stretched and yawned the word, "Better."

"Sit down. Kathy put out some breakfast. There's cereal and cinnamon rolls, coffee—"

"I'll take it all," he said. He couldn't get enough to eat.

"We're going to go bring your sled over to the garage," Sandy said, rising from the table.

George nodded. "I have to change the runners," he said. "Just wait a bit, I'll go with you."

"No," I interjected. "I can change them, George. You rest."

Sandy turned to me. "The laundry's not done," she said briskly. "You'll have to stay and do the laundry."

I shook my head. "I just have to get George's boot liners dry. Everything else is just about ready to go back to the sled."

"It's too cold out for Kathleen," she continued.

I looked at her. What was this, I wondered. She didn't want me to help my own husband?

"I can go and get handwarmers now," she said to George.

"All right," he told her. He was oblivious to the tension. He finished up a bowl of cereal and clenched a cinnamon roll in his teeth. He grabbed his parky off the beam and laced up the spare boots I'd brought for him.

"Let's go," he said through the roll.

"Well, come back in a couple of hours," I said. "I'll have the laundry done by then, and Kathleen will be dressed. You can sleep and I can change your runners."

He popped the roll out of his mouth. "Will do." He popped it back in.

Sandy and Dave filed out the door behind him, leaving Kathleen and me at the table.

I had trouble getting the boot liners to dry. I ended up sticking a hair dryer into them and praying that the closed-cell foam they were made of didn't melt. When they were finally free of all moisture, I stuffed them back into the shells. Then I sorted all the clean booties by size and put them into their sacks, making something of a game of it to amuse Kathleen. I returned all the gloves, underwear, and socks to their bags and waited for George to arrive.

At eleven o'clock, I began to get anxious. His thirty-six hours would be up at four-thirty that afternoon. Given his position in the race, he couldn't afford to leave a minute past the appointed time. I estimated it would take perhaps two hours to work on the sled and, by the time we got all his gear reunited, an hour to load it. He should have another nap and another good meal. He'd have to harness the team. Booties alone could take forty-five minutes, and then he'd have to sign out.

At one o'clock, I phoned the checkpoint.

"Any of you seen George Cook?" I asked.

"He was down here earlier. He got a trail update from the race marshal."

"Do you know where he went after that?"

"No," was the reply.

I considered and reconsidered walking downtown to look for George, but the temperature was still an even fifty below and I knew Kathleen couldn't make the trip in that weather. The walk to the campground was nearly three miles, too much for most adults when the mercury was that low.

At a quarter to two, I found Kathy's phone book and looked up Dawson City's only taxi company. I dialed the number and got a recording stating that the taxi only operated May through September.

"What the hell good will that do me?" I shouted as I slammed down the phone. "And what the hell is Sandy *doing?* What the hell is going on!"

Fifteen minutes later, I saw our truck pull into Kathy's driveway. George got out and walked up to the house.

"What are you doing?" I asked sharply as he walked in through the front door. "I thought you were going to take a nap. I haven't got much time to fix your sled."

"I fixed it," he said.

"Why you? *I* could have fixed it."

"Well, Sandy brought me over there and I figured I could do it."

Silently, I counted to ten. In a more composed manner I said, "Did you get anything to eat?"

"No."

"I'll make you something now."

"I need to get my clothes over to the campsite."

"*Sit,*" I said, ushering him into a kitchen chair. "I'll take care of it." I gathered the stuff sacks in my arms. The whole lot of them at once was too much for me to carry, but I was angry enough to overlook that. I hauled them down to the truck.

Sandy was sitting in the driver's seat. She did not see me coming, but Dave saw me and was obviously alarmed by the expression on my face. He touched Sandy's shoulder and motioned to me. Sandy rolled down her window.

"Take these things over to the campsite," I rasped, "and come right back with my truck!" Dave raced around the truck to help me lift the sacks into the backseat. I did not look him or Sandy in the eyes. I turned and stomped back to the house, breathing in the cold, stinging air to calm myself.

Above all, I could not let Sandy, her behavior, or my reaction to her behavior get in the way of George's race, so it was with a false sense of camaraderie that we saw George off at exactly four-thirty that afternoon. The thirty-six hours had flown by and we found ourselves rushing to get the dogs harnessed in time. We led the team to the riverbank. Rules stated that handlers had to drop the lines at the first on-trail marker, but the instant George pulled his snow hook, the team was traveling faster than we could run. Minnie and Kirk had seen the marker and were guiding the team onto the trail, so we opened our hands and let them go on their way. In one fluid motion, they hopped the bank. They looked like a roller coaster climbing up, then swooping down. George rode the sled as if he were a part of it, never turning back to look at us.

On the way to the campsite, I'd been filled with anxious thoughts: *If only Sandy had let George sleep while I changed runners; if only I'd been able to get more food into George; if only I'd spent more time with the dogs that day.* As I watched the team lope off into the fading light, those thoughts faded, too. It occurred to me that whatever had happened or not happened in Dawson made little difference, because the team I saw before me had changed. They were complete and strong. They had matured on the trail. Their fast, easy strides were the strides I'd seen in newsreels of Quest teams. I'd always been in awe of the matter-of-fact attitude of long-distance dogs and their drivers. Now I realized that it was their confidence that set them apart, a confidence that comes from experience. The race was not by any means over, but getting to the finish line was now a more tangible goal. At this point, skill and determination seemed to outweigh luck on the scale of what would be.

I saw the look of surprise on Sandy's face.

"He's gone," I said, and she startled when she heard my voice. She hadn't realized I was in the room. "He left this morning. Caught a ride with someone else's handlers. Going to get a look at the front-runners when they come into Carmacks."

Sandy stood by Kathy's sofa, gazing at the cushions where Dave had slept. She crossed her arms over her body, rumpling her night-gown.

"You didn't expect him to stay, did you?" There was just a hint of scorn in my voice.

"No," she whispered. She turned slowly and walked upstairs.

I envisioned Dave as a vagabond. He was a freeloader, a ne'er-do-well, I supposed, but I couldn't dislike him. He was full of romantic stories about Alaska and, for a meal and a place to hang his hat, you could hear them all. Charming and entertaining he was. Certainly not the sort of man a smart woman ever depends on, but Sandy seemed to think we needed him. She'd solicited his opinion on how to set up our campsite, how to care for our dogs, and then sided with him if I'd had any other opinion. In his presence, Sandy decided my fifteen years as a handler counted for nothing. Needless to say, this chafed me.

The night before, after George left Dawson, we'd joined other handlers for a dinner at a good restaurant. Halfway through the meal, Sandy had pulled me aside.

"I told Dave you'd invited him to dinner," she'd said. "He doesn't have much money, so I said you'd pay for his food and drinks. You know, like a thank-you present, since he's been such a help."

I couldn't decide whether Dave had conned her or she'd learned a trick from him. Either way, I knew that while he was a variable in our equation, there would be no solution. Things could not balance out. I paid the bill to avoid embarrassment, but inwardly I vowed it was for the last time. I did not need the Daves of the world, and I was be-ginning to wonder why I'd ever thought I needed Sandy.

Vagabonds always know the future. They can sense it in the eyes of the people around them. True to his kind, Dave had disappeared into the clouds just before a gathering storm.

Carmacks lies between Dawson City and Whitehorse, a single outpost on desolate Klondike Highway 2. During the Yukon Quest, the cost of one bed at Carmacks's ten-room motel skyrockets to $103 dollars per night. Nevertheless, reporters and spectators quickly fill the rooms. Handlers, who must wait two to four days for their mushers to complete the three-hundred-mile trek from Dawson, drive on to Whitehorse in search of less expensive accommodations, then return to Carmacks just long enough to see their teams through a mandatory six-hour layover.

Travel on Highway 2 is not for the faint of heart. Extra-wide ore trucks, whose length is often doubled by tandem trailers, roar up and down the road unimpeded. Other motorists are expected to cower to the side of the road. Darkness and bad weather complicate these already difficult encounters, and accidents are numerous. Unfortunately, some fatalities occur, not only because of the severity of injuries that result, but because of the lag time between the occurrence of an accident and the arrival of medical help.

After bidding Kathy and Matthew a fond good-bye, Sandy, Kathleen, and I left Dawson to do battle with the rolling ore monsters.

We stopped only once on the eight-hour trip, when we refueled the truck in Carmacks. The morning's drive was quiet. Sandy and I said little to each other, though we shared certain profane exclamations each time an ore truck barreled past us.

In the afternoon, Sandy initiated conversation, and I found myself holding back, not answering much. As her friend, I'd always been her sounding board and confidante. Throughout her adolescence, I had listened to her gripe about her mother. In her college years, when academics or relationships disappointed her, I comforted her, but now I heard her moody talk with different ears. I could barely recall a time when she was happy. There seemed no end to her disappointments. I wondered if she truly believed all her troubles were someone else's fault. Since we'd been in Alaska, I'd become the one to blame. Why did she seem to think that it was my fault the truck was behaving poorly? It was my fault the roads were rough and the wind was cold? It was my fault she hadn't made some lasting friends? Was I supposed to wave a magic wand and make everything perfect, comfortable, and easy? I couldn't do that, but more importantly, I *wouldn't* do that. It was completely against my nature, because I actually enjoyed the imperfections of life. It never occurred to me to assign blame for the bumps and hurdles along the way. I figured they just happened and it was my obligation to get over them and keep going.

For the first time, I saw the enormous difference in our personalities. Our common interests created only a flimsy bridge between us. She could control me by putting on a long face. I was always guessing what she wanted, guessing what would make her smile, but now I understood that this was a futile game. Just outside Whitehorse, I tuned back into her dreary monologue.

"I feel like I'm in two different worlds," she was saying. "I want to go home. I just can't think about the race anymore. I'm not into it. The whole thing just isn't *me*."

Her words hit me hard. I wanted to shout at her. I wanted to yell, "Of course it's not *you*. It isn't *about* you. It never was. It is about a dream and an adventure and working together." I wanted to tell her to put herself aside and look around at the land and the snow and all the astonishing beauty. Look at what George and we and our dogs were accomplishing. Instead, I held my tongue.

"The race is almost over," I said quietly. "We'll talk about going home when we've finished the race."

The Quest headquarters in Whitehorse was full of people that afternoon. The front-runners were through Carmacks, and their times were close. The winner was still anybody's guess. I leaned into the office and glanced at the standings board.

"Cook?" asked an official who recognized me. "He's coming. He'll be into Stewart River soon."

"You wanna leave a message for him?" asked a woman seated at a desk. She waved a phone receiver at me. "I'm talking to Fairbanks. They can relay."

I hesitated. "No," I said finally, and turned back to the standings board. There was a note chalked in next to the Stewart River heading that read DOG DROP.

"Stewart River is a dog drop?" I asked the official.

"Yeah."

I knew George had traveled over 3,800-foot King Solomon's Dome after leaving Dawson. He had then faced 3,550-foot Eureka Dome. After that, there was a mining area known as the Black Hills, consisting of some up and down trails. Stewart River was the last place he could turn an injured or exhausted dog over to veterinarians until he reached Carmacks, some 180 miles to the south. The local news station had reported that Dawson City was the coldest spot in the northwest that day. No doubt Pete's arthritis was being aggravated by the extreme temperatures. I wondered how he was holding up. Dogs dropped at checkpoints were examined, then flown to Fairbanks or Whitehorse, where they remained in the care of race volunteers until their handlers could retrieve them. Although the dogs are well treated, they recover best in familiar surroundings. I suspected George might be reluctant to drop a mildly injured dog, simply because he had no way of knowing how soon that dog would be delivered into my hands.

I walked over to the woman behind the desk. She was still on the phone.

"Still talking to Fairbanks?" I asked.

She placed her hand over the mouthpiece and said, "Changed your mind?"

"Yeah."

She handed me a small notepad. "Write what you want to say here. I'll send it on."

I wrote, "We are in Whitehorse. Can receive dropped dogs if necessary. I love you. Ann."

19

315 MILES

The cabin at Stewart River was hardly a cabin at all. The eight-by-ten wood-frame building had walls of thin boards. Here and there the boards had separated, leaving gaps so large that one needn't look in through the single window to see indoors. After a night in the bitter cold, George was glad to see any structure sporting an active chimney. The low temperatures had rendered the snow more abrasive, making it harder for the dogs to drag the sled. It had been slow going through the Black Hills.

Jim's team caught and passed George not far from the cabin. When George pulled up to the tiny building, Jim greeted him with a butler's bow.

"Welcome to the Stewart River Hilton," he said.

George hooked down his team and walked up to the cabin. He entered through a flimsy painted door. Inside, light beamed through the openings in the walls, creating such a contrast with the otherwise dark interior that, at first, he could see nothing. When his eyes adjusted, he spotted a large cookstove, a small tent stove, and a man seated on a trunk operating a ham radio. The radio unit was balanced on a dilapidated homemade table. In the darkest corner, another man was perched on an upturned plastic bucket. He held an anxious-looking sled dog by the collar.

"Cook!" the radio operator growled. He turned to look at George, and George nearly took a step backward. The fellow looked more like a bear than a man.

"You need ta see a vet?"

"No."

"Got any dogs to drop?"

"No."

"Okay." He turned back to the radio. "This is KL7XYK," he barked into the receiver, "calling KL7VMP, come in, over."

The radio snapped and sputtered. A faint reply was broadcast along with a deafening whistling sound. "This is KL7VMP, over."

"Yeah, we got Cook here. He reports no dogs to drop. That's negative dog drop. We'll wrap it up here now. If the plane's on time, we'll be in the air by . . . o-nine-thirty, over."

"How is he?" the radio piped. The question was so informal, as if a friend, not a radio operator were asking.

The operator looked at George again. "You good?" he asked, nodding before George could answer. He seemed to think George looked fine.

"I'm okay," George said.

"KL7VMP, this is KL7XYK. Condition on Cook: normal. Over," he reported.

The radio popped and squealed. " . . . message . . ." was the only intelligible word.

George was starting out to tend the dogs as Jim stepped into the cabin.

"Wait a minute," the operator said. "I think we got a message for one of you guys. I can't read you, KL7VMP. Come again?"

". . . message . . . Cook . . ."

"Go ahead, KL7VMP. Read message."

A wave of static began, followed by more whistling. Then ". . . you!" came through loudly.

"Come again?"

"Mrs. Cook says . . . you!"

George exchanged nervous glances with Jim. She doesn't say things like that, George almost said.

The operator turned some knobs on the radio unit. "KL7VMP, this is KL7XYK. Come again. You're breaking up." He listened closely to the noise. "Cook, I think it's from your wife," he said with annoyance. "She says she loves ya."

George felt a twinge of embarrassment, but Jim lifted a mittened hand to pat him on the back. "Cool," he said.

"Lee, go out an' shut down the generator, will ya?" the operator said to the man in the corner. "Let that dog pee and we'll be on our way. John'll be here any second."

As the other man rose and helped the limping dog out the door, the operator began to break down the radio and box it up.

"I haven't got anything much to offer you guys," he told George and Jim. He held out a crumpled paper bag. "There's a little bologna and bread in here, if you like."

Jim shrugged and took the bag. The operator walked over to the tent stove. Opening the stove door, he checked the wood box. It had just a few live coals in it.

"I'm gonna dump this thing now. I'm sorry, but it's got to go with us. The big stove there— well, I wouldn't use it. It's pretty well broke. I think it'd be dangerous." He began to disassemble the stovepipe and placed it in the metal trunk he'd used for a chair.

George could hear a plane landing somewhere close to the cabin. He stepped outside. Down on the river, an orange ski plane was taxiing in. The prop whirred and echoed in the trees.

"Good luck, you guys," the operator called to George and Jim. He motioned to the other man to follow him. The two hoisted their gear and hurried toward the plane. The limping dog followed on leash behind them. Within minutes, they were airborne. The plane reduced to an orange speck in the sky.

"I'm soaked," Jim told George as the speck vanished into a cloud. "I don't know how I'm going to get dry."

"Let's look at the big stove," George said, but after he'd gone inside and examined it, he saw that the back plate and stovepipe could be pierced with a touch of a finger.

"It's no use," he told Jim.

"It doesn't matter," Jim said. "The radio guy told me it's forty below and that even with the stove, they couldn't get it any warmer than twenty below in there."

Jim and George were both starting to shiver. Their icy clothes were stiffening when they noticed a large pile of cut, split wood a short distance from the cabin.

"I got some extra fuel for my stove," George said.

"Me, too," Jim said. "Let's do it."

With desperate frivolity, they doused the woodpile with fuel and set it ablaze. As soon as they warmed their fingers against the flames, they stripped off their wet clothes and hung them in the trees near the fire. Jim had to struggle to remove his huge green parky. It had frozen solid.

"Man, that coat is enormous," George said, watching Jim lash the parky to a branch. "It looks like a dress!"

Jim laughed. "It felt like I was wearing a big bell last night. It froze straight out."

When they'd pulled dry clothes from their sled bags, changed, and fed their dogs, the two men settled back by the fire to eat their meals. Their conversation was witless and repetitive due to their exhaustion, yet, somehow, George felt entertained. There he sat, in cold and squalor that would befit a caveman, smoking his clothes over a fire, trading salmon snacks and silly jokes with a man whose lot, at the moment, was no better than his. In "real life," George dimly recalled from some *News-Miner* article, Jim was a physician, a fellow scientist. Now it seemed they'd slipped into some time machine and been blasted back to the Ice Age. It was all very funny, except that it hurt so much. It was even somewhat sad, until they looked at the bright beauty of the land around them. Either way, George knew this journey was worth it. Despite its anxious moments, it had brought him to a simple peace. From now until some indeterminate time, his world was limited to himself, his dogs, and the land. The physicality of this plan, the repetition of it, was strangely comforting.

· · ·

Sandy had abandoned me. I couldn't get over the thought. She was physically present, but she was emotionally elsewhere. I had to get used to knowing that she no longer cared about me or the dogs or George or Kathleen or anything we cherished. Her support had been paper thin and her encouragement insincere. In Whitehorse, as we drove to our hotel, she angled for a plane ticket back to New Hampshire. She showed no concern for how our family and our dogs would manage the return trip without her.

In the lobby of our hotel, the profound hurt I felt suddenly converted to anger. As I turned from the reception desk to hand Sandy a key to our room, I saw her throw her arms around a man. It was Richard! Somehow he was there, a thousand miles from Fairbanks. Surely he had no car. Probably no money. No doubt I would be expected to chauffeur him around and pay for his meals. His needs and his priorities would be pressed on me when clearly I had other commitments.

I snapped. A charge went through me as real as an electric shock. I threw the hotel key at Sandy, grabbed Kathleen by the hand, and left the building. Sandy followed me, screaming obscenities and accusations.

"You ask too much of me. You never let up!" she bellowed at me as we stood in the parking lot. "I've had it with you!"

The charge in me subsided slightly. "Look," I began, "we're both under stress—"

"I quit! I quit! I quit!" she raged. She opened the door of the truck and gathered up her suitcases. Shouldering all her luggage, she headed off down the street. I didn't see Richard anywhere. He'd stepped off into the shadows, a coward to the last.

After she'd gone, I noticed that her shouts had caused a small crowd to gather. Most of the people were handlers and race officials who were staying at the hotel. Perhaps I should have been embarrassed in front of them, or embarrassed that I showed such a temper in front of my daughter, but what I really felt was absolutely nothing.

A handler I recognized leaned out from behind his dog truck, mimicking a soldier's caution when rising out of a foxhole. "Is it over?" he asked with a twinkle in his eye.

"I guess so!" I replied. He walked up to me and put his hand on my shoulder.

"Don't worry," he said merrily. "It's the pressure. Some handlers can't take it. They space out. It happens every Quest."

"Really?"

"Sure. Forget it. She obviously wasn't cut out for our kind of work." He waved a pooper scooper in the air.

I started laughing. For a while, I couldn't stop. The other handler laughed with me. It was the most wonderful release. Soon I noticed everyone in the crowd chuckling. I was surprised to see Dave standing there, smiling with them. He stepped forward and gave me a little hug.

"This happens every Quest?" I said to him.

"Every Quest," he assured me.

In dry clothes and in good spirits, Jim and George turned their teams onto Scroggy Creek Road, a notorious ninety-mile stretch of trail that has been the undoing of many a Quest team. The road is used to access mining claims south of the Black Hills. Mushers must negotiate the narrow, winding road even while "cat trains"—bulldozers or graders that push the snow aside for the following trucks or trailers—share the way.

If a musher escapes chance encounters with heavy equipment, he cannot escape the surface of the road, which, constantly frozen and rebroken by huge plows, is carpeted with boulders, jagged ice cakes, sharp rocks, and clods of frozen dirt. Passage is a jarring affair, leaving sled dogs bruised and mushers weak from pushing, pulling, and walking behind the sled. Each year the Yukon Quest organizers attempt to negotiate a brief cessation of activity on the road, but if weather permits, mining in the area stops for no one.

George and Jim followed the road, pushing up the short, steep inclines and fighting to steer on the treacherous downhill runs. Gradually, Jim pulled ahead of George until at last he was out of sight. Throughout the night, George continued, stepping up and down, pulling, hauling, and encouraging the dogs to do the same. By 2:00 A.M., the team was tired. George stopped and towed them up off the edge of the road, hoping to camp far enough from the roadbed to avoid any passing traffic. A light snow was falling. Temperatures had climbed considerably. It was no longer a fight just to keep warm.

In the early hours of morning, George woke the team and resumed the depressing run. His heart skipped when he saw the headlights of a giant fuel truck moving toward the team. For a moment, he feared the driver didn't see him, but then the truck turned its wheels to the left side of the trail, stopped, and flashed its lights. George gave Minnie and Lightening a go-ahead command and they trotted up to the truck, steering toward the two-foot-wide "lane" on the right side of the road. As his sled passed the cab of the truck, George saw that three more double tanker trucks were stopped behind the first one. Their engines idled loudly as the dogs inched past their wheels.

One false move and we'll be crushed, George thought. He hoped he wouldn't hear the sound of air brakes; his heart might not be able to take that. His sled bumped one of the tires as it rode over a boulder, and just as he was sliding by the last truck, he caught the shoulder of his parky on the license plate. He heard a tearing sound and almost lost his balance, but he found his feet just as the truck started up. He wanted to stop and catch his breath, but he didn't dare. Keep on putting distance between you and them, he told himself, and hope no more are coming up the trail.

He passed a fresh campsite. Jim's, he thought. So Jim couldn't be far ahead. He pushed along, climbing, bouncing, walking, sliding. The road presented so many obstacles that he became mentally drained as well as physically tired. Each bump required some thought about how to skirt it, and each thought required an action.

At noon, he saw the red plane he'd seen outside of Eagle. It buzzed over the team, and he forced himself to wave at it, though his arms felt leaden. He began to feel jabbing pains behind his kneecaps.

His legs swelled up and he had trouble bending them. He wondered if he should stop to put on his knee braces. After a while, the thought of strapping on the braces, of forcing his kneecaps into a correct position, seemed a painful proposition, too. He tried changing his position, putting weight on one foot or the other, or leaning over the handle bow to take pressure off his lower body, but the trail never allowed him more than a few seconds in any relaxing state.

Finally, at about 3:00 P.M., Scroggy Creek Road came to an end. The team stepped onto a snow-covered trail that wound through a stand of tall, full spruce trees. George was bathed in relief. What he noticed most was the absence of sound. The sled made just the slightest whirring noise as it slid over the snow. The dogs' feet, padded in the powder, made no noise at all. No more crunching and grinding over rocks and dirt. Just quiet, quiet woods. It was heavenly, except for the pain in his knees.

At four o'clock, he came to a cabin on the Pelly River known as Stepping Stone. Once a stopping point for Quest drivers, the cabin was closed that year. Nevertheless, there was evidence that many teams had stopped in a nearby clearing. At that moment, Jim's team occupied that spot.

"Hey, it's my buddy!" Jim called out cheerfully as George approached. "Wasn't that road a beauty?"

"Hell couldn't be worse."

"The best part was getting off of it."

"You gonna stay a while?"

"Just snacking my dogs, then I'm going on. You?"

"I'll catch up with you," George said.

The two men tended to their teams, but George found it difficult to bend over his dogs. When he was not moving around, his legs felt numb and full of fluid. If he tried to walk, he felt jabbing agony.

He managed to snack the team and medicate their paws, then he searched in his sled bag for his own medicine—anti-inflammatory pills that he should have been taking all along. One pill was the recommended dose. He swallowed two and then sat down stiff-legged on his sled. He couldn't follow Jim. He wasn't going anywhere if he couldn't stop the swelling in his knees. "Get them elevated," he said aloud. Grasping his thighs with his hands, he swung his legs up onto the driving bow of his sled. He remained in that position for four hours, drifting in and out of sleep and bad dreams, waking when snowflakes fell on his face and when the dogs stirred.

Finally, he opened his eyes and saw Orah. She was in lead, standing on her feet, looking at him. For a brief moment, he thought he was seeing Dan. That was enough to truly wake him. He rolled off his sled bag and landed facedown in the snow. Slowly, he pushed himself up on one hip, then he swung his legs forward and stood up, testing. His legs were no longer numb. They were throbbing. He searched for his knee braces. He hadn't worn them since the first day of the race, and they had slipped to the bottom of his sled bag, but he dragged them out, pulled off his pants and long underwear, and put them on. They barely fit over his puffy legs. He had to pull them into place, even with the straps fully loosened. When he was bundled up again, he took two more anti-inflammatory pills and prepared to hit the trail.

Carmacks was not far, but every step was measured in pain. To avoid complete incapacitation, he changed his race cycle to one hour on, one hour off and made slow progress into town.

Less than an hour after Sandy left me, I decided to search the local pubs and restaurants for her. I thought perhaps I could smooth things out with her, even if she no longer wanted to work for our team. Hoisting Kathleen in my arms, I wandered down a few brightly lit streets, but quickly changed my plan when I realized that Whitehorse's Rendezvous had begun.

Supposedly, the finish of the Yukon Quest marks the start of the Rendezvous celebration, but with the front-runners less than one hundred miles from town, many residents had figured the teams were close enough to begin raising glasses.

Traditionally a time when fur trappers headed in from their cabins and congregated with traders to sell their winter's catch, the Rendezvous has always been associated with wild entertainment, free spending, and drunkenness. Modern Rendezvous includes more formal events. Musicians and entertainers roll into town for their gigs, but the old style of reveling persists, and the streets become filled with tipsy people, some dressed in 1890s dance-hall garb, others in Native finery.

I wove my way through the pickup trucks that were cruising the main street of town, and all the while I was cringing at the sound of whoops and raucous laughter. I was happy to see the front door of my hotel, happy to arrive at my room, and even happier when Kathleen was safe asleep in bed.

Late that night, I received an angry, hysterical phone call from my aunt, Sandy's mother. She hurled insults at me, but few of the insults made sense. I could only conclude that Sandy had described her work as enslavement, complete with daily floggings, and my aunt had believed her. After tolerating a few minutes of verbal abuse, I informed her that I was going to politely hang up the phone. I did not wish to be provoked into saying something I didn't mean. I put the receiver back in its cradle. The phone began to ring again, but I didn't answer it. Eventually, the ringing stopped.

Around 1:00 A.M., I was visited by two RCMPs whom my aunt had contacted with the bizarre story that I posed a threat to Sandy's well-being. I think the two men were surprised to find nothing but a sleepy mother and child in my hotel room. They were evidently braced for an ogre with an ax in hand. After ascertaining my identity, they asked if I was armed.

I kept a rifle in the truck in case of collisions with wildlife, but it was not on my person and I had no intention of using it on Sandy, so I told them I was unarmed. They likely guessed that I was well over twenty-one, but I answered that question, too. They glanced at each other, apologized for disturbing me, and promptly left. I closed the door and leaned against it, remembering that Sten's Quest handler had been arrested by the RCMP.

"It happens every Quest," I breathed. "Only I didn't expect it to happen to me."

       John Schandelmeier won the 1992 Quest when he crossed the finish line that next morning at 11:40, posting an elapsed time of eleven days, twenty-one hours, forty minutes. Though the finish banners were clearly visible from my hotel room, I slept through his triumph, unaware that history was being made just below my window. By the time Kathleen and I had awakened, bathed, and dressed, Sonny Lindner had completed his race, too, claiming second place.

       I stopped by the Quest headquarters hoping for news of George, but his column on the standings board remained unchanged. Since there was no radio contact past Stewart River, there was no way to know how he'd fared on Scroggy Creek Road. The standings indicated that no more drivers had a chance of finishing the Quest that day, so there was nothing to see at the finish line. Impatient, I decided to leave for Carmacks. Kathleen and I would face the ore trucks alone.

       Carmacks, named for the successful Klondike gold prospector, looked to be a town in a ditch. Coming upon it by roadway, I saw nothing more than a convenience market at the height of land. The rest of the town, constructed on an incline behind the market, was obscured by enormous roadside snowbanks. Just north of the store, an opening in the left bank led to a narrow street. I steered the truck onto the street and spotted a square brick building with a yellow banner. This was the community center, the checkpoint location.

       After parking the truck, Kathleen and I went inside for a look around. We walked into a big, square gymnasium. The doors, glass and metal with push bars, rattled when we opened them, causing the handful of people gathered in the room to turn and look at us. Some of those people had been dozing in corners on the floor, others were slumped in chairs. One woman sat at a radio unit. She was evidently the on-duty race official. She smiled at us, a sweet sympathetic smile. No one spoke a word.

I pulled a chair out from a long table, removed my parky and Kathleen's parky, and draped them over the chair. We walked over to check the standings board. No news on George. No more finishers. We tiptoed around the room viewing crayon and newsprint murals of the Quest made by Carmacks's schoolchildren. The name of each Quest driver was written on the murals, along with encouraging slogans such as "Good luck to all teams." I looked for George's name on every poster and felt sad when I saw the names of drivers who had dropped out of the race.

Jim Kublin's handler sat at a table at one end of the room. She was wrapped in a big quilted parky, her arms crossed over her chest and her head bowed in an attempt at sleep. Her blond hair stuck every which way out of a black knit headband. When I returned to my chair, she looked up and met my eyes. She gave me a little wave and I acknowledged it. A few minutes later, she plopped down in a chair near mine.

"They must be together," she said.

"George and Jim?"

"Yeah. I heard they went through Stewart River together, so they can't be too far apart. I think they'll be here pretty soon."

"I hope so." I hunted for something else to say.

"I'm Jenny," she said, "and you are . . . Ann?"

"Yeah, and this is my daughter, Kathleen."

"Where's your friend? Weren't you traveling with someone?"

"It's a long story."

"Oh. So it's just you and your daughter out here?"

"Yeah. The girl I was with . . . well . . . we had a . . . disagreement."

"Yeah?" Jenny smiled. She leaned forward as if wanting to hear more. I saw that she was a young woman, no more than Sandy's age. "I'm just asking because I wondered if you have any room in your truck. Could I get a ride back to Whitehorse with you? I mean— whenever you're going?"

"Sure," I said. It was an unwritten rule that handlers helped other handlers.

"Great."

"Did your truck break down?" I asked.

"No, I was sharing a truck with another handler and her team's faster than Jim's, so she's gone on to the finish line. I've missed Jim at some of the checkpoints on account of this, so I just told her I'd find a way back to Whitehorse somehow. I didn't want to hassle her, but I came to see Jim, you know? I figured it was easier this way because I was kinda getting angry at her."

"Yeah, well, it happens every Quest, I guess. Handlers getting angry, that is."

"It's a lot of pressure."

"Yeah, it is."

"So, is that what happened to your friend?"

"Yeah, she kind of blew up. I kinda helped her do it."

Jenny and I spent two hours talking. We discussed a wide range of subjects, but always got back to wondering if our teams and drivers were all right. I learned that she was Jim's girlfriend and that she had followed him to Alaska after meeting him in the lower forty-eight. Our conversation ended when a dark-haired woman and a young child came through the doors. The woman announced, "Team coming." She looked at Jenny. "I think it's Jim," she said.

Jenny jumped up from her chair, gathered her clothes, and rushed outside. I followed her, vaguely hoping that the woman was mistaken, but once outside I could see the dark faces of Jim's dogs and knew it was not George. I waited and watched Jim's arrival anyway.

Jeff Bouton's team was hooked down in front of Jim's, sleeping through their six-hour layover. They barely stirred as Jim fed his own team. I realized that the woman who'd spoken to Jenny was Jeff's wife. Standing guard over his team, she looked terribly tired and worn. Her arms hung at her sides as if she had no energy to lift them. Jenny didn't look much better, and I, in my parky (dirty from dealing with the truck) and my snowpants (battered from nonstop wear), I certainly wasn't going to win any beauty prizes. Zombies, I thought. We were all handler zombies. Too many days on the road, too many nights spent worrying.

Jenny escorted Jim to the community center. "I'll find out if he saw George," she told me as she passed.

Jim's six-hour layover came and went. He slept, ate, organized his team, and left the checkpoint just after darkness fell that evening. He told Jenny he'd seen George at Stepping Stone and that George had indicated that he planned to rest awhile.

For those six hours, I lived on the idea that George was just a few minutes, an hour, or two hours behind Jim, but when Jim departed, I could no longer fool myself into thinking all was well on the trail. Something had happened out there, something bad. Though my mind raced, turning over the possibilities, I was unable to move my body from my chair. Kathleen chattered at me, expecting attention, but I couldn't answer her.

The radio operator came over and sat with us. She was a pretty woman who seemed genuinely concerned. "He's probably just very tired or the dogs are tired. They might have needed a long rest," she assured me.

A pile of parkys, sleeping bags, and assorted down-filled items moved in one corner of the room, and two sleepy people emerged from it. They were veterinarians, just coming on duty. They joined me and the radio operator at our table. Soon Jenny came along and we all sat together saying little, keeping a nervous vigil.

By 9:00 P.M., I thought I would explode. There seemed no more room in me for all the worry. I could hear my own heart beating. All I wanted to do was see George. My mind played cruel games. It asked me which dog I was willing to give up to an accident. Which dog I could let die. It asked me if I wanted to be the wife of an invalid, or if I wanted to be a widow. Though I could not suppress my fear, a tiny spark of hope remained in me. It could not be extinguished, because for so long I'd made a habit of keeping it going. George and I had both wanted this Quest. We both knew the risks and we agreed to take them. But if only—if only—I could see him again, I thought.

An RCMP walked into the community center and the radio operator spoke to him. "Sid, we've got a team that's really overdue. Do you think you can get Paul to go out on his snowmobile and look for him?"

"I'll try."

Overdue. Another half hour passed and Paul appeared with a friend. The two men were clad in raggedy snowmobile suits that smelled of crankcase oil and bore ten years of decorative sew-on Quest patches. They were trailbreakers, part of the force that packed and marked the entire race trail. One of them guessed I was the missing driver's next of kin. He touched my arm with a grubby hand and said in a voice filled with conviction, "Just relax, we'll find him."

He strode out of the building with all the purpose of a sheriff leading a posse. His friend followed. In a few seconds, I heard the engines of their snowmobiles start, then the noise faded as they drove off. I sat down again to wait, but soon the engine noise returned, so I hurried to the door to see what was happening.

"He's here!" Paul cried out over the roar of his machine. "That's his headlamp down there!"

About a quarter of a mile down the trail, a headlamp beam bobbed up and down. The bobs were slow, deliberate, and not in the rhythm I associated with George.

"Is he all right?" I shouted to Paul.

"Yeah. He said something about his knees hurting."

His knees! I hadn't thought of his knees. They were his Achilles' heel, his limiting factor in shorter races, his braces had kept the hyperextensive joints in line. We hadn't really known what prolonged punishment would do to them. I watched George's headlamp come closer and winced each time it moved. Soon I could see Orah and Minnie, then the whole team trotted into the floodlights of the community center. George stood on the runners, a vague smile on his face.

"Hi," he said quietly when I walked up to him. I put my arms out and hugged him. The radio operator, the RCMP, the trailbreakers, the veterinarians, Kathleen, Jenny, and a few residents of Carmacks all stood behind me in the parking lot, gaping.

"Welcome to Carmacks," the radio operator said, switching on a note of enthusiasm.

George tipped his head. "It sure is good to be here," he sighed.

If I ever had any doubts about the humane aspects of the Yukon Quest, I had them at Carmacks. My concerns were not for our dogs, who settled into that layover unharmed by all they had come through. They still managed to eat heartily, to wag, to greet me with cheerful canine bows. They hadn't lost much weight. They were hard, muscled up under their fur, and their heads seemed hard, too, figuratively speaking. They were not merely responding to George's commands. They seemed to know they were on a mission, a mission that was nearing an end. They seemed determined.

George, on the other hand, looked haggard, frostbitten, and filthy. He walked stiff-kneed into the community center, balancing like a bad imitation of Frankenstein's monster. He stripped off his gear in a corner of the room. When he pulled his shirt off, I could see every vertebra in his back. He had lost a good twenty pounds off his already lean frame. When he tried to remove his knee braces, some of his skin came away with them. The steel hinges and stays had worn bloody holes in his legs. His ankles and knees were puffed out and bruised. Several times I had to turn away from him to hide my eyes, because he'd know what I was thinking. I wasn't sure anything was worth this much pain.

While George slept, the entire checkpoint was still. The radio operator dozed in her chair. Jenny slumped down at the table and buried her head in her arms. Two remaining trailbreakers crawled into the pile of sleeping bags. I carried a chair out of the building and scooped up a sleeping Kathleen in my arms so she could stay on my lap while I watched the dogs. Bandit and Scamp were making quite a din with their snores, but Orah seemed to sleep very lightly.

She has one eye on the finish line, I thought.

In the sky above the team, a curtain of northern lights began to form. First it was pale and white. Then it turned green. It stretched from the noses of the leaders to the runner tails of George's sled. I hoped it was an omen, a parenthesis of finishers in which our team would be included. The lights flickered, waxed, then waned. I checked my watch. Before I knew it, it was time to wake George. Jenny would wake him for me, since, as his handler, I could not lend even this assistance. Hoisting Kathleen, I went into the building to fetch her.

At 6:00 A.M., George hobbled around his sled, preparing to leave the checkpoint. It had been difficult to pull his braces on over yesterday's wounds, but he could not otherwise support his weight, so he'd taped his scabs, gritted his teeth, and done the job. Jenny, the radio operator, and I watched him call up the team. He walked from dog to dog, patting and encouraging them, scratching their ruffs. They stood up and leaned into their harnesses, waiting to feel the sled release. Mentally, Minnie and Orah were already on the trail. They positioned themselves somewhat obliquely, indicating that they saw the first trail marker and knew where they'd be headed. Mother and daughter, they focused identical pairs of blue eyes on that distant point. George stepped on the runners and held out one arm to draw me close. I rested my head against his chest, smelling the now familiar stench of salmon, meat, and dog wool.

"Only a hundred and fifty miles to go," I said.

"Piece of cake," he told me.

"See you there."

"See you there, George," Jenny called out.

George pulled the hook and the team scampered off down the trail. For a long while, Jenny and I remained in the parking lot. When there was no more evidence of the team or of George's headlamp, Jenny turned to me and said, "He'll make it. He left smiling. I know his knees looked rough, but he'll do it, I'm sure."

"Jim will, too. I know it."

We exchanged a quick glance that belied our reassurances. We both knew there were no guarantees, but we hoped, for ourselves, for our teams, and for each other, that the last stretch of trail would be kind.

. . .

After the sun rose, Jenny, Kathleen, and I packed up and drove to the Carmacks convenience market. The truck needed gas. When I attempted to turn the gas cap on one of the tanks, it didn't budge. It was locked. Sandy had the key! I walked into the market to pay for the one tank of gas I'd been able to fill and wondered what I was going to do if I could not fill the other. In the doorway of the market, I came face to face with four tough-looking young Natives. They looked me up and down. Carefully I stepped aside and let them come out the door.

"Nice boots," one of them said to me, glancing at my Native-made mukluks.

"Yeah, very nice," another agreed.

They smiled pleasantly at me, the darting smile that I associated with their culture. I considered asking them if they could break the locking cap on the gas tank, but then thought better of it. There was a little gas in the locked tank, and with the other tank full, at nine miles to the gallon, I could just make Whitehorse . . . maybe.

"Is there any place to get gas between here and Whitehorse?" I asked the cashier.

Her expression said What do you think? but she answered, "Nope."

"Do you have a mechanic or locksmith or somebody who can get a locking gas cap open? The key is gone."

"We just sell gas. There's no mechanic here. The locksmith comes up from Whitehorse. He's expensive. Maybe you could talk to the RCMP and see if he can do it."

"No, thanks," I said. I'd been enough trouble to the RCMP already.

I left the market and fiddled with the gas cap for a while. I couldn't see how I could remove it without severing the hose that led to the tank. Recalculating my nine miles to the gallon formula for the fifth time, I decided to make the run for Whitehorse. The sun was out. It was a bright ten-degree morning. We still had food in the cooler and dry sleeping bags. We could make it. I climbed into the cab and looked at Jenny and Kathleen.

"It may be a hell of a trip, but we're gonna get there," I said. I advised Jenny of the situation, but it hardly mattered. Since George was the last team through Carmacks, she had no choice but to ride with me. I started the engine. It was relapsing into its former illnesses. I noticed a frown on Jenny's face as she listened to the rattles and thumps.

"Look at it this way," I said. "At least we're moving."

Twenty-two miles from Whitehorse, the truck coughed out the signal that I'd drained the left gas tank. I threw the switch for the right tank. The truck picked up and kept moving, though the needle on the fuel gauge rested at the edge of the zone marked E.

Jenny looked a little worried. Given what I had learned about her in the course of casual conversation, I had her figured for a free spirit. Life, as she described it, was a long adventure. Jim was just a part of that adventure. When she spoke of him, her words reflected no expectation of permanence. I assumed that anyone taking so big a risk with her heart wouldn't mind me taking a calculated risk with our lives, but her level of anxiety on the drive proved my assumption wrong. I began to wonder why I, a generally cautious person, did not feel concerned. I knew that if we ran out of gas, no one would find us for hours. If we stopped in the middle of the road, the ore trucks would run us down, but George was on his way to the finish line of the Yukon Quest and I felt lucky, as if nothing could stop me from sharing that moment with him.

Eleven miles out of Whitehorse the truck sputtered again. I switched back to the left tank. We drove four miles before the engine balked and I flipped the lever back to the right tank. That carried us four and a half more miles. I switched again. Miraculously, we were still moving. We began to pass a number of fishing cabins. All of them were boarded up for the winter.

"We're coming into civilization," I told Jenny. "Look for a gas station—any one we can find. I've got cash, so just any station."

"There's got to be one soon," she said.

"Well, even if the truck dies here, we're only about a mile from the city limits. Look—there's a traffic light!"

At the junction of the Klondike Highway and the Alaska Highway, there was indeed a traffic light, a symbol of Whitehorse urban life that jarred one out of the bush. The light turned green as we approached it, and we cheered.

"There's a station. There's gas!" Jenny cried.

I saw a little building with gas pumps. A sign advertised some frontier brand of petroleum. We rolled up to the tanks just as the truck stalled. I put my head down on the steering wheel and giggled uncontrollably.

"See, nothing would dare stop us now," I told Jenny.

20

133 Miles

The Chain of Lakes is an aptly named stretch of country lying between Carmacks and Whitehorse. The last link in the chain is Lake Laberge, a forty-mile-long body of water made famous by Robert Service in his chilling poem about death in the Yukon, "The Cremation of Sam McGee." The Quest trail crosses the frozen surface of these lakes and makes small portages through tall spruces. There, traveling almost due south, sled dog drivers experience rapid changes in the climate and geography. The sensation is one of blinking: first one is on an open lake with a certain character, then plunged into darkened woods, only to emerge on another lake of quite different character.

Whirlwinds stirred the snow as George and the team neared the first lake. There was evidence that this was the last of a ground storm that had moved in during the previous night. George began to encounter downed trees, some so sizable that he had to cut away the branches with his ax and lift the dogs and sled over the trunks. Such tedium seemed ordinary by now, and George went about the work in a pleasant sort of daze. He thought about how nice a team he had. Good dogs; not fast, but steady and very healthy. They functioned like a big interlocking puzzle. They were so used to traveling as a unit that he could hitch any dog next to any other in the team and they all seemed to fit, each one as dedicated as the next. He'd put Lightening back in lead with Minnie and moved Orah to the improbable position of second swing with Boomer. She was happily trotting along. He liked that Boomer was white with touches of black and Orah was black with touches of white. Opposites. Pieces that fit. Then he saw they were not dogs, but an engine with moving pieces.

He was jolted out of this hallucination by the sight of a team coming head-on. He recognized the driver, a Quest musher named Doug Hutchinson.

"It's wild out there on the lake," Doug told him as he pulled his sled alongside George's. "Storming. I went only six miles in seven hours. I'm gonna run out of food. I can't feed my dogs."

George stared at Hutchinson. The man was every inch a specter from Sam McGee. His eyes were wide and his complexion was ghostly white. He gripped the handlebar of his sled as if it would get away from him.

"I don't have enough food," he repeated. "It might take two to two and a half days to cross these lakes. Are you sure you have enough food? Better be sure. You've gotta have food. I can't feed my dogs."

"Where are you going?" George asked him.

"To Carmacks."

George was confused. Had Hutchinson finished the race and decided to mush back to Carmacks? Was he turning back to get more food? Maybe he lived in Carmacks and this was his way of getting home.

"I've got food enough for two days, I think," George said a little weakly.

"Just be sure. Be sure," Hutchinson rasped. He pointed a finger at George and then slowly recoiled his hand. "I'm going on." He called up his leaders and continued toward Carmacks.

George moved on toward Whitehorse feeling unnerved. Once out on the lake, he could feel the force of a warm, unfamiliar wind. The trail was sketchy and disappearing quickly, filling with drifting snow. Though he could not see the far bank of the lake, George hurried the dogs along, hoping to cross before all trace of the trail was lost to him.

Half an hour passed. Drifts were mounting. Orah was tiring, though Minnie continued to push on. George moved Kirk into lead, but to no avail. Eventually he had to strap on his snowshoes and stomp in a trail for the team. He navigated using mere hints of Hutchinson's tracks. Not a marker in sight. Was he lost? He agonized. How could he be lost? Sooner or later he'd reach the south end of the lake. The trail had to go on from there. Finally, he saw some obvious trail and resumed his position on the sled runners.

As the team started up, Moose attempted to turn around in his harness. The dog became tangled in his lines and struggled for a moment before falling to the ground and allowing himself to be dragged by his teammates. George slammed on the sled brake and rushed up to the dog, fearing he'd been injured. As Moose slowly came to his feet, George untangled him and patted him. Moose accepted the affection and seemed ready to go on, but when George called up the team again, Moose repeated the entire sequence. Again, George untangled him. Again, Moose turned and entangled himself.

George was puzzled. What was causing this strange behavior? Moose gazed at George with an expression of equal bewilderment. Perhaps Moose needed a rest, George decided. He unhitched the dog and loaded him into the sled bag. No sooner was the team under way than Moose was asleep. Apparently, in his weariness, Moose had become focused on George as front-end commander. He had followed along while George snowshoed ahead of the team. When George had returned to the rear of the sled, Moose had attempted to stay behind him. He had completely lost his bearings. He could not remember in what direction the team was headed.

While Moose slept, Kirk began to act up. He kept looking back at the team, searching for Moose. The two dogs were brothers and inseparable friends. Kirk was clearly concerned that something had happened to his buddy.

"Kirk, go on. It's okay. He's just overtired," George told the dog, but Kirk didn't understand. So George swapped Kirk out of lead, replacing him with Lightening.

When the far bank of the lake came into sight, George spotted a trail marker and felt a tremendous sense of relief. As he pushed his sled onto the bank, Moose awakened and began fidgeting in the sled bag. George stopped, lifted the dog out of the bag, and examined him. He looked fit to run again, so George hitched him back into the team next to Kirk. Both brothers seemed pleased and continued down the trail as if nothing had happened.

After a portage littered with blown-down trees, George faced the second lake. The wind had not subsided, but the markers on this stretch had remained in place. The trail was clear, but soft and punchy from the heat. As the team approached a second marker, Lightening stopped, bringing the whole crew to a halt. In a matter-of-fact manner, she lay down on the snow, crossing her front paws before her.

"Lightening, c'mon. Lightening, let's go," George told her.

She stood up, gave herself a shake, and led the team all the way to the next marker, then she laid down again, causing the team to overrun her and tangle.

What in the hell . . . ? George wondered. He fixed the tangle and started up again. Everyone trotted along smoothly for another quarter mile, until Lightening stopped at yet another marker. George set his snow hook and walked up to her. He patted her for a moment. She wagged happily, but somewhat wearily. She was completely unaware of the trouble she was causing.

Warm weather, mushers going crazy, dogs acting up, George said to himself. He switched Lightening with Orah, and, at last, the team moved on. Hours after the incident, George realized why Lightening had been stopping at the markers. He wasn't sure how he came to understand her behavior. No particular notion seemed to trigger the thought, but he recalled that Ron had once trained Lightening to work a trap line. Caches on the line were marked by wooden stakes that resembled the Quest markers. Lightening was accustomed to stopping at the caches so the sled could be filled. The poor dog was so tired that she'd had a flashback to her former life!

All that afternoon, the team slogged along the deteriorating trail.

The sun moved over them, warming George's face and heating up the dogs' coats. George shed his parky and wore only a wind shell. The gnawing fear of freezing to death that had accompanied him throughout the race had now given way to a worry that the dogs would suffer heat prostration. He guessed it had to be close to forty degrees. Though his knees were barely functional, George helped the team as best he could, lightening their load by walking or pedaling. He let the dogs gulp mouthfuls of snow to cool themselves.

Even when the sun sunk below the horizon, the strange weather continued. George imagined he had mushed all the way back to New Hampshire, where the weather cycles brought on similar conditions. Carefully, he guided the dogs over Frank Creek. This was a stretch that had ended many mushers' Quest, but that night the creek was benign. No open leads. No missing trail markers or insurmountable drifts. Just a winding trail that led to Coghlan Lake cabin, where it was rumored that ice cream and homemade pies awaited the mushers.

Jim Kublin and Jeff Bouton were finishing a late-night meal when George hooked down at Coghlan Lake.

"Well, I was wondering when I was going to see you again," Jim called, his grin illuminated by his headlamp. "Weren't those blowdowns something?"

"Something," George said. "Something terrible."

"I confess, it wasn't the storm that brought those trees down, it was Jeff and me. We had our axes going. Had to try to stop you somehow."

The joke struck all three men silly. They giggled like overtired children. Suddenly, Jeff was serious again.

"Did you see Hutchinson?" he asked.

"Yeah. What's going on with him?"

"Got caught in the storm on the big lake there—Mandana. You must'a been at Carmacks when the storm went through here. There was thunder and lightning, snow and rain. Trees crashing down around us on the portages. It was *spooky!* Chinook winds, you know. They bring a lot of weird stuff."

"So, did Hutchinson finish, or what?" George asked.

"No, he turned around at Laberge."

"But that's only seventy miles from the finish!"

"I know. Jim and I both met him. He was real freaked out. We tried to convince him to come along with us. He wouldn't go. He thought he didn't have enough food for his dogs. He was gonna scratch at Carmacks."

"But it's seventy miles back to Carmacks from Laberge. And anyway, he could have finished in less than a day. Then he could feed his dogs at the finish!"

"I know. It's awful, huh?"

"I didn't realize he was going back for good. I didn't really know what he was doing. Maybe I should have talked to him more. Talked him out of it."

"Naw, we tried, believe me."

George wandered away from the conversation. His headlamp flashed over a pile of empty ice cream boxes that lay near the door of the cabin.

Inside the cabin, he found a woodstove, a table, chairs, and an iron-framed bed. There was a note on the table that read "Sorry, we ate all the ice cream." It was signed by musher Tim Mowry. George turned the note over so he wouldn't see it again. There was no water heating on the woodstove, so he stepped outside to start up his cooker. It was time to water his dogs.

George's watch alarm beeped around 4:00 A.M. and he awoke in the iron-framed bed. He hoped that this was his last day on the trail, but he pushed the thought aside just in case that hope would not become reality. Hearing the wind outside the cabin, he gathered that the weather had not changed. If it was his last day, he knew it was going to be a long one. The balmy temperatures—perhaps climbing into the forties—would mean a slow march to the finish. If the sun brought too much warmth, he might be forced to rest the dogs all day and approach Whitehorse at night.

By 6:00 A.M., George and the team were on Lake Laberge. They were buffeted by almost tropical headwinds on the unsheltered ice. Some gusts were so powerful they brought the dogs to a standstill.

"Robert Service was a liar," George told the team, but he knew that if these same winds had shifted to carry arctic air, he'd be ready to take Sam McGee's route to warmth.

In the distance, he could see the glow of two headlamps. Jeff and Jim, not far ahead of him. Perhaps he could catch them. If not, he would be the last team to cross the finish line. He tucked that thought away, to keep it from discouraging him, and concentrated on negotiating the slushy trail.

The headlamps faded when the sun rose, and George lost track of Jeff and Jim. By noon, Lake Laberge was awash with overflow.

Pedaling in the slush was useless. It only served to jolt the sled about, interrupting what little momentum the dogs could gain. George could only ride the runners, hoping to get some flotation. He was dead weight. His spirits sunk along with his sled.

"It's unfair," he said to the team. "Unfair after all you guys have been through. Now I can't even help you. You have to just keep pulling. But tonight, I promise, you'll be in your beds in the truck. I'll think of a way."

An unevenness in Bandit's gait caught George's attention. The old fellow was wobbling. His back legs looked weak. George wondered if he should load Bandit into the sled. Fifty more pounds in the sled in that heat would slow the team to a crawl. Stopping, George went up to examine Bandit.

"Can you make it fella?" he asked the dog. Bandit flattened his ears and bowed his head in loving submission. He was panting hard. George put a hand on the dog's thigh and checked his pulse. It was high, but not abnormally so. He unhitched Bandit's tugline, so that the dog could walk along with the team without having to pull.

"We'll try it this way," George told the dog, as he headed back to the runners. "All you have to do now is keep up. We're going home."

• • •

On the Yukon River at Whitehorse, Quest finish line banners flapped in the breeze. A two-by-four supporting the main banner stood askew, knocked off kilter by shifting ice. It waved about and tore at a Canadian flag on another post. Over the past two days, race officials had made attempts to reset the post, but that day no one bothered. It was nearly time to remove the banners completely.

The ice had opened up not far from the banners, and trailbreakers had been careful to warn approaching teams away from the long line of black water. That day, as I stood watching the banners puff and twist, I saw that the lead had grown to dangerous size and that a small diversion had been made in the course, bringing the last hundred yards of trail up onto the riverbank. Still, I worried. If the Yukon was open here, what did it look like upriver on its feeder, Lake Laberge?

Evidently, race officials were wondering the same thing. I spotted the race marshal and a trailbreaker as they zipped past me on snowmobiles. They waved to me, and I felt a little ashamed to be recognized, standing there, waiting like a seafarer's wife on a widow's walk. I turned away from the bank and heard a terrific crash. When I looked back, the banners were floating downriver, trapped in a jumble of ice floes. The last section of Quest trail had been erased by rushing water.

George was closing in on Jeff and Jim. Their tracks were very fresh. He followed them through a small settlement and onto the headwaters of the Yukon. With perhaps fifteen miles to go, he might still catch up and pass them. There was still a chance. He passed some riverboats, beached and frozen into the bank for the winter. Suddenly Minnie pulled the team right up to one riverboat and promptly entangled the team in the huge bronze blades of its propeller.

"Minnie, what the hell did you do that for?" George demanded. Minnie looked away vaguely.

"Even *you're* spacing out," George muttered as he worked on the tangle. He felt an irrational sense of hurry and dread, as if the engine of the boat might be started by a phantom and his team would be chopped to bits. As he was turning his team back onto the river, he noticed blood and crumbs of meat. Some team had stopped there to snack. Minnie was apparently demanding a snack break, too.

"At Burma Road, Minnie," George told her. "You'll get a snack there."

Located eight miles from the finish line, Burma Road is the last radio check on the Quest trail. Handlers and spouses know that ham operator's call letters by heart and rejoice when their own musher's name is transmitted along with that code.

Mushers know the check as merely a truck parked on the river ice. A yellow light flashes from the top of a vehicle, a beacon, a light-house, proving that home shores are near. When the race is over, Burma Road is a forgettable location. It does not have the color or warmth of the cabins, nor the beauty of the open trail. For George, Jeff, and Jim, however, Burma Road was to hold special meaning.

Early in the afternoon of the sixteenth day of the race, the race marshal leaned in the door of the Whitehorse headquarters and said, "It's over."

Jenny, Kathleen, and I sat crowded around the standings board, elbow to elbow with race officials, reporters, handlers, and fans. We were the faithful, hanging on, waiting for the final report from the ham operator.

"What do you mean it's over?" I asked.

"We're moving the finish line to Burma Road. The last eight miles of river is impassable. Not safe. I couldn't even get a snowmobile out there."

On this note, the faithful rose to their feet and stampeded out of the room. Reporters shouldered TV cameras, fans threw on their coats. Jenny and I watched the commotion without moving. We both seemed unable to react.

Finally, Jenny let out a scream of joy. Before we hurried out to our trucks, I snatched a message addressed to George that I'd spied on the bulletin board. The lone Quest official left in the office handed me a long, slender box and said, "This also came for George." I didn't think about the contents of the box, I just tucked it under my arm and headed out the door.

George was just receiving the news that he had finished the race when I pulled our truck up to the riverbank. Kathleen burst out of the truck and ran down to her father. "Daddy! Daddy!" she yelled. He caught her up and held her in his arms. He saw me coming and smiled. His eyes looked fiery, peeking out from a swarthy, now-bearded face.

"We did it!" we said as we embraced.

For half an hour, an odd assortment of people reveled on the ice. The fans passed out beer to the people and dog cookies to the teams. A few Quest drivers who had finished the race ahead of the last trio arrived to express their congratulations. Reporters lingered, seeking closing statements from the mushers. People hugged one another and hugged dogs. The race marshal presented finisher's medals to all three drivers, and to George he gave a red lantern, the type that hangs from a train's caboose. In mushing, this lantern is the prize reserved for the last man off the trail. In the crowd I saw Walter Therriault, the man I considered a dog murderer. He came up to George and shook his hand.

"I knew Siberians could do it," he said, and patted George on the back.

I felt a wave of satisfaction. The man is haunted by what he has done, I thought.

When the crowd dwindled down, Jenny, Jeff's wife, and I began the business of loading our teams into our trucks. George called Minnie up one last time, directing her to lead the team up the bank. She stood up proudly and marched across the ice, her cool blue eyes squinting slightly in the light. I watched each of our dogs file past me, their faces bright, their ears up. For just a moment, I saw the secret place in their hearts, the place known to man but not fully understood by him. It is the place that makes sled dogs want to run through cold and storms and heat and hell. It is the place that celebrates the delicate beauty of survival. Somewhere in that place, our dogs knew what they had done.

Light

21

I sat in our Whitehorse hotel room savoring the quiet. I could not remember when I'd last heard something so subtle as the tick of our travel clock. It seemed there had been noise all the time, for months on end. If not the noise of people, dogs, and trucks, then the noise of loud, urgent thoughts. Suddenly, I was free to hear and to think nothing at all.

The drapes in the room were closed to block out the February sunset. Kathleen napped on one bed, her hands gently tucked under one cheek. George slept on the other bed. He lay flat on his back, his hands folded over his ribs. After an epic shower, he'd stretched out on the clean sheets and passed into a state of unconsciousness only slightly this side of a coma.

The box I'd taken from the race headquarters to the finish line had contained twenty-five long-stemmed roses. They were a congratulatory gift from friends back east. Such exquisite symbols of victory were not overlooked by the citizens of Whitehorse. After the press enjoyed the opportunity to photograph George with the roses and his lantern, our hotel manager instructed a staff member to place the roses in vases on our bedside table. The roses were joined by gifts and mementos from all sorts of people. The staff neatly arranged everything around our bed. Bottles of champagne chilled in a variety of silver ice buckets, readied for a celebration that George and I were too tired to start.

Cards, faxed messages, and notes from friends were piled on a large table at the foot of the bed. When I looked quickly at the scene, George appeared to be lying in state. The lush flowers and gleaming silver contrasted eerily with his gray, frostbitten skin. I walked over to view the messages again. The little note I'd snatched from the Quest bulletin board rested on the top of the pile. It read, "To George, the unstoppable: You did it! No one appreciates what you've been through more than I do." It was signed "Mike Conolly."

It took over a week for new pink skin to replace the crusty scabs of frostbite on George's cheeks, nose, and chin. As he checked the progress of his healing in our bathroom mirror at Two Rivers, he noted that there would be just a bit of permanent scarring at the top of his cheeks. He glanced at his hand, the one he'd injured in Central. It, too, was healing. Most of the numbness was gone, but from now on he would likely have to guard it with a glove even in temperate weather. His knees were back to their normal loose but painless condition.

For a few nights after the race, he had been repeatedly awakened by terrible leg cramps, and when he did manage to sleep, he dreamed that he was still racing, that some team was sneaking up on him or getting ahead of him, and he had to hurry. The dreams had subsided now, along with the pain.

Still, he had a feeling that he was assessing damage. Emotionally, he was emerging from another world. He had to walk slowly back, because some thoughts left him mildly depressed. His great adventure was over, and the places it had taken him were behind him. Even if he were to go to those places again, they would never be as wondrous as they'd been the first time. Worse, he could not find words to explain what his solitary voyage had meant. Other Quest drivers understood implicitly, and he felt comforted when in their company, and somewhat alone when he was without them. These sad thoughts were akin to his scars: minor in the overall picture, but there, and likely to stay. They existed alongside a new confidence.

He felt as if he would never fear anything again. Nothing seemed impossible. All things could be accomplished. In a long relay race of planning, preparation, and execution, he had been the anchor man. He had carried the last baton without fumbling or failing. In the mirror, he saw the person he had always hoped he could be.

Everything in his life seemed suddenly more valuable. His wife, his daughter, and his dogs. They were bonded together by choices, choices they had all made. The adventure was over, yes, but it had opened the door to the possibility of many more. He looked into the mirror again.

The Quest and the Iditarod races follow a pattern that is familiar to all Alaskans. They must be planned and prepared for in the fall. The racing takes place at the toughest part of the year, when the land is still cold and dark. By the time the mushers cross the finish lines, light has returned to the land—a sure sign that spring will follow.

More light and more leisure time lifts Alaskan spirits. While there is still plenty of snow on the ground, it is sometimes warm enough to mush in T-shirts. Attention turns to training new puppies while the seasoned dogs get a rest. Post-race parties are held all over the state. People gamble on the exact timing of "breakup," the moment when the ice fractures in the rivers. Everyone feels a sense of relief. They have survived another winter.

The Alaskan term for a newcomer is "*cheechako*," and one remains a *cheechako* until he has successfully wintered over in the Great Land. Then he becomes a "sourdough," tough and crusty and able to renew himself, just like the bread the original prospectors made.

In the eyes of Two Rivers, George and I had outdone ourselves in our pursuit of the sourdough title. Completing the Quest was far beyond the minimum necessary effort. We received the congratulations of our community in so many ways. Our sled dog club printed a cheerful acknowledgment of George's finish and included it in a meeting notice. Friends welcomed us home. Strangers stopped by our house, hoping for a chance to meet us. Invariably, they had followed the media's accounts of the race and cheered for George.

Dave Rummel happened by one afternoon. He admitted that he was one of several of our neighbors who had engaged in informal betting on the Quest. He didn't say he'd bet against George finishing the race, but his firm handshake told George that he had.

Sten was less subtle, mixing his usual caustic comments with open-hearted joy. "Aw, I knew you'd finish. Those damn Siberians. Slow as hell, but they always get there," he grumbled.

For a wonderful six weeks, George and I put aside all notion of leaving Two Rivers. We neither spoke of staying nor of going home. We lived as Alaskans, entirely comfortable and familiar with our surroundings.

Jack Patterson completed the Iditarod that season, and he came over one night to share frostbite stories with George. Neighbors gathered to hear the two men talk. It was that evening, amid all the merriment, that I asked Lila Patterson if she wanted our houseplants.

"Why?" she asked. "Don't you want them?"

"They'd never make the trip home," I said.

"But I thought—we all thought—you weren't going."

"Well, we are. On April first. We have to," I said, though a little voice inside of me asked why.

It was the same everywhere we went. The cashiers at the store frowned when I told them Kathleen would not be laying waste to their supply of nickel-a-box raisins any more. Steve, the postman, sighed when he handed me the forwarding address form I'd requested.

Karen and I sadly watched our children play together, knowing it was for the last time. True to the Alaskan spirit of recycling, people quickly answered the ad I tacked up on the bulletin board at the store. It listed various household goods we had for sale or for giveaway. Everything disappeared. The house was emptied. Still, friends visited, sitting on the floor and eating off paper plates.

Two days before our scheduled departure, George and I talked seriously about canceling our plans. It was not too late to buy our Alaskan house.

"I don't know why we're leaving," I said. "I don't really want to leave."

George sat on the bare linoleum. Pink streaks of light filtered through a curtainless window and touched his face with sunset. "What if we stay?" he asked.

"Kathleen will grow up differently," I said.

"Our parents will miss her and us," he offered. "I'll be out of a job."

"But there's lots of work here for geologists."

"I know," he said. "I've read the *News-Miner*."

"The dogs would be happier," I said, only half kidding.

"We'd have to go home for a while, anyway, to settle things. We can't just run away."

"I know," I said. "I guess this is the way it has to be."

The next morning, I was packing some linens when my attention was drawn by motion outside our kitchen window. I expected to see the snowshoe hare that had taken up residence under our sauna. I was used to his comings and goings and had often enjoyed watching him.

I was surprised when, instead of the hare, I saw a cross fox intently hunting around the sauna. I saw him poke his head into the hare's hideaway. Apparently, the hare wasn't home, a lucky turn of events for the hare. The incident was not so lucky for me, though. The Natives claim that a cross fox sighted near a house means bad luck for the house's occupants.

Only hours later, Sol called to inform me that our house had been sold. He was making sure we were leaving on the date we'd specified in our lease. I made arrangements to turn over the keys to him. He offered me the moose rack on the shed as a souvenir of our stay. Now I knew I was going back to New Hampshire, but I could no longer think of New Hampshire as home.

Our phone was to be disconnected on March 30, so we were puzzled when it rang at seven in the morning on April 1. I recognized the heavy Native accent of the caller.

"Martha, how are you?" I asked.

"Okay. I want you to know you will have safe trip. I went to church early today to pray for your safe trip. I tell God how you buy my sewing and that help me pay for my grandchildren. I tell him you are good friends and to help you, now."

"Thank you, Martha. That's very kind of you."

"How far New Hampshire?" she asked.

"Far. In the eastern United States."

"Farther than Yellowknife?"

"A lot farther."

"Oh. I once go to Yellowknife. Farther than that is *far!*"

Neither of us spoke for a moment.

"Maybe I see you again," Martha offered.

"No doubt. Someplace. We might come back . . ." My voice trailed off.

"For now, we say good-bye. Don't forget to dance."

"I won't, Martha. I promise."

I hung up the phone when I heard the dial tone come on. A few minutes later, I thought I'd make a last call to Karen, even though we had already said good-bye. When I picked up the receiver, there was no sound. The service had been disconnected.

Our truck was loaded when Sten arrived and handed George and me a folded flag. When we opened it, we saw it was the state flag of Alaska. Its dark blue field was emblazoned with the eight stars of the Big Dipper. To those who have lived under the northern sky, no explanation of its symbolism is necessary. The Dipper is huge from the Alaskan vantage. One can almost reach up and touch it.

"If you are ever lonely for this place, you can tack this up on your ceiling," Sten said.

I walked one last time to the potato field and saw the ravens there at play. I took a long look at the trail, at the slope of the field, and at the trees beyond, before turning to view our dog yard. The yard was empty and still, but I saw a dog there. I did not conjure his image. He simply appeared. It was Dan. Mentally, I let him off his tie-out. He was free to run down the trail. I saw that he had caused me to come here and I had carried his spirit to this place. I walked back to our truck, leaving him to chase the ravens.

Returning to New Hampshire, I saw my life as a stranger might view it. I could not get used to so many houses, so many neighbors, so many social demands. Everything in my life had been redefined in only seven and a half months. If I felt the adjustment to Alaska had been bumpy, the readjustment to New Hampshire was worse. George and I went back to our jobs and our lives. We enrolled Kathleen in preschool.

I got used to living in a large house again, though it took months to shake off a feeling that the house owned me. It had too many rooms and too much furniture. I was obliged to clean it, take care of it, as if it were some sort of shrine.

I stopped putting the coffee on for just anyone who happened by. I started wearing skirts again and caring what I looked like when I stepped out to the store. Outwardly, I was an easterner once more.

Inside, though, there would always be Alaska. I knew that for sure one day late in June. I was driving down the interstate passing a low-lying area. Shallow ponds rimmed the shoulders of the road and a beaver dam was visible near a culvert. At the edge of the right lane lay a beaver. I steered my car onto the shoulder and got out to examine him.

He was dead, no doubt bumped by a car, but there wasn't a mark on him. His pelt was in perfect condition. The fur rippled in the breeze. I immediately thought I'd lift him into my car and take him to someone who could use the pelt. Someone like Martha, who prided herself on utilizing every bit of any hide she sewed. She'd shown me how the pattern trimmings from beaver mitts could be used to edge the top of mukluks. She never wasted anything that nature gave her.

Standing over the beaver, I came to my eastern senses. I didn't know anyone here who could skin a beaver. I didn't know anyone who would want the pelt. The sun was high. The beaver's carcass would soon be rotting. It wasn't like Alaska, where, much of the year, natural refrigeration would have preserved him.

I walked to my car and drove away from the beaver. I felt sad at first, but then could not repress a soaring sensation. *I* knew the beaver's value. I would always know it, just like I knew the low angle of the sun on a winter's day in Fairbanks. For a moment, I returned to the pink and gold light.

About the Author

Ann Mariah Cook was born and raised on a farm in New Hampshire. She graduated in 1976 from the University of Rochester with a B.A. in Fine Arts/Art History. She's been a graphic artist, an antiques dealer, and a contender for the U.S. Women's Rowing team.

In 1986, Cook became a freelance "dog writer," working as a columnist for *Siberian Husky Club of America Newsletter* and contributing to the *American Kennel Gazette/Purebred Dogs.* She has also cowritten and coedited several books about Siberian Huskies.

Ann Mariah Cook lives in New Hampshire with her husband, her daughter, and thirty-five purebred Siberian Huskies.